BAPTISM BY FIRE

OCTOBER 4, 1967

My second mission I flew copilot with Latimer on a gunship. We were flying in support of the 101st Airborne in a small valley near Tam Ky. Being basically new and still remembering what I'd been told in flight school, I was incredulous when Latimer approached the intended strike area very low and very slow. In training, you were taught to start your gun and rocket runs at 1,000 feet, break off prior to the target at 500 feet, and try to maintain an air speed of 80 knots.

Latimer flew over the target "down and dirty," allowing his airspeed and altitude to drop off to about 50 knots and 100 feet so that he could maneuver in the confined valley. Immediately, the shoot-out turned into a wild west gunfight. Over the staccato drone of our own door gunner's machine guns, you could also hear the rapid clacking of enemy guns. With a sudden jolt, I took a .30 caliber round through the floor into the bottom of my armored seat. We were being hit from all directions. The helicopter was being riddled with bullet holes. Luckily, we were able to nurse it back to friendly territory. As I gingerly stepped out of my seat, I felt faint. Astonishingly, the rest of the crew was laughing and joking.

After only two combat missions and six days in Vietnam, I had concluded that all gunship pilots were nuts and that my chances of living twelve more months were absolutely zero.

"Let the F............ you .... lly ride. . . . This is .... eir war in helicopters .... age, unbowed by the .... n their own country .... Mr. Carlock is unspa..................... d often hilarious detail. It is a great war story."
—LIZ TROTTA, NEW YORK BUREAU CHIEF, *The Washington Times,* AND FORMER VIETNAM WAR CORRESPONDENT

*The best
first-person
account
of helicopter
combat in
Vietnam ever
written*

FIREBIRDS

Chuck Carlock

Bantam Books

*New York   Toronto   London
Sydney   Auckland*

This edition contains the complete text of the original edition.
NOT ONE WORD HAS BEEN OMITTED.

FIREBIRDS
A Bantam Book / published by arrangement with
The Summit Publishing Group

PUBLISHING HISTORY
The Summit Publishing Group hardcover published in 1995
Bantam mass market edition / August 1997

Library of Congress Catalog Card Number: 95-50005.
No part of this book may be reproduced or transmitted in any form or by
any means, electronic or mechanical, including photocopying, recording,
or by any information storage and retrieval system, without permission in
writing from the publisher.
For information address: The Summit Publishing Group, One Arlington
Centre, 1112 East Copeland Road, Fifth Floor, Arlington, Texas, 76011.

ISBN: 0-553-57705-0

Published simultaneously in the United States and Canada

Bantam Books are published by Bantam Books, a division of Random
House, Inc. Its trademark, consisting of the words "Bantam Books" and
the portrayal of a rooster, is Registered in U.S. Patent and Trademark
Office and in other countries. Marca Registrada. Random House, Inc.,
New York, New York.

PRINTED IN THE UNITED STATES OF AMERICA

OPM   16 15 14 13 12 11 10 9

CONTENTS

P. 19, 21, 22, 102, 104, 132, 170,
174-175, 216-217, 215-216

PREFACE

· ·

THE DATE WAS FEBRUARY 12, 1993, AND THE TALES OF combat were flying as thick and fast as the bullets had been twenty-five years earlier. At a reunion of flight buddies from the Seventy-First Assault Helicopter Company in Vietnam, the time reeled away. The gray and the bald once again became the young and the brave. The atmosphere of the room was jovial, irreverent, and gratified. I think that what had happened in our lives after the war was still overshadowed by the accomplishment of just having survived experiences that most people will never comprehend. We had a mutual bond; we were helicopter pilots and crew members in the "Vietnam Conflict."

We fought in the war that was never a war. Funny, to us the feelings we had were the same. We ran the gamut of fear, exultation, grief, disgust, frustration, exhaustion, and terror. Death was a part of our daily lives. We were young. Some pilots and crew members were but nineteen years old. Entrusted with expensive machines, powerful weapons, and other people's lives, we grew up fast or not at all. We fought daily; while back home, people made judgments about this war based on what they saw on the TV screen in the safety of their living rooms.

I remember the special forces motto: "You have never lived until you have almost died, and life has a flavor the protected will never know."

I realized that those of us at the reunion had an account

to tell. We had been in 'Nam tasting of life and flirting with death. We could once again feel the exhilaration of being young and strong. I truly felt that we had met eye to eye with destiny and escaped from the edge of the grave. Over fifty-eight thousand men and women did not escape. This narrative belongs to us all: those at the reunion, and those whose names are found on the Wall.

I would like to express my thanks to the members of our reunion association who provided inputs to the manuscript and without whose help this book would not have been possible. Accordingly, all royalties from the sales of this work are to be donated to the association. Thanks are also due to V. M. Owens for her long hours of help in bringing the book together. Most of all, I would like to thank my lovely wife Kathy and my daughters, Krissy, Deanna, and Joanna, for their encouragement and support.

PROLOGUE

....

MARCH 11, 1968

THE INFANTRY UNIT WAS IN A BATTLE TO THE DEATH. Having already repelled two human wave attacks by North Vietnamese Army (NVA) soldiers, Lieutenant David Zbozien's infantry platoon was in grave danger. The platoon was almost out of ammo, time, and luck. Hope of assistance was quickly fading as eight antiaircraft guns and tenacious small arms fire had already downed two troop-carrying helicopters and one gunship that were trying to rescue his troops. Zbozien had sustained thirteen separate wounds during the battle and had already been pronounced dead by his radio operator when he temporarily lost consciousness.

Zbozien peered into the heavy cover surrounding his position. The bushes were moving! Heavily camouflaged NVA soldiers were preparing for what would be their final assault against the tired and outnumbered Americans.

Hearing a sudden noise during the lull, Zbozien lifted his head slightly and glanced over his left shoulder just in time to see a "Firebird" helicopter gunship beginning an attack on the enemy positions. The attack was divinely timed and Lieutenant Zbozien lived, thanks to the efforts of the Firebirds.

I was the pilot of that gunship, and it had only been six months since I first stepped into the country of Vietnam. Oh, what a difference six months had made.

First Mission

OCTOBER 3, 1967

"Did you see them? Did you see them?" Anton screamed
into the intercom as we flew over three armed Viet Cong
fleeing into a wooded tree line. Since this was my first
mission after arriving in Vietnam, I failed to realize that
the frenzied question actually meant, "Why the hell aren't
you shooting, stupid?" McCall, who was flying lead gunship at the time, swung around, fired his rockets, and
"punched the ticket" on the three Viet Cong, sending
them straight to commie heaven!

We were supposed to be giving air support to a marine
infantry unit during a "blocking mission." The ground
troops had come up on the village from three sides, and
our job was to maneuver over the hamlet and shoot any
Viet Cong that ran. Being copilot, my job was to fire the
miniguns. But when we came up over the rice paddy near
the village, everything happened too fast for me. I did answer Anton as he spotted the Viet Cong. Instead of shooting the guys, I just shouted back, "Yeah! I saw 'em—they
looked right at me!" This was the inauspicious beginning
of my Vietnam combat experience. After we arrived back
at base, the lead pilot received credit for three kills. Anton, who was screaming all the way to camp that he had
the "dumbest copilot in Vietnam," spent the next several
weeks riding me hard. I just kept thinking that only a
week before, I'd been doing the two-step and drinking
cold long neck beers at Rustler's Rest in Fort Worth,
Texas. How life had changed!

Baptism by Fire

OCTOBER 4, 1967

My second mission I flew copilot with Latimer on a gunship. We were flying in support of the 101st Airborne in a small valley near Tam Ky. Being basically new, green, and still remembering what I'd been told in flight school, I was incredulous when Latimer approached the intended strike area very low and very slow. In training, you were taught to start your gun and rocket runs at 1,000 feet, break off prior to the target at 500 feet, and try to maintain an air speed of 80 knots.

Latimer, who was completely fearless, flew over the target "down and dirty," allowing his airspeed and altitude to drop off to about 50 knots and 100 feet so that he could maneuver in the confined valley. So much for flight training! Immediately, the shoot-out turned into a wild west gunfight. The door gunners began peppering the space directly below us. I looked around and saw muzzle flashes from numerous automatic weapons. The area was total bedlam. Over the staccato drone of our own door gunner's machine guns, you could also hear the rapid typewriter-like clacking of enemy guns and the metallic impact of bullets passing through the helicopter's skin. With a sudden jolt, I took a .30 caliber round through the floor into the bottom of my armored seat. Simultaneously, the door gunner, who was sitting on an armored plate, took a .30 caliber round directly on his seat. We were being hit from all directions. The helicopter was being riddled with bullet holes. It looked as if someone had stitched it from one end to the other. Luckily, we were able to nurse it back to friendly territory. As I gingerly stepped out of my seat, I felt faint. The adrenaline was still pumping, my legs were rubber, and I felt as if I had just awakened from a horrible nightmare. Astonishingly, the rest of the crew was laughing and joking.

After only two combat missions and six days in Vietnam, I had concluded that all gunship pilots were nuts and that my chances of living twelve more months were absolutely zero.

OCTOBER 6, 1967

My third mission I flew as copilot with McCall. We were flying north out of Chu Lai to support an infantry company that was engaged in heavy combat. On the way, we headed out at a low level. McCall dipped toward a rice paddy full of Vietnamese who were working. We were approximately eighteen inches above the ground. Everyone scattered or dove into the mud except for one kid about ten years old. Defiantly, he stooped over and, at the last second, came up with two handfuls of mud and rice plants. The mud hit the Plexiglas window in front of me with a booming sound. Instinctively, I ducked. McCall nearly crashed the gunship when he started laughing at me.

Chapter One

THE MAKING OF A CHOPPER PILOT

···

AUGUST 16, 1966

After a weekend conference with General William C. Westmoreland, President Lyndon Johnson announced that American troops "will not be defeated" in Vietnam.

I JOINED THE ARMY FOR THE sole purpose of becoming a helicopter pilot. A friend of mine, Garland Lively, talked me into it by telling me what great fun it was to fly these things. As it turned out, we wound up in the same battalion, flying UH-1s in Vietnam. Twenty-five years later, he came to my office to show me a picture of one he was flying that took twenty-seven bullets during the Tet Offensive. He also showed me the scars from a bullet that went through his arm. I told him thanks for talking me into becoming a helicopter pilot.

I didn't realize that army helicopter training would be little more than preparation for becoming cannon fodder. I recall my meeting in August 1966 with the review board—those men who screened personnel for enrollment into helicopter flight school. A colonel asked me if I fully realized that being a helicopter pilot in Vietnam was a very dangerous profession. I recall smiling and confidently telling him, "I will do my duty." I was thinking how much smarter I was than him. I would have two months in boot camp, nine months in flight school, and one month on leave. By that time it would be October 1967, and everyone knew that the war would be over by then. My training would merely enable me to become a peacetime pilot.

This was only my first big mistake.

I was formally introduced to the army by being invited to partake in the induction physical. Hundreds of guys stood in line buck naked. Our valuables were carried in a sack hooked to our wrist. We were all told to face the wall; and a doctor, apparently checking for a rupture, told a guy to lift his sack. The next thing I knew the doctor was screaming at the guy, "Your other sack, stupid!"

My next memory is of my first day in boot camp. They stood about ten of us at parade rest in front of the orderly room. There was an open window in front of us which could not be seen into because of the sun shining on it. After ten to twenty minutes, I started to look around and admire my new home. Suddenly, I heard a booming voice scream, "ATTENTION!" I must have jumped at least four feet off the ground. The distorted face in the window yelling out the order, our top sergeant, looked exactly like a creature from a late night horror movie. We subsequently heard that he had suffered severe wounds to his face while serving in Korea. One whole side of his face was nearly gone.

As boot camp progressed, I became the company truck driver. Each morning, I had to go in to the top sergeant's office and get papers authorizing a jeep, truck, or ambulance for the day. I suspect that he remembered me as the recruit who could jump so high, because he was always nice to me. Sadly, he never returned a smile—I suppose that was because of the injuries to his face.

One buck sergeant, who had just returned from Vietnam, was apparently an alcoholic. He bunked in the same barracks with us. Occasionally, this particular sergeant would come in late at night, wake us up, and stand us at attention. He would then make us get into bed still holding the position of attention, order us to close our eyes, and tell us to go to sleep at his command. One Sunday, he was mad at someone, so he made us go run with him. We trooped along at full speed for around five miles. Half of the platoon just passed out in the middle of the road. We didn't have an ambulance following, so we just left a trail of soldiers lying along the road. Much to our relief, the sergeant became a private the very next day.

After boot camp, they bused us—now warrant officer candidates (WOCs)—from Louisiana to Fort Wolters, near Mineral Wells, Texas. My father drove over from my hometown of Joshua, Texas to meet me. While he was waiting for us to arrive, he spent several hours visiting with the drill sergeants and had the impression that these were pretty nice guys. They told him to stick around and he would soon see some real fun when the guys from boot camp showed up. When we arrived, these "really nice guys" screamed and bellowed the whole time we were unloading the buses and trying to check in. My father thought the situation was hilarious. I personally did not see the humor in it.

During preflight training, before being allowed to fly, the senior WOCs would come down each night to harass us. One night, I made the mistake of grinning while they were going through their act. They took me into the latrine and made me do chin-ups on a water pipe that ran across the ceiling. By that time, I could do chin-ups or push-ups until they got tired of watching. But I made the mistake of grinning again, and they asked if I smoked. I told them no, so they promptly lit one and stuck it in my mouth while I was still doing the chin-ups. One guy smarted off, "Try it, you'll like it!" Before long, these sadists had six or seven cigarettes lit and dangling from my mouth. The smoke was barreling straight up my nose, and breathing was absolutely impossible! They still had me doing chin-ups even though I closely resembled a chimney. I did get rid of the smile and learned to show proper respect in the future. At least, I was a quick study!

Early in flight school at Fort Wolters, I discovered that I was not cut out to be a career military officer. Maybe it had something to do with my body chemistry, because my starched uniform always looked like I had slept in it, even if I'd only worn it for thirty minutes. My boots could never keep a shine, and my military brass, belt buckle, etc., seemed to tarnish in a matter of minutes. I am certain I would have been booted out of flight school posthaste, except for the fact that I had a friend—a very influential friend!

Warrant Officer Candidate Charles Bootle was probably the most powerful warrant officer candidate who ever went through helicopter flight school. He was about twenty-nine years old and had a wife and kids. He also was gifted with an incredible arm that he used quite well in the art of softball! Generals all over the country tried to get him assigned to their commands. He was the Nolan Ryan of softball pitchers, and could hum that big old ball into home plate at 100 mph. For some reason, he took a liking to a fellow farm boy—me. When I asked him, twenty-five years later, why he took me under his wing, he merely replied, "I knew you were just a peanut farmer, and all of us farm boys needed to stick together." I used to tell Bootle that I was so poor down on the farm, that I was very lucky to be born a boy. Otherwise, I wouldn't have had anything to play with. He always called me "Skippy." I assumed it was in honor of Skippy Peanut Butter. All I know is that I had hoed and combined plenty of peanuts, and I was very happy to have this guy as a mentor. He rescued me from more than one run-in with my commanding officers.

One night, having become discouraged by my constant disheveled appearance, I was trying to shine up all my gear in order to earn a weekend pass. I was frustrated and about ready to give up the whole idea of flight school, but Bootle talked me out of it. He had a sure answer for me: "Skippy, don't worry, I'll put you on the softball team." I did not realize until later that WOC Bootle had cut a deal with the officers at the base. If they kept winning, the team kept getting regular weekend passes.

Now, I was not a bad athlete, but in comparison to most of the other guys on this team, I didn't have a clue! I had been an all-state football player in high school, but some of these jocks had played professional baseball. Bootle had an arm like a whip. I was, to put it nicely, in over my head. The coach kept needling Bootle as to why in the hell he had put me on the team. I could not hit anything and was slow turning double plays. Bootle would always say, "I can just pitch better knowing Skippy is backing me up." It was a ritual at batting practice for him to chunk a 90 mph fastball straight at my head. I would cuss, and the coach would fuss. The coach figured I would never learn to hit as long as my friend was zeroing in on me. Maybe Bootle was just preparing me for Vietnam. Eventually, I got to be pretty good at dodging .50 cal. tracers coming at me. Dodging softballs was good practice.

Bootle used his persuasive powers several times to my advantage. One Saturday morning, during inspection, the commanding officer found a fingerprint on the back of the belt buckle in my display drawer. The commanding officer (CO) and the sergeant literally tore my room apart, throwing my stuff everywhere. I was given enough demerits to keep me from receiving any weekend passes for the next twenty years. After they left, I just sat on my bed in a state of shock. Then Bootle walked in. I told him about the incident and moaned that I would never see the outside of Fort Wolters again! He turned around, walked out, and came back a short while later with my pass!

On another Saturday (my "lucky" day of the week), Bootle got really steamed at our CO because he had ordered a late morning parade inspection which would cut into our leave time. The official order stated that the inspection would be in the company area, but didn't specify precisely where. Bootle decided we would mess with the officers a little bit and teach them a lesson. He arranged for the entire class of WOCs, about 350 men, to fall out in formation on the roof of our barracks. From my point of view, there was one slight problem with this ingenious plan. I was the temporary flight commander and therefore was technically Bootle's boss for the week. Both the commanding officer and the sergeant would immediately know who thought up this joke, but they would take their wrath out on me. I begged Bootle not to follow through with his plan.

I should have received my first Purple Heart there at Fort Wolters for the butt chewing I endured. Bootle thought the whole thing was hysterical, but I knew I was about to get my walking papers. As I was loudly voicing my concerns, Bootle left and, sure enough, soon showed up with my weekend pass in hand.

During the actual flight instruction, I fared much better. I could tell I was doing well because of the way my flight instructor treated me. His other students were always complaining about him whacking them on the sides of their flight helmets as they flew. If they made any mistakes—Wham!

One day, several of the guys in our flight shared that they were going to solo the next day. Because I had already shot my mouth off about what a hot pilot I was, I was determined to solo first. The following morning I raced up to my instructor and informed him that I was ready to give it a try. He proceeded to take me up for my chance. As I turned base leg in the traffic pattern to descend from 500 feet to 300 feet, the lights went out! Wham! He hit me on the side of the helmet, hard! Well, I decided to show him a thing or two. I turned loose of the controls. This type of small helicopter had a tendency to burrow into the ground nose first, then burn. We came close to successfully completing this maneuver! As the instructor landed the chopper, he just kept staring at me trying to figure out if I had let go on purpose. That fiasco ended my flying for the day. My friend, Gary Beck, was the first to solo. That afternoon, back at the flight operations building, my instructor kept on staring at me, so I glared straight back! He didn't speak to me the rest of the day. The next day, we flew one traffic pattern without exchanging a word. Then he barked out, "Pull over, I'm getting out!" I never flew with him again.

I ran into him after I returned from Vietnam, and we had a good laugh about the fact that I nearly killed us both. I also learned that he had suffered a heart attack and was restricted to teaching ground classes. I hope our little escapade wasn't to blame.

My diversions with the softball team continued—we never lost a game at Fort Wolters. The "Amazing Bootle" kept on performing his magic, both on and off the diamond. When we transferred to Fort Rucker, Alabama, for advanced helicopter training, he got me on the team there, too. At Fort Rucker, we played some good softball teams from other bases. Against these guys, I rarely made contact with the ball. The bat seemed to have some internal device that repelled the softball. Our new sergeant was asking the same old question, "What's he doing on the team?" Again Bootle would reply, "I can just pitch

better with him behind me!" He said I was his bodyguard
and was supposed to protect him if any of our opponents
took offense to a fastball "up and in." For a number of
years, I kept the newspaper clippings of all our impressive victories. Bootle would always tell the reporters, "We
could not have won without the hitting of Skippy Carlock." They never questioned him, but just printed what
he said. Maybe he was referring to my bodyguard abili-
ties. It certainly was not my batting prowess!

At Ft. Rucker, I earned the nickname "Kamikaze Carlock," because of my fearless nature and general tendency to showboat. We were one of the first flight
classes to receive direct training in flying helicopter gunships. I was quite brave during training flights and
thought my new nickname was pretty accurate. In fact, I
was anxious to hurry up and get into battle against the
"godless commie barbarians." Thank goodness only one
man in Vietnam knew my nickname from flight school.
After only a few actual combat missions, I concluded
that my nerves were of a mediocre variety which allowed
fear to override my tendency to show off. One day in
Vietnam, in a fit of machismo, I told my crew chief to
paint "Kamikaze Carlock" on the front of the gunship.
He thought maybe "Chicken Liver Carlock" would be
more appropriate. Instead of being classified as chicken
liver, I preferred to say that I had strong genetic traits
that created a definite instinct for self-preservation.
However, I can say that on certain particular days, for
whatever reason, I *was* macho!

In my last month at Fort Rucker, Bootle informed me
that I was now on the battalion WOC staff. He said it was
because I was such a "sharp soldier." Nobody in the company could believe it. He merely handed me a little book
and confidently told me that in two weeks, I would or-
ganize and conduct a battalion parade and review. My

mouth fell open in shock! I could barely march myself, much less conduct a parade of four WOC companies. Each of these companies contained about three hundred and fifty men. Any mistake in timing an order would result in mass confusion. Several hundred guys would end up marching all over several hundred other guys! For two weeks, I constantly begged Bootle to find someone else to handle this responsibility. I begged each WOC who had been a sergeant to come to my aid. They all refused. I knew the key to pulling the parade off successfully was to measure the field and compute and mark each location where the proper commands were to be given. The idea of being in charge of all this petrified me. I told Bootle that all his previous jokes and shenanigans were funny. This one was not. I needed help, and I needed it fast!

The dreaded day arrived. Bootle came by the barracks to inspect my uniform and make sure my normally sloppy appearance was sharpened and shipshape. He also mentioned nonchalantly that he had asked one of the other guys to take over my job. He told the guy that he thought I might be in the process of having heart failure. For a fleeting moment, I wondered what might happen to me if I murdered the army's best softball pitcher.

This turned out to be a perilous time for me. After my scare about the parade, I should have learned my lesson. Maybe I wasn't such a quick study after all. Being on the battalion staff, another guy and I had a barracks to ourselves. Bootle had informed us that there would be no inspections. For some insane reason, I believed him. I immediately indulged myself and began to keep my room like a civilian. My bed was unmade, and I had stuff strewn around the area. One day, a sergeant walked through. He made a beeline to the CO, and once again, I could have received a Purple Heart.

I graduated, tied for fifteenth in my class of three hundred fifty men. I had slept through my share of classes and messed up my share of the rules, but my flight grades were pretty good. On the afternoon of the ceremonies, we were supposed to attend a formal function wearing our dress uniforms. We had been given three hundred dollars to purchase these uniforms to wear at this party to show off our flight wings. Having finally become a warrant officer, I definitely knew a career in the military was not for me. I took my money and headed out for home. I was going to celebrate my accomplishment by drinking some of those cold long neck beers back in Texas. I figured the worst they could do to me was to pack me off to Vietnam, and they were going to do that anyway.

Between boot camp and the flight schools, I learned many things about life and about myself. There had to be training. That training would include the tedious and the thrilling. I learned about friends, how to take orders, and how to think for myself. I played hard—all the guys did. Somewhere in the back of our minds, we knew that this training and these experiences could be the beginning of the end. Every single one of us would wind up in Southeast Asia. Some of us would earn medals. Some of us would lose a part of ourselves—if we were real lucky, it would only be our innocence. Some of us would find courage. Tragically, some of us would never make it home. We approached our careers and our lives in a cavalier manner. Thank God for the COs, the sergeants, and all the others in charge who made it tough to succeed. Thank God, they stretched us to the limits of endurance. We would need everything we learned, and then some, to make it back to the "world."

Chapter Two

HELLO, VIETNAM

• •

SEPTEMBER 30, 1967

California Governor Ronald Reagan began a highly successful nationwide speaking tour amid growing speculation that he would run for the presidency. Reagan denied that he was a candidate, claiming that his only intention was to gain "favorite son" status in the California delegation. Most analysts agreed that the former actor had little chance to take up residence in the White House.

IN LATE SEPTEMBER 1967, I HAD orders to report to a helicopter company in the delta region of South Vietnam. One of the instructor pilots at flight school had mentioned that this was a fairly passive area. That sounded fine to me.

After a long flight over, with too much time to think, we arrived at Cam Ranh Bay and then flew directly to Nha Trang, where I spent one night. At the time, I thought it was a little strange that there was no one to direct me to the delta region or tell me where to go. On October 1, 1967 (my first full day in Vietnam), while waiting around the processing center at Nha Trang, we began to hear word of two big "shoot 'em up, blow 'em ups" involving a helicopter battalion up north at Chu Lai. One engagement was at a place that was afterward called Million Dollar Hill. On September 12 and then on September 29, during a Romeo Foxtrot (RF = rat fuck = combat assault led by a battal-

ion officer), the helicopter battalion was decimated. We
heard they had landed a flight of choppers in a mine field
under fire on Million Dollar Hill. They had thirteen helicopters damaged, five totally destroyed, and quite a few
human casualties. On September 29, they had twenty-two
helicopters that took hits. Four were shot down, eight pilots wounded, and one crew chief killed. Million Dollar
Hill got its nickname from the wreckage of four helicopters that were abandoned there. Later on in the war,
this same hill saw heavy action. Rocky Blier, the future
Pittsburgh Steeler running back, was injured near there.
Also, in 1969, a huge conflict was brewing at the Hill
when, for one of the first times in Vietnam, an infantry
company refused the order to attack.

    After hearing about all the action around Chu Lai, I
wondered if my luck would hold. The delta area was looking better all the time. But it was never to be. Later that
same day, I was told the next chopper in would be deliv-
ering me to that very battalion at Chu Lai. I was stunned
as I boarded the chopper and headed north. So much for
my "safe" orders.

Firebirds

Officially, I was now a member of the Seventy-First As-
sault Helicopter Company assigned to the Fourteenth
Aviation Battalion in support of Task Force Oregon. Task
Force Oregon was a combination of the First Brigade of
the 101st Airborne Division, the Third Brigade of the
First Cavalry Division and the 196th Light Infantry
Brigade. The 196th was later to join other units to become
the Americal Division.

    My company had three platoons. Two of them flew

troop-carrying UH-1Ds and UH-1Hs, called "slicks" because of their lack of externally mounted weapons—their only armament was two machine guns fired out the door. These two platoons were known as the Rattlers. The other platoon—the one I was assigned to—flew UH-1C gunships. We were known as the Firebirds because of the large red bird painted on the side of the chopper. My first thought upon seeing it was what a nice target that large red bird made!

Because helicopters can perform so many different tasks, each platoon had a variety of missions. But in a nutshell, the slick's basic job was to haul troops in and out of combat. The gunship's primary mission was to support the slicks by attacking and clearing out the enemy from landing and pick-up zones.

The unique relationship between gunship and slick pilots included a lot of good-natured bad-mouthing between the two groups. The gunship pilots were loud, cocky, and boisterous. I believe that the slick pilots really liked gunship pilots to act like that because, while sitting in a landing zone (LZ) with tracer bullets flying everywhere, it was comforting to look up about twenty to thirty feet and see those boisterous loud-mouths blowing the hell out of Charlie. The whole company (other than some commanding officers) liked the bravado of the gunship pilots. That cockiness gave a feeling of security—what little there was!

While I was still new, I felt that some slick pilots didn't like a twenty-one-year-old greenhorn like me moving into the gun platoon. As far as I can determine, I was the only pilot who first flew gunships in Vietnam and then moved over and flew slicks. Most gunship pilots started out on the troop carriers.

A gunship platoon had eight helicopters and ten to sixteen pilots. We had twelve pilots when I arrived, but seemed to always be short of aircraft. It was impossible to get all eight helicopters flying at once due to combat damage, normal repairs, and lack of spare parts.

Two gunships were called "Hogs" and were equipped with forty-eight rockets, besides the two machine guns manned by the gunner and crew chief. Two were called "Frogs" and had a 40 mm cannon on a swivel on the nose of the chopper, in addition to the two door guns. The 40 mm grenade explosive head looked like a bullet about one inch long and one and a half inches wide that exploded on impact. The Frogs also carried fourteen rockets.

The rest of the copters were equipped with fourteen rockets and two miniguns (similar to the Gatling guns seen in some old cowboy movies). These guns each had six spinning barrels and two electric motors. One motor pulled ammo into the gun, while the other pushed it in. The miniguns fired 6,000 rounds per minute. They didn't sound like a regular machine gun, but made a wailing noise just like Godzilla in those cheap Japanese movies.

The UH-1Cs carried a crew of four—a pilot, a copilot (called the peter pilot), a crew chief, and a gunner. The pilot fired the rockets, the copilot fired the cannon (on the Frogs) or the miniguns (on the basic helos). The miniguns were aimed with a hanging gunsight, which could be snapped in an up position, out of the copilot's face, when not in use. One day Steven Buzzell, who was flying as Frank Anton's peter pilot, turned on the miniguns' electrical power, then reached up to unsnap the gunsight to lower it in front of his face. In the process, he accidentally hit the trigger and fired off a blast, just missing one of our Rattler helicopters!

Crew chiefs and door gunners were an important part of the gunship crew. These were the men who covered your butt as the gunship maneuvered around during combat. An experienced door gunner could make life a little safer while all hell was breaking loose. One of the most vital duties he performed was to put a cover of gunfire under the other gunship (we usually flew in pairs) as it attacked the target. The goal was not to shoot at anything specific, but to spray the area totally with bullets. This made the enemy take cover in the surrounding shrubs, brush, and trees. While crouching down with bullets flying all around them, the enemy would not normally return fire at the helicopters. After we determined the location of the friendlies, we then let the door gunners shoot in the areas adjacent to the attack location.

The ammunition fired in the miniguns was standard army issue—metal belts of ammo, four lead shells (we called them "lead" even though they were made of steel with a copper jacket) with the fifth round being a tracer. The guns shot so fast that at night, the tracers looked like a solid beam of light shining down to the ground. Our door gunners fired from ammo belts that were straight tracer rounds. I found it interesting that firing a door gun from the left side required a different aim than firing from the right. The twisting of the bullet meeting the rushing air as the copter flew forward caused the bullets to react differently. The bullets fired from the right door curved and dropped to the right. Bullets fired from the left rose and veered to the right. For this reason, the door gunners needed straight tracer bullets in order to "walk" the rounds up onto the target.

We had plenty of discussions concerning tracer bullets. If the bullet did not hit a vital area of the body, it would pass through and actually cauterize a wound, burn the flesh and seal the blood flow. Sometimes we would hit enemy soldiers so many times that they resembled Swiss cheese, but they just kept on running for cover.

Chu Lai

The Seventy-First was based at Chu Lai, on the South China Sea, fifty miles south of Da Nang. The provincial capital of Tam Ky was about halfway between the two. The US military had divided South Vietnam into four areas of operations. Chu Lai was located in the northernmost area, known as "I" Corps (pronounced "eye core"). It is interesting to note that the Vietnamese still refer to the place as Chu Lai today. I wonder if they realize it was named after a US marine general. The general's name was Krulak and Chu Lai is his name in Chinese characters.

My first week at Chu Lai was a real "experience." Getting used to this way of life wouldn't be easy for me. I was shot at, surrounded by lunatics, and even had to get used to taking public showers.

I arrived during the rainy season. It was cool, and we did not have the luxury of hot water. A person would only shower when he couldn't take the stink anymore. I finally gave in and decided I had reached that point. As I walked toward the shower area, I saw a bunch of old Vietnamese women squatted down polishing boots, using the run-off to rinse the boots. After some hesitation, I decided "what the hell" and dropped my drawers. I jumped into the shower as quickly as possible, but it seemed to me that the mamasans' chattering got louder and faster when I got naked!

Because I was a new guy, the old hands went out of their way to torment me. Soon after I went to the flight line, a big gunner stepped in front of me, looked me in the eye, and said, "Death is our business, and business is good." I'm sure my hair stood straight up. I was thinking, "Who are these nuts?" When I went to put up my gear, I was introduced to a pilot named Ager Davis, who lived in our hootch. (A hootch was where someone lived, except when we blew it up or burned it down. Then we called it an "enemy structure.") As Davis walked out of the hootch, someone mentioned that he didn't fly anymore. I asked "What does he do?" He answered, "He builds shitters" (restrooms). I asked why, and the reply was, "He went nuts one day and got a machine gun and was going to kill the commanding officer." I started laughing because I thought it was a joke. It wasn't!

That same day, I was introduced to Clarence J. Dammitt. Mr. Dammitt was an alcoholic monkey who had become our company mascot and had a cage at the Officers' Club. Every once in a while some drunk would attempt to pet him, and would invariably get bitten for his efforts. Next to the cage was a tent pole to poke poor Clarence whenever that happened. My introduction to Mr. Dammitt furthered my doubts about the nature of my new companions. Shortly after I arrived, Clarence had been in a grouchy mood (possibly a hangover), so two Firebird pilots (Ken Wiegand and Gary McCall) decided to give him an attitude adjustment. After a hard night of gorging on drink, Wiegand grabbed a two-by-four piece of wood and told McCall to hold the door to Clarence's cage open so he could give the monkey a thumping. Clarence, not one to take his thumpings lightly, scrambled up the board and bit Wiegand on the arm. As he went down Wiegand's back, he bit and scratched him again. Clarence had fangs about an inch long. Wiegand and McCall ran to the Firebird hootch, snatched up their hand artillery and their army helmets, and paraded around the company area saying over and over "We are going to kill that son-of-a-bitch." After a fruitless search for the hapless Clarence, they went back to the club. In a few minutes, the company commander came storming into the club dressed in only a T-shirt and underwear. He had his pistol belt on and his

.38 pistol drawn. "Where are the guys that want to kill me!" he bellowed.

In addition to our inebriated ape, there were always several dogs around. Later in my tour, we befriended one at LZ Baldy. He was affectionately tagged with the name "Shithead." One of the guys rigged a special harness for him that connected to a parachute from a flare. A slick would lift Shithead up to 500 or so feet, and out he would go. Geronimo! He would always be so badly scared he would piss all the way down. The crazy thing was, as soon as he landed, he was ready to go again!

Before I got to know them well, I thought that my fellow pilots were a pack of reprobates who intended to lead me astray. The first night I was in the company area, several of us went to the Officers' Club and proceeded to get smashed. I noticed right away that some of them used language unbecoming officers. Then they started singing songs. One was something about "dropping napalm in the schoolyards, watching the kiddies run and shout, you will really laugh your ass off when they try to put it out." The song went on to talk about the difficulty of shooting kids because they could run so fast you had to lead them further (shoot in front of them). I'm sure my eyes were as big as fifty-cent pieces the first time I heard this song. I remember part of another song that went like this:

Away in a sampan
All loaded with rice
A young VC warrior
Sat picking his lice
When out of the dark sky
A Firebird came
And blew him to hell
That's the name of the game.

And another one:
> *If I die in Vietnam,*
> *Send a letter to my mom,*
> *Tell her that I died with a grin,*
> *Putting smoke on Ho Chi Minh.*

One of our favorite songs was:
> *O' Chu Lai, O' Chu Lai's a hell of a place,*
> *the organization's a fucking disgrace.*
> *There are captains and majors and light colonels too,*
> *with thumbs up their asses and nothing to do.*
> *They sit on the runway, they scream and they shout,*
> *about many things they know nothing about.*
> *For all of their worth they might as well be,*
> *shoveling shit on the South China Sea!*

The funniest thing about this song is that many of the singers became majors and light (lieutenant) colonels. One became a full bird colonel—and he didn't even have a good singing voice. But back then, we were sure that all field grade officers (majors and above) spent twenty-three and a half hours each day eating, sleeping, drinking, and copulating, and the remaining half hour planning idiotic ways to get heroic warrant officers killed.

Bob Parsons, a fellow pilot who checked into the Firebirds a few days after me, recalls having similar feelings on his first night at the Officers' Club. These are his words:

> *My first evening in the club you (Carlock) had been with the platoon for several days. You, me, Anton, McCall, (Andrew) Sutton, and I believe Davis, were at a table. Either Sutton or Davis blew our minds with the following story and the new guy "set up."*
> *He was pretending to be in a solemn mood, kind*

of withdrawn. One of the older "gunnies" drew us into the trap by asking him, "What's wrong, Sutton?" Slowly, taking a sip of beer, Sutton responded. "This business of being in the guns is really hard. Hairy night missions back in the mountains in bad weather, taking hit after hit from small arms, RPGs (shoulder fired rockets) and antiaircraft fire . . . losing your friends . . . killing people . . . yeah, it's tough killing men. And sometimes killing women . . . it's even tougher killing NVA (North Vietnamese Army) women." He is still gazing down into his beer, looking as though he is about to cry when he says . . . "but man, occasionally kids are out there, and then it is really hard. Boy, is it hard on you when the kids come into it!" (Everyone is dead quiet now.) Sutton looks you in the eye and then me in the eye and says with a big smile . . . "the little sons of bitches are so small and they run so fast it is almost impossible to hit them!" Everyone breaks out laughing except you and me, the new guys. I was shocked and didn't know what to think. I know you felt the same way because your jaw was down to your belt buckle and your eyes were wide with disbelief. We had the same thought—"what kind of crazy people ARE these guys?" It didn't take us long to adopt the same kind of "graveyard humor" and warped understanding.

As we soon discovered, this sort of macabre humor was a way of coping with the pressure and anxieties that ensued from the unique and deadly form of combat we had stumbled into. Combat humor, on the ground and in the air, could seem cruel, unbalanced, and in total disregard for human life. But it was part and parcel of the times and the circumstances in which it was born. The twisted humor took the edge off of some dicey situations. These guys would even joke about who would get the other's stereo equipment if one of them was killed. The main purpose was to keep from going crazy. Sometimes it was the only thing that worked.

Unfortunately, there was a lot more to Chu Lai than evenings at the Officers' Club. Although the songs were certainly exaggerated, the facts of battle were indeed brutal. The VC (Viet Cong, also called Charlies) south of Chu Lai put out "wanted posters" for any war criminal flying the helicopters with the red bird on the side. The lucky Charlie was to receive a bicycle and a thirty-day leave for catching one of us. During my tour, I had two friends from flight school who were last seen alive on the ground and were assumed to have been executed after capture. Charlie's hatred of the Firebirds was said to go back to an incident in which some marines found their dead buddies skinned and cut into pieces. Enraged, they radioed the Firebirds to use the area as a free fire zone. That meant to shoot anything that moved—people, chickens, water buffaloes, anything.

There were plenty of stories of VC atrocities. Later in my tour, I heard about a VC woman who tied up American soldiers, put baskets around their necks, filled them with several rats, and sewed a lid over each poor guy's head. When you were twenty years old and believed all the atrocity stories, it did not take long to harden your attitude. Tales of this type (and the effect they had on young men's minds) allowed us to cope with the degrading butchery and incited some to return outrage for outrage.

One of the gunners told me about the time his helo was running a VC down a rice paddy dike, and the guy tripped. The dink looked up, and saw the gunship diving on him. He came up to his knees praying. I asked, "What did you do?" He replied, "He was the only one I ever shot while he was praying." I was at that time positively sure I had been assigned to a loony farm. "Dink" was another term for the enemy. Some soldiers used it in referring to all Vietnamese. The rumor was that the term actually meant "hairy creature from the jungle" and was originally used by the Vietnamese to describe Americans. They also called us "big nose" and "cat eyes."

The Pilots

During our down time at the company area, we would all spend the hours in various ways. Parsons and I remembered Wiegand being a "Jesus nut freak." The "Jesus nut" held the rotor head on the helicopter. When he preflighted, postflighted, or had any spare time between missions, Wiegand was always on top of the mast scrutinizing the nut. We never were really sure why he did that. Also, he and Sutton were always fighting over the volume of Sutton's Beach Boys music. When they did this, I would rip up the volume of my Ray Price country and western music. All the Yankees would go berserk. They hated it. While we were occupied with our music, we had one unfortunate Firebird pilot who always had a terrible case of hemorrhoids. He sat naked in a pan of medicine to soak them. I assumed he had even more severe pain when the "pucker factor" increased during a hot gun run! Every time I saw this pilot squatting in his pan of medicine, I was reminded of where the Firebirds got their name. A previous commander's wife had named the gunship platoon from Stravinsky's 1919 version of "the Firebird." We were, after all, men of culture. We were so sophisticated, we actually stepped out of the showers before we peed!

Parsons spent quite a bit of his spare time at the Officers' Club. It was run by a young Vietnamese girl named Mary, who nicknamed Parsons, "Mop." The word *mop* is Vietnamese for large or fat. She told Parsons it meant "big guy." Parsons also had the nickname of "Killer Whale." One day Parsons was lying on the beach, and Wilber Latimer and Leopold took him some "alcoholic resupply." Leopold told him, "Jesus Christ, Parsons! I could not tell if that was you or a beached whale lying there. You had better get back in the club before someone comes along and harpoons your ass!" From then on, the nickname stuck.

Richard Taylor was the resident connoisseur of liquor for the Firebirds. He only drank the best booze—until it ran out. Then he would lower his standards and drink "rot gut" with the rest of us. He also had a penchant for lobster. He kept boiled lobster in the icebox and was constantly trying to get me to try some. Being a country boy from Texas, I had never seen one of the critters before. They resembled a grown-up version of what we found in muddy ditches back home, and I damn sure was not going to put any of that in my mouth. The hootch maids could supply lobster for about two dollars a sackful. I just did not know what I was missing!

Carson and Parsons were the intellectuals of the Firebirds. They knew how to play chess and spent hours contemplating their respective moves. Since I was just an old Texas farm boy, I was impressed. Only the smartest guys back home played checkers.

Shawn Hannah, as far as I recall, was the only religious man we had in the Firebirds. He regularly spent some of his time in prayer and reflection. He prayed before each flight. On May 5, 1968, Hannah was shot down in flames. While he was hiding and trying to evade the NVA, he really put the prayers into high gear. I was proud of him. It must have worked, because he made it back OK.

Some of the pilots drank hard every night. After several missions, I concluded that I was too scared to be flying with a hangover because it made me feel less secure. I did drink on the nights I didn't have to get up early or was not on standby. Even though I was sober, I would still stay in our Officers' Club to watch the action. On a busy night, the beer cans would start flying through the air like mortar rounds. Many of these guys were not old enough to drink back in the States. This beer, usually a Filipino brand, was rumored to be laced with formaldehyde. The heavy drinkers put enough away that there would have been no need to embalm them if they were killed.

Our club was just a few feet from the South China Sea, and on some days it had a beautiful view. Notwithstanding the tremendous view, the aroma of the place was a whole different matter. The odor was similar to an old soiled bar towel. Even the strong ocean breeze could not mask the stench of stale beer and puke!

We had some low tables which were placed end to end and wet down with beer. The poor fool that drank too much was given lessons in "carrier landings." Being held by four strong guys, arms and legs, and slung down a beer-slicked table was really good fun—if you were not the one being thrown. One night, we had a new pilot who apparently did not appreciate this activity. He ran and got his pistol for protection and came back into the club. On the ocean side, we had a wide opening and at least one large window with no glass. It was amazing how fast people exited the club through every available opening when they saw the pistol. This new guy took a bullet to the foot while flying a slick shortly after this incident. He was sent to Japan and later returned to the company. He was really a nice guy; he just had no appreciation for carrier landings.

In our club, we also had a slot machine that, to my

knowledge, never paid a penny in winnings. One night a drunk executed the slot machine with his pistol. Years later, I figured out why the slot machine never paid off and why our food was so mediocre. After my tour, they had a huge scandal involving a bunch of sergeants, including the head sergeant of the army. At his trial, he accused General Westmoreland of being involved in the rip-off of officers' clubs and mess halls. Chu Lai was one of the three places they were ripping off, stealing the money that should have been spent on our food! This is one of the reasons I went to Vietnam weighing 185 lbs. and came home weighing 142 lbs. A bad case of nerves also contributed to my weight loss.

The Enemy

The kind of missions we flew (and the level of risk) depended on where we went after taking off from our base. In the area surrounding Chu Lai, we would confront small, poorly trained VC units that would often break and run. Usually, they were about as lethal as a bunch of school girls throwing marshmallows.

To the south, around Quang Ngai, we would encounter a Main Force VC unit that shot pretty straight and usually held its ground. But the terrain they held was flat, so they were at a distinct disadvantage fighting gunship helicopters. We fought this unit around the area where the My Lai massacre took place.

In the vicinity of Tam Ky and to its west, was another Main Force unit, just as good as the one around Quang Ngai. Occasionally, you would also bump into an NVA unit from the Second or Third NVA Infantry Divisions in this area. NVA regulars were highly disciplined, lethal opponents. I only saw the NVA break and run once. That was during the Tet Offensive when they were taking unbelievable casualties. Even then, they eventually stopped running and fought.

Northwest of Tam Ky was the Que Son Valley. The mountains surrounding it were so steep and rugged that it was said that goats would detour around them. But there were several NVA base camps on these steep mountains. In this valley, we would fight the regulars of the Second and Third NVA Divisions in some of the fiercest combat of the war. It was called "Death Valley" by many people, and helo pilots entered it at grave risk. Of the twelve pilots in my platoon from October 1967 through May 1968, eleven were wounded and one was captured. Most of this action took place in and around Death Valley. By late 1968, the remnants of at least forty helicopters would be scattered around this valley and adjacent areas.

The NVA divisions were stationed in the hills around Que Son and would emerge for approximately a week of fighting every month. It took about three weeks for them to haul in enough ammo, men, and material for one week of "Bang Bang." After that, they would retreat back into the mountains to resupply and regroup for the next battle. One reason why the fighting in Que Son Valley was so heavy was that it had the greatest concentration of population in the northern part of South Vietnam. This population was an important source of rice and soldiers, so the NVA was able to sustain more combat here than it could in other areas.

Up in the Air

Flying gunships consisted of a routine of "five minute standby" one day and "fifteen minute standby" the next. Every third day was supposed to be a day off. On fifteen minute standby, you could leave the flight line area and did not have to be ready to go at once; but on five minute standby, you were required to be dressed in clothes and have on boots at all times. We were also required to stay at the "standby hootch" located at the flight line. The company area, where our living hootches were located, was approximately three hundred yards from the flight-line. On most nights in Chu Lai, it was nearly impossible to get any sleep while on five minute standby. Jets were continually launched throughout the night, and the runway was directly in front of the standby hootch. Since the helicopter had to be in the air in five minutes when a call came, all the switches were set on these gunships. That way, all that was required for takeoff was to flip on the battery switch and hit the starter button.

Eight of us—four pilots and four crewmembers—slept in the standby hootch. When we were on five minute standby, the ringing of the phone always set off a frantic burst of activity that would have been comical, had it not been such a serious matter. Generally, the two aircraft commanders took the phone information in order to get map coordinates and radio frequencies of the ground unit under attack. Simultaneously, the other six would run to the gunships. To this day, Joe Bruce (one of my crew chiefs) and I laugh about how six people, half asleep, would simultaneously hit the small doorway at full speed. We really looked like the Keystone Cops! These phone calls caused the adrenaline to start pumping and the nerves jumping because you knew you were about to become a moving target. My normal reaction was to jump straight into the air when the phone rang, and my heart would always start beating wildly. One unforgettable night, we were dead asleep when a truly compassionate cook called down, offering to deliver something for us to eat. McCall gave this poor cook a ferocious cussing and offered to go to the company area and personally put holes in him with his .38 pistol. Simply by using the phone, the cook had set our nerves on edge. So many years later, it is difficult to relate the effects that a ringing phone had on the nerves at 3:00 A.M. It was even more alarming on a dark rainy night when we were covering the ground units operating in the mountains. One night, when some others were on standby duty, one poor pilot had an attack of nerves and vomited all over the hootch when the phone rang.

Kamikaze Carlock, the terror of flight school, did not exactly overwhelm the combat-experienced Firebirds. On my first mission (described in the prologue) I got so excited that I forgot to fire at the enemy. Anton, the aircraft commander on that mission, spent the next several weeks riding me hard. He told anyone who would listen that the military had spent a bunch of money training me for combat, but forgot to tell me to shoot the enemy.

Aside from the danger, flying in Vietnam was a lot different than what I'd experienced in flight school. One thing I had to adjust to during the first few missions was becoming familiar with the radio and the use of different frequencies. I avoided too much talking and found it somewhat confusing when a grunt commander would direct us to change our frequency to another grunt radio. The commander would inform us of the change by saying something like, "Change to Jack Benny," plus or minus a number. This "code" left me completely in the dark, because I was not familiar with Jack Benny! I had no idea that this comedian was "forever 39." Once this little detail was explained to me, and after I was screamed at by the aircraft commander a couple of times, I finally realized that, "Change to Jack Benny plus two," meant go to frequency forty-one. Apparently, the enemy did not know old Jack either, so they could not follow our conversation to the new frequency. Later on, after I made aircraft commander, a grunt once radioed to me to change to "Winchester," plus another number. I could not figure this one out and finally had to ask him outright what number he meant. He sarcastically shot back, "30-30." These codes weren't very complicated, but they worked. I should mention that infantrymen acquired the name "grunt" from the sound they made as they picked up their heavy packs. This is not a derogatory term, in any sense. I have only the highest regard for anyone who served in any infantry unit in Vietnam.

The Crews

Working with gunners was another new experience for me. Since the entire crew bunked together when on standby, we got to know each other fairly well. The enlisted guys thought there were several pilots who had single digit IQs. In return, the officers felt that most of the door gunners could easily be suicidal psychopaths.

Door gunners on the gunships suspended their M-60s on a rubber cord (called bungee cords) which allowed them to shoot the gun anywhere in any direction. The gunners had a safety strap that allowed them to move around in the gunship at the same time. They could stand on the skids and shoot under the helicopter or, on a Hog, stand out on the rocket pods and shoot. Bob Burroughs tells the story of how a gunner with muddy feet was standing on a skid shooting. As he made a hard break, the gunner's foot slipped, and the gunner was dangling from the side of the helicopter with his finger still pressing on the trigger of his M-60. While hanging precariously out of the door, he shot the pilot's armored seat and through the window past his head.

Greg Palazzo, a gunner, got tired of the rocket motors burning his leg as he stood on the skid shooting his M-60. He wrote home and got his baseball catcher's shin guards sent to him in Vietnam. He wore them to help keep his legs from being burned.

After the war, my crew chief Joe Bruce once asked me if I remembered a certain captain that he didn't care for. His dislike went back to one night that he and Mike Aker were flying with this guy. All gunners and crew chiefs on gunships carried two or more barrels for their M-60s and an asbestos glove to take out the hot barrel and replace it with a cool barrel. In the dark of night, I have seen the crew shoot until the barrels glowed white. (Bruce has actually seen barrels become so white hot that he could see the bullets going down the barrel.) During the night attack, Aker pulled his red hot barrel and accidently threw it on a greasy rag which he had been using to clean the M-60 before takeoff. The rag caught fire. Bruce said, "You know, Aker never was that smart, and instead of kicking the burning rag out, he jumped on it trying to stomp out the blaze. Unfortunately, he forgot he had just refueled the ship and had fuel on his pants!"

When I heard that, I started laughing because I knew exactly what the captain said that upset Bruce so badly. Bruce admitted, "Yeah, I guess he was right, maybe I should have thrown Aker out." Instead, Bruce helped his friend put out the fire. With all the hydraulic fluid, tear gas (CS) grenades, frag grenades, smoke grenades, and ammo, a fire inside a gunship could certainly reduce life expectancy. A night landing, in an enemy area with your gunner serving as a lighted flare, could also present a few problems. After Bruce and Aker put out the flames, the captain told everybody over the radio what a dumb crew he had.

Bruce once got chewed out by our CO for painting a slogan on the bottom of my helicopter. His art work consisted of the words, "SAT CONG" in big bold letters on the bottom of the gunship. "Sat Cong" was Vietnamese for "kill VC." The CO admonished Bruce and told him his actions were "very unmilitary." Bruce merely said that was what he thought he was paid to do. Because the gunships were always overloaded, the skids were bent out. It was a real trick to write anything on the underside of one of these gunships. Maybe that slogan was the reason the VC were always trying to shoot the crap out of us. I guess they were insulted.

Burroughs once had a difficult time with a new gunner who had recently come from an infantry unit. One day, in the middle of an attack, Burroughs noticed the guy was just standing at the door and not firing his M-60. After they landed, Burroughs asked him if something was wrong with his machine gun. The inexperienced man replied, "I didn't see anybody to shoot at." Burroughs patiently explained to him that most of the time he would not see anyone. His job was to "make Charlie duck." He was to just keep them down and occupied with saving their skins. That way, they would not be able to make life dangerous for our side.

The next day they went out again, and once more the door gunner saw only trees and bushes, not human targets. Burroughs, using stronger language than the previous day, spelled out the door gunner's duties. He also threw in an added comment for emphasis. "You don't fire the gun, and your ass is back out there humping through the rice paddies with the infantry units." Burroughs remembered that this particular explanation worked like magic. Afterward, the only problem they had was to get the guy to quit shooting. He fired non-stop!

We had a door gunner from Tennessee who appeared to be very young. From a prior conversation with him, I knew he was about two beers short of a full six pack. When I first met him, he told me about his girlfriend at Chu Lai village. After talking to him, I asked someone else where the village was located. To this day, there is not a real village called Chu Lai, just a few hootches. Chu Lai, the military base, was a huge complex in 1967 with an army division, marine infantry, Korean infantry, army and marine aviation units. However, at that time, the enlisted men swore there was only one house of ill repute anywhere around, and it had one little fat Vietnamese girl about fourteen or fifteen, plus the old mamasan who ran the place. They said when the line got too long, the old woman would pitch in to keep the customers happy. I have to admit I did go down, one time, just to check on the rumors of immorality. Sure enough, there was a line of soldiers down Highway 1 out of this one hootch. This guy from Tennessee was in love with the young hooker.

For some reason, this lovesick kid from Tennessee could not keep his M-60 machine gun working while flying. It was sort of like a single shot machine gun. Anton, Wiegand, and McCall told me to stand him at attention, chew him out, and tell him that his machine gun better operate on the next mission. (Twenty-five years later, they had a good laugh when they finally revealed to me that this same gunner had previously threatened to kill Wiegand. They neglected to tell me this small detail prior to me standing the kid at attention!) I did as I was told, and the next day, while flying with Anton and me, the gunner's machine gun worked just fine. When we landed back at Chu Lai, the gunner told me over the intercom that he had a "slight problem." As we shut down the helicopter, I turned my head and saw he had nearly shot the aluminum door pole completely in two. This demolished door pole was inches from my head! Wordlessly I passed him upon exiting the helicopter. As I glanced in his direction, he had a smile on his face. This actually scared the other pilots and our commanding officer. The CO had the kid shipped out of the company immediately, and from that day forward, I religiously wore a ballistic flight helmet (allegedly a bullet proof brain bucket). Most pilots did not wear it because of the weight. To keep from getting neck pain, I then had to wear a flak jacket so the collar would help hold up the helmet. Also, I never stood anyone else at attention in my army career.

I had another unsettling "initiation" during those first few days that I had completely forgotten about until twenty-five years later. At our reunion, Ray Foley, a crew chief, was telling me a story about how he gave a new peter pilot a warm welcome to Vietnam. A crew member could position the M-60 machine gun in such a way that the brass casings would spray out on the pilots. This brass was so hot, it would stick to the skin as it hit. It would also burn a smoking hole in a uniform. One day, he decided to welcome a new peter pilot to the Firebirds. Foley fired his machine gun in the required position, and this poor new peter pilot suddenly had hot brass sticking on his neck like ticks. The new pilot promptly and loudly, with extremely colorful language, raised holy hell. The pilots were strapped in so tight to the armored seats that it was impossible to get the searing bits of metal off their skin. They just had to wait until the stuff cooled!

As Foley told his story, he started to slow down and think. Suddenly, it dawned on him. The peter pilot he had pulled this stunt on was me!

Chapter Three

FIREBIRD TALES

••

"It seemed like a war to me!"

I HAD BEEN IN THE COUNTRY A COUPLE OF WEEKS WHEN I HAD MY MOST TERRIFYING MISSION WHILE IN VIETNAM. OTHER MISSIONS CAME CLOSER TO COSTING ME MY LIFE, BUT NONE CAME AS CLOSE TO SCARING ME TO DEATH.

WE WERE GIVING AIR support for a unit of the First Cavalry. During this particular engagement, the medical evacuation helicopters (medevacs) had been hauling wounded all day. Medevac helicopters were regular Hueys modified to carry stretchers. There was a huge red cross painted on the side which was supposed to mark it as a noncombatant, but which actually made a nice target for enemy gunners. As a result, the medevacs were all shot up and unflyable due to combat damage. As night approached, there were no more available medevacs, and they had already hauled out forty wounded. I was flying peter pilot with Wiegand in the lead gunship. Anton and Parsons were flying wing. Suddenly, we heard the First Cavalry commander crying and sobbing over the radio. He had to move his remaining men

OCTOBER 9, 1967

Latin American guerrilla leader Che Guevara was shot and killed by Bolivian army troops near Vallegrande. Guevara was 39 years old.

out of the small valley back into the Que Son Valley. With nightfall coming, time was running out for the ground troops. Wiegand immediately made the decision to jettison his rocket pods. These rocket pods were held on the helicopter with explosive bolts. You could merely flip a switch and—no more rocket pods. We had already expended all forty-eight rockets on the known enemy positions. I asked him, "What for?" and he said he was leaving Vietnam and needed a Distinguished Flying Cross! I gaped at him in disbelief. I know my heart stopped. For the rest of my life, I will never forget the big grin on Wiegand's face as he made that statement. He was going in to get the wounded. Our gunships were not routinely used for rescue missions because of a lack of power, even with the rocket pods gone.

Wiegand and I both remember the grunt who was crying over the radio saying that all his people were in the tree line, and he had the only friendly troops in the area. Wiegand understood that to mean the "wounded" were in the tree line. I understood it to mean "all Americans" were there which put all our guys to my left. After jettisoning the rocket pods and starting a nearly inverted descent into the landing zone, the NVA automatic weapons opened up on us. I was so scared, I nearly went into convulsions. A few seconds later I stopped breathing completely! As we flew into the small rice paddy, Wiegand had me on the flight controls with him in case he was shot.

I glanced to my left and saw that the grunts were knee deep in mud and were attempting to carry four shattered bodies to the helicopter. Then I glanced to the right front of the helicopter facing the jungle, and at about the two o'clock position, I saw a rifle sticking out of the jungle. The rifle was about twenty yards from our helicopter. Instantly, I tensed so violently that I either tore or strained a chest muscle. My butt was so "puckered up" that it would have taken a sledgehammer to drive a finishing nail up my ass. I just knew the infantry commander said all the friendlies were to my left. We had only been on the ground ten to twenty seconds by now. The seconds seemed like hours! I attempted to pull the intercom button to scream, "Gooks! Two o'clock!" but my finger would not budge. I sat there completely paralyzed and glared wild-eyed at death! I thought I was going to die. As I tried to focus, I could see three or four rifles jutting out from the darkened jungle. To this day, I am convinced if I had screamed my message, the door gunner on the right side of the gunship would have killed whoever was there behind the rifles. Later we realized that several of our grunts were standing there. I did not know this until after we had cleared the area.

To further add to my horror, as Wiegand made a hover check, he decided we did not have the power to clear the jungle ahead. He then calmly hovered backward in the LZ and all the while, I still could not make the radio call. My finger wouldn't move! Wiegand coolly proceeded to mow down the jungle as we left and cracked out a chin bubble (the Plexiglas in front of my feet). This entire time Anton was shooting the hills all around us.

Twenty-five years later, Wiegand said that any dumb-ass should have known if you saw a rifle it had to be an American or else they would have shot the hell out of us. I did not realize this, because it was the first time I had ever sat in a rice paddy. Wiegand also asked if I remembered Anton buzzing around over us strafing the area with bullets and singing a tune over the radio the whole time. Anton was always singing during missions. All I did remember was being petrified, and my chest hurting for several weeks from a pulled muscle after this experience.

As we pulled out and gained altitude, I remember the

crew chief saying, "Don't look around!" Of course, I did. My wife, who was my fiancée at the time, was a Catholic and had given me a Saint Christopher medal to wear for good luck. One of the grunts we had picked up was wearing a medal identical to mine except that his chest below it was blown away. I remember thinking that his medal didn't bring him much protection. Apparently, the blood had stuck the medal to what was left of his chest. That was the first time I looked at a mangled body. Wiegand had taken me on one hell of a joyride! I could not believe it, but we did make it back to Chu Lai all in one piece.

P and L Missions

We weren't always shooting VC when we were in the air. Sometimes we were "killing time" in the choppers. In Fort Worth, Texas, there is a Certified Public Accountant who was a Green Beret in Vietnam at a special forces camp southwest of Chu Lai. One day (clearly forgetting that I was a helicopter pilot), he said the hardest part about living with the Vietnamese was trying to calm down the irate dads after those crazy helicopter pilots scared their daughters who were bathing in the creeks. This brought on a good laugh when it dawned on him that I was a helicopter pilot in the same area.

My first month in Vietnam, I was nearly killed in what could have been a low level mid air collision of four gunships. My comrades at arms were spooking the girls out of the creeks during their evening baths. The Vietnamese girls were terrified by the noise the helicopters made and would generally break and run instead of staying in the water. On this particular day, we had four gunships out nosing around. As two of the gunships were low level buzzing the young maidens, we popped over a tree line. The other gunships were low level on the other side. Had we had a four-helicopter mid-air collision, I can only imagine the letters the army would have sent home to our mothers:

> *Dear Mom:*
>   *We regret to inform you that your courageous son was turned into a crispy critter in a flaming mass of helicopter debris. His actions on a top secret P&L mission were over and above the normal call of duty.*

Hopefully they wouldn't have told our moms that P&L stood for Peep and Lust! I have a vague memory that whenever the guys would go chase the bathers, it would shock my pious soul! I have assured my three daughters that I never did this after I became an aircraft commander.

You could do this kind of nonsense in the VC areas, but in the Que Son Valley, it would have taken a certified nut to mess around close to an NVA unit. Once we started flying primarily in the Que Son Valley, we did not chase the girls around. We worried more about staying alive.

Fatal Errors

On October 13, I was flying peter pilot in lead with Mc-Call. He told a grunt commander over our FM radio about some female woodcutters we had spotted. Our wing man in the other gunship, who I will leave unnamed, did not have an operating FM radio. This proved fatal. The grunt commander told us to mark the workers with smoke so he could catch and interrogate them. Dropping smoke by a gunship was usually a signal that you were taking fire in the vicinity of the smoke. The wing man, seeing the smoke, proceeded to blast the woodcutters with the miniguns.

OCTOBER 12, 1967

The St. Louis Cardinals won the World Series, defeating the Boston Red Sox in seven games.

Quite a few were killed or wounded before we got things straight.

Our helicopters had FM radios for communicating with the grunts and any ground bases. A UHF radio was used for communicating with other helicopters and airports. The gunships generally used VHF frequency for talking to each other. Many times in the pandemonium of an air strike with NVA bullets blasting through and around the helicopter, my headphones screeched with the garbled noise of up to three different intercom voices and three radio frequencies at the same time. Sometimes my own voice was added into the confusing mixture. Eventually, I got to where with one hand, I could turn all the external radios off with a flick of my wrist.

I actually began to get used to being shot at—if one can ever really reach that point. I remember Anton telling me that it was a great experience to be shot at and missed. I even decided I was macho again. I purchased an M-2 carbine from a slick crew chief. It was cut down in pistol form and carried in a holster that swiveled to allow you to push

October 16, 1967

WE HAD TWO RATTLER CREW MEMBERS PRACTICING QUICK DRAWS WITH THEIR PISTOLS. AN ACCIDENTAL DISCHARGE KILLED ONE OF THEM.

down on the handle, flip the safety and blast full automatic. It had three custom made banana clips that held thirty rounds each. I believe it added to my invincible image!

This, along with my bowie knife strapped to my leg, allowed me to strut around like John Wayne. The company commander spotted me at breakfast with the wicked-looking weapon on my leg and could not believe it. I agreed to do a real quick bargain sale outside the company to stop him from confiscating the thing. Then I bought a .44 magnum pistol from Crew Chief Bruce to go along with my .38 pistol. (I later replaced the .38 with a silencer-equipped 9 mm sten machine gun.) With my two pistols, I looked like a wild west gunfighter. I also had a .45 caliber grease gun (a World War II machine gun) that I sometimes carried. Looking back, I believe I carried the nasty ornaments as a security blanket. Some days I had the feeling that I was "bad to the bone." In my mind at least, all the weapons made me look bad and feel good. Every few months, the brass would crack down and threaten everyone with a court martial for carrying unauthorized weapons. We would hide our guns in a bunker until the heat was off. A few weeks later, we would dig them out and carry them again. In several of my letters home, I stated that I used to shoot the pistols out of the window at target areas while flying. I have no memory of this but Hannah said we used to do it all the time. I do remember blasting the .45 caliber grease gun out the window because I had straight tracer rounds for it and the big .45 caliber tracer round would ignite the enemy structures (hootches) in a second. It was like shooting flaming arrows at them.

A Close Shave

I was sent to get my first haircut since my arrival in Vietnam. It was not a pleasant experience. The old man, whom we called Mr. Charles, wielded a thin straight razor to do his dangerous work. He would insert this blade into the ear to clean it out.

OCTOBER 17, 1967

Hanoi announced they were forming an organization in the United States to encourage the war protesters.

I swear it felt like he pushed it in all the way to my eardrum. Then, he would stick the same razor deep inside the nose to thin the hairs in each nostril. This was more excitement than I enjoyed, so the next time I went to the old geezer, I took my .38 pistol. I unsnapped the holster and kept my hand ready the whole time. I only hoped that if he tried to do me in with that razor, I could at least get off a dying shot! After I had endured a few of these "trim-ups," I always had my hair cut at either Hill 35, LZ Baldy, or the special forces base in Da Nang. They had American barbers there, and my nerves just could not take making an adventure out of every haircut. The whole time that I was in 'Nam, I only got a haircut when I received a direct order to do so.

I might mention that Mr. Charles never returned to work after the Tet Offensive. They found his body entangled on the perimeter wires at Chu Lai. He was apparently a VC officer.

Friendly Fire

I was hit by friendly fire several times, often from our own helos. This was a real risk when making a combat assault (escorting slicks that were landing troops) into a rocky LZ area. With fifteen slicks (thirty M-60 machine guns firing), two gunships, and all the bullets and rocket shrapnel they put out, the metal ricocheted everywhere off the rocks.

October 17, 1967

MY GUNSHIP TOOK SEVERAL HITS FROM THE DOOR GUNS OF A SLICK HELICOPTER.

On one mission, we were providing close support for some grunts close to Hill 35. Because of the location of our ground troops, the Firebirds were forced to make attack runs directly over several army tanks and APCs (armored personnel carriers). Empty bullet casings and metal links from our guns dropped onto the tanks and APCs as we passed overhead. The Americans thought we were firing at them and immediately started shooting at us. Fortunately, a grunt commander frantically radioed for everyone to stop—NOW! He probably saved us all from a real "internal conflict," since it was our unofficial policy to return friendly fire with friendly fire—we smiled as we shot back!

Another time, a grunt at LZ Ross shot a round into the tail boom of my gunship as I was on final approach to refuel. I saw the muzzle flash and could identify the actual bunker where the shot was fired. I circled back out and lined up on the bunker for a rocket run, then radioed in to the infantry commander that I was going to "fix that dopehead." He started screaming, "Don't shoot!" and assured me he would handle the problem immediately. The Firebirds had a reputation of always returning fire—no matter who did the shooting! At the time, I really did have every intention of firing my rocket. This was in January, after a lot of heavy fighting and my nerves were not in the best condition. For some reason, that grunt infuriated me!

The ARVN (Army of the Republic of Vietnam, pro-

nounced Arvin) was a great source of friendly fire. One
of the first night missions I flew in Vietnam, we passed
over the province capital, Tam Ky, at around 1,500 feet.
The friendly South Vietnamese soldiers (ARVNs) shot
about 100 friendly tracer rounds at us. McCall said that
they did this every night. The ARVNs always claimed to
be clearing their rifles. I asked him why didn't we shoot
back? He said that if they ever hit him he would, that he
didn't give a damn if they court-martialled him or not. On
clear nights, we flew around the town. We always turned
our lights off, so they could only shoot at the sound.

Eventually, I had enough of this. One night (after I
made aircraft commander), I was flying a single gunship
along Highway One to Chu Lai. In a foul mood as I approached Tam Ky, I told my peter pilot, "Put it on hot and
get ready." When the ARVN soldiers unloaded on us out
of their compound, we returned about 2,000 rounds of
miniguns right back at them. Miller said he was about ten
miles behind me and saw me go low level with no lights
and land at Chu Lai without calling the control tower.
This ensured that there would be no record of the time I
landed. As far as I know, the ARVNs never shot at a helicopter at night again. At least, they tried not to shoot at a
Firebird gunship.

Tam Ky also had a lot of VC. Several weeks after I arrived at Chu Lai, a Chinook (large two-rotor helicopter)
accidentally dropped a sling load of artillery shells there
and started a fire which ignited a VC grenade factory in
the town.

One day I took a hit as we flew across Tam Ky, and my
gunner saw the muzzle flash at the back of the Catholic
church in town. I assume that some Charlie decided to
use the church for cover. The round tore up a bunch of the
electrical equipment in the chopper.

The most frustrating kind of "friendly" fire was that we

received from the VC who would fire at us from
"friendly" areas, knowing we wouldn't shoot back. Many
times as we came in on the final approach at night to the
refueling point at Tam Ky, the VC would sneak one of
their men into an area of hootches near the perimeter to
shoot at us. I always refused to let Bruce or Aker return
fire because we were so close to the provincial capital
headquarters building. One day, as we were coming in on
final approach to Tam Ky for refueling, I felt the helicopter lurch. Bruce and Aker, frustrated at being shot at
and not being able to shoot back, began to laugh as they
told me they had shoved a large hunk of metal out the
door of the gunship. It was a link from a tracked vehicle's
drive train and was extremely heavy. Bruce made a perfect hit on the hootch which the sniper used, and it caved
in the entire roof.

As we sat on the ground and refueled, I could actually
peer around my armored seat and see the damaged hut
just outside our perimeter. I vividly remember sitting
there and thinking how I would feel if I was sitting at
home with my family at the evening meal, and the whole
top of my home came crashing in around me. However, I
do not remember ever getting shot at while landing there
again.

One time, the Firebirds were actually chewed out by
our CO for firing at a village which higher powers had
decided was friendly, even though Charlie was constantly
shooting from it. My gunship had a .30 caliber round
fired up through the ammo chute that ran to the miniguns.
Still, two gunners and two crew chiefs were grounded for
shooting back at Charlie. The pilots were responsible for
where the gunners fired, but we were probably short of
pilots because none of them was grounded.

Later (in late December), we received maps that indicated "no fire" zones. In these areas, we could not shoot

at anyone even if they stood in the open firing at us. We would have to make a radio call and receive permission to shoot back. Actually, we paid about as much attention to these maps as we would to a hummingbird fart! I am real sure the VC got a good laugh, too. The brass needed to get real!

Foo Gas

On October 18, the NVA attacked a fire support base and were able to get inside the perimeter. We fired the mini-guns at the top of the bunkers to knock them off. This fire support base was located in the Que Son Valley. This was the first time I saw "foo" gas used. Foo gas consisted of a fifty-five gallon drum filled with naptha and diesel fuel. At night, when ignited with a blasting cap, it made quite an impressive fireworks show, killing anything in a fifty-yard radius.

Fire support bases were surrounded by several rolls of barbed wire and trip wire flares. Land mines and foo gas were added between and under the barbed wire. All this usually slowed down anyone trying to sneak in.

One night, while flying with McCall in a minigun gun-ship, it was pitch dark and raining. I could not see a thing. McCall could see like a bat in the dark. He told me to shoot outside the perimeter of the fire support base. I did as I was told and promptly hit a barrel of foo gas. The grunts at the base were highly pissed. They thought the commies were crawling around the wire checking for weak points. The foo gas I set off lit up their entire position. The next day they had to go into the mine field and bury another barrel.

Later on in my tour, when I was an aircraft comman-

OCTOBER 20, 1967

An all-white federal jury convicted seven Ku Klux Klan members with conspiracy in the 1964 murder of James Chaney, Michael Schwerner, and Andrew Goodman.

der, I never let my peter pilot shoot close to Americans when it was dark and rainy. I should have admitted to McCall that night that I could not see a thing. Instead, I blasted away.

On October 19, the weather was miserable. We were told to stay at the company area and haul sandbags up on the roof of our hootch. A typhoon was expected to hit, so we were trying to keep everything from blowing away. I wrote home that I hoped the storm would blow all the choppers away. I had already grown tired of this combat hero stuff. The following morning, the area north of Chu Lai was pretty well torn to pieces. It looked as if a giant lawnmower had chewed up about a two-mile-wide strip. I was disappointed, myself. Neither the hootch, nor the helicopters were damaged, much less blown far, far away.

Frogs

On October 20, I was flying with Anton in a Frog gunship. Prior to this day, I had flown the Frog several times while making airstrikes and also had some experience with it in flight school. On this mission, we caught a Charlie running down a rice paddy dike with a weapon. Anton screamed, "Get him!" I put a perfect box on him. I shot short, long, left, and right. Since everything missed, my effort only speeded up the guy, who now resembled O. J. Simpson dashing through an airport. Anton got really steamed because neither I nor the door gunner could hit the guy. Naturally, the lead helicopter got credit for the kill. Suddenly, we took a hit in the tail boom and turned toward a village where the automatic weapons fire was located. By this time, all gunship tactics were forgotten, and we once again engaged in a wild west shootout. As we ripped low level down main street (the only path through the village), I was doing real damage with the 40 mm cannon. I knocked out the top of a hootch about seventy-five yards in front of us and saw a flock of chickens scrambling in all directions. For some strange reason, I went for the chickens with the 40 mm, and we passed low level through the feathers. Anton was completely furious by then. He stormed for a week about his stupid peter pilot who massacred chickens. My only response was that I was going for the VC food supply. At least to my knowledge, the helicopter wasn't hit by a drumstick.

By this time, Anton and I had become good friends.

Anton had 40 mm grenades explode inside the grenade launcher mechanism two days in a row. They finally discovered that the cannon barrel was bent. This could have blown the pilot's legs off. In certain areas, we were told to shoot all water buffaloes because the VC used them just like trucks to haul supplies. I remember one day, I made a perfect 40 mm shot on the rump of a big buffalo. I told everyone that sucker could have won the Kentucky Derby.

Parsons told an interesting story of his shooting the 40 mm grenade launcher from a Frog gunship. This is in his own words:

> *I remember one of only three or four times that I flew as peter pilot in our Frog with the M-5 40 mm grenade launcher. Again we were west-northwest of Tam Ky in a village. We were directed to hit the vil-*

lage and bunkers around it. I was with Anton. There were NVA running through the hootches and coming out of the bunkers and di-ding (Vietnamese for running) back into the jungle. We thump-gunned several before they got to the thick jungle. Then we set the place on fire. After about three or four passes, my round counter indicated about five rounds left. There was one hootch burning furiously by itself which was a great distance from the main village and within about a hundred yards of the rice paddies.

As we broke around, I spotted this one NVA (whose uniform and attached brush camouflage was smoking from the fire) as he came running from the hootch and straight for the rice paddy full of water. We were out of 2.75s (rockets) so it was up to me, and I knew that there were not many forty mike-mikes (40 mm grenades) left. I deflected the sight back behind him and added some elevation (better known as wild ass guess and Kentucky windage). I squeezed the twin handles and trigger . . . CHUNK, CHUNK, CHUNK . . . and that was all that was left. The guy kept running and was almost at the edge of the lake-like rice paddy. It seemed as though it took about five minutes for those rounds to impact. Just as the guy leapt in the air at the edge of the paddy, intending to douse out his fire, the rounds impacted. One hit about ten meters back from the edge, the next simultaneously at the spot from which he had leapt, and the third just over the edge of the dike. Dust, gray smoke and a water plume obliterated the area for a minute as we dove down and over the spot. We skimmed the impact point and saw that the only evidence of the NVA was the red stained area of water in the paddy.

Vertigo

I soon had another scary incident that nearly resulted in my demise. We were flying at night. It was raining, and there was no visible horizon. McCall always flew the lead gunship at night in the rain with his red rotating beacon flashing. Wing gunships did not use their lights. When it was a rainy night, the peter pilot (myself) watched the instruments in case the aircraft commander got vertigo. Vertigo is a condition in which you lose all sense of balance and cannot tell whether or not you are upside down, turning, or straight and level. If you get vertigo, you naturally have a tendency to crash.

As we flew through the driving rain northwest into the Que Son Valley, I kept peering up at the rotating beacon of the lead helicopter. We should have been following at least several hundred meters behind the lead gunship. I glanced up at least five or six times before I relayed over the intercom, "How close are we?" The aircraft commander (A/C) said, "Can you tell?" Sensing disaster, I grabbed the cyclic (main control) and jerked it full against the stop. Our rotor blades where about to hit the tail rotor of the lead gunship. Needless to say, I nearly had another strained chest muscle. The aircraft commander said, "We were close, weren't we?"

Later, I was told the reason I made aircraft commander so fast was that they knew I would not go out and kill my crew in some goofy accident. I made aircraft commander in three months—the same day Anton got shot down and captured.

I always figured good pilots never got vertigo. Then, near the end of my tour, I was flying a slick at night to make an emergency resupply of ammunition to an infantry unit under attack. It was out in the middle of the Que Son Valley and a thin cloud layer was about 800 to

1,000 feet off the ground. A flare helicopter was making a drop to light up the area for the grunts. I was above the clouds and was going under them to decide if I wanted the flares shut off and do the resupply in total darkness. This was the preferred method. However, you would not have good night vision immediately after the last flare died out. Also, you had to watch for burned-out flares still suspended from parachutes. We always dodged them, and I never heard of a chopper hitting one with a rotor blade. As I was getting ready to descend through the clouds, I saw a hole which gave a very strange sensation. The flares underneath the clouds let a glow penetrate from this hole in the clouds. It was like a pillar of light shining up. I had a brand new peter pilot, and I told him to watch the instruments as I ripped a hot rod, spiraling turn and descended into the pillar of light. The next thing I felt was a severe vibration through the cyclic. I glanced at the instruments. I had the helicopter nearly inverted in a nose down position. I managed to pull the nose up before busting into the ground. I radioed the grunt commander to tell him to turn on his strobe light and flew straight into the LZ. Then we kicked off the ammo. I figured that if I could live through that maneuver, I would not worry about Charlie shooting me at that time. Every nerve was stimulated. I was told later that some helicopters did not vibrate through the cyclic in a nose down banking maneuver. I am convinced that this vibration saved my life.

On the way back, I asked the new peter pilot what he thought of my flying. He said I was really hot! I did not hide anything from the new kids whom I trained and proceeded to tell him that I had nearly killed his ignorant ass. It was his job to watch those instruments and take the controls if there was a problem. Some helicopter pilots shared that they had been told in flight school never to descend through a hole in the clouds because it was easy to develop vertigo while inside the cloud. No one had ever told me that!

Damaging Government Property

Firebird crew chief Ray Foley was wounded and then nearly court-martialled for damaging government property—himself! While in a gunship during an airstrike, he was shot slightly below the knee with a lead bullet. Most military rounds are steel. His wound bled a little, but didn't hurt so he didn't bother to go to the doctor. After several days, he developed blood poisoning. When he finally went to the doctor, the flight surgeon threatened to court-martial him. The lead bullet had shattered, and small pieces were lodged under the kneecap. The battalion flight surgeon then threatened to cut the leg off to teach him a lesson.

An incident occurred on October 28 that nearly led to my undoing at a later date. The gunships were scrambled and as Anton and I fired up our helo, with the gunner and crew chief standing outside as safety observers, I noticed that the turbine engine temperature gauge was past its maximum limit. I kept glancing at Anton and looking over my shoulder at the crew chief. I as-

October 23, 1967

A HOMETOWN FRIEND WHO WAS STATIONED AT CHU LAI CAME BY TO SEE ME. HE WAS A TOUGH MARINE WHO HAD ALREADY BEEN WOUNDED TWICE. AS WE TALKED, HE BEGAN TO CRY AND TOLD ME A COUPLE OF HIS FRIENDS HAD BEEN GRAVELY WOUNDED. IN THE MIDST OF THE FIGHTING, THEY GRABBED HIS ARM AND BEGGED HIM NOT TO LET THEM DIE. I COULDN'T THINK OF ANYTHING TO SAY.

OCTOBER 24, 1967

Back in the World, hippies staged a big protest against Dow Chemical for manufacturing napalm. The police came in and knocked a few of them in the head.

sumed that the gauge was incorrect, but read the temperature to Anton over the intercom anyway. He immediately tried to shut the engine down, but couldn't. We later found that a fuel control valve was stuck open. As Anton kept trying to kill the engine, I saw the crew chief break and run. Being convinced that safety was the better part of valor, I bailed out of the gunship at a dead run. Apparently, Anton did not see me exit because I was waving at him from across the taxiway before he bailed out. The crew chief had seen the turbine engine get so hot that it burned the paint off the metal engine cowlings. Naturally he figured that the chopper was ready to explode.

Later, maintenance personnel repainted the cowling, waved their magic wand, and declared the gunship okay to fly without any major repair of the engine. On December 3, 1967, that same engine exploded in flight with me flying the helicopter.

The Demise of Dammit

Not all the minutes of all the days were so exciting. One boring day, on standby at the flight line, I built a gallows to hang the company commander. It was pretty sturdy and stood next to the flight line for several weeks until the CO heard about it and ordered its destruction.

The intended hanging was in retribution for the barbaric execution of our alcoholic monkey mascot, Clarence J. Dammit. Mr. Dammit lived on beer and C-rations.

Occasionally, some drunk would let him out of the cage and let him roam. One morning, I got up early to shave before flying. In the dark, I rounded a hootch and encountered Clarence J. Dammit sitting on the edge of the roof about twelve inches from my face with his fangs

October 28, 1967

WE HAD A DISCUSSION ABOUT HOW BAD THE FOOD WAS IN THE MESS HALL. SOMEONE PROPOSED THAT WE EAT CLARENCE.

fully extended. Under these circumstances, this damn monkey resembled a miniature King Kong. My heart stopped and I fell over in the sand.

Another day, I heard my puppy, Missey, screaming and howling. I ran out of the Firebird hootch and caught Clarence in the act of attempted rape. Parsons was concerned about Clarence's deviancy and somehow arranged for some nearby marines to bring their female monkey down to our club for a romantic interlude with Clarence. Clarence, who was probably drunk or hung over, could only muster enough energy to look at the marine monkey and play with himself. Some pilots considered it a disgrace to our unit to have such a perverted mascot.

On another occasion, Clarence got into Patrick's SOI bag. We used these to carry our code books, radio frequency books and morphine for our medical kits. When he was discovered at the scene of the crime, Clarence had his paws pointed up in the air and was happily dreaming about the land of the big bananas. He had eaten Patrick's morphine.

Parsons recalls that one night Clarence bit a pilot. The two drunks, Clarence and the pilot, fought it out. The pilot finally managed to attach a chain to Clarence's collar. He then drug Clarence to the edge of the South China Sea and, with Clarence hanging on the chain, began to twirl him around. He launched Clarence into the sea and made it clear that this was the end of Clarence J. Dammit, pervert. Parsons said he later stood next to the ocean, in the dark, and saw Clarence swim out, still drunk and plenty mad, looking for the pilot who had whirled him.

A lot of people were offended that the company commander, who had a separate hootch, had installed a flush commode. All of us peons used crude wooden outhouses that had half of a 55-gallon drum under each hole. A slick crew chief put Clarence into the commanding officer's hootch to greet him upon his return from a hard night of hanging out at the division Officers' Club. When the commander entered his hootch, Clarence frightened him badly. In a drunken state, he whipped out his pistol and promptly shot the commode to pieces in an attempt to eliminate Clarence. The monkey made a quick exit out of the hootch. He then made the fatal mistake of spending the night on top of the roof. The next morning, the CO came out with a pump shotgun. Each time Clarence peeked over the top, the commander ripped off a shot. After several shots, poor Clarence's luck ran out, and he and the roof suffered permanent damage.

Twenty-five years later, this commanding officer said that being our boss was the worst experience of his entire life! Carson wrote a poem after poor Clarence's demise entitled "Ode to Clarence," which was posted in the Officers' Club. This poem expressed our sorrow over poor Clarence's horrible ending. We made our mourning over poor Clarence obvious every time the offending officer entered the club. After he noticed the poem, the CO promptly had it taken down. Someone else wrote Clarence up for a Distinguished Flying Cross for his heroic bravery under fire from the enemy. The CO had this taken down, too. We then spent a lot of time looking for someone with taxidermy experience to stuff Clarence and enable us to mount him over the bar. Unfortunately, he started to smell fairly rank before we found anyone.

Camping Out

On October 30, while flying with McCall, we escorted a medevac helicopter into a grunt unit of the 101st Airborne. The NVA shot up both gunships with automatic weapons fire. The grunt commander took our names and promised us big medals. All we got was the lead the NVA put in our gunships.

An aviation company moved into Chu Lai to help support the 101st Airborne or the First Cavalry. They were such "bad dudes" they decided to rough it and set up their camp outside our base perimeter, even though there was plenty of room to park their helicopters inside the safety of our base.

That night, the VC made a diversionary attack, swooping down on two bridges that were manned by guards. The Firebirds flew out of Chu Lai in order to help the troops being attacked. Then other VC crept into the camp set up outside the perimeter and blew up five of the "bad dudes'" helicopters. Seven others were damaged. The next day some holes were dug outside the camp. The wrecked helos were pushed into them and then buried.

The Firebird crews actually

NOVEMBER 1, 1967

Secretary of Defense Robert McNamara, who bore much of the responsibility for getting us involved in Vietnam, turned against the war. President Johnson later nominated him as president of the World Bank, claiming that this was neither a demotion nor a shift in policy.

November 1, 1967

VICE PRESIDENT
HUBERT HUMPHREY
STOPPED BY CHU LAI.
HE HAD BEEN AT
YESTERDAY'S
INAUGURATION OF
NGUYEN VAN THIEU
AS PRESIDENT OF
SOUTH VIETNAM. WE
HAD TO STAND NEXT
TO THE GUNSHIPS THE
ENTIRE TIME FOR AN
IMMEDIATE LAUNCH IF
HE WAS ATTACKED.

had a good laugh. Our fellow aviators had been pretty stupid and had paid the price. At Chu Lai, we were not fighting a bunch of inexperienced farmers.

Around this time, I was flying with Wiegand, and McCall was lead. McCall got shot up on a gun run. He took a bullet through the floor and through the crew chief's water can. This can, used for drinking water, had a cork liner in it. Wiegand called McCall over the radio and asked "Are you O.K?" McCall answered "Yes, but we have some brown stuff flying around in the helicopter." Some smart mouthed slick pilot heard the radio calls and said "Check your pants." It was the cork flying around.

Commie Frogmen

Before dawn on November 2, I was flying peter pilot with Wiegand south along the coast to Duc Pho to engage in a large Romeo Foxtrot. Suddenly, our fire warning light lit up the entire cockpit as it started flashing. The gunner and crew chief stepped out on the skids checking behind the helicopter for smoke. McCall, in another gunship, fell back beside us and said over the radio that everything looked fine. He thought it was probably a defective warning light and told us to fly on to Duc Pho. I asked Wiegand what he was going to do, and he said he would rather take his chances on the ground. I totally agreed, so we landed on the beach next to the jungle. Being stranded on the lonely beach, I was worried about a human wave attack out of the trees and kept glancing at the ocean expecting any second to see a commie frogman. A slick flew in, picked us up, and later inserted troops until maintenance fixed the helicopter. Apparently, it was too early in the morning for Charlie to start any action.

Airbursts

On November 3, we were back down south at Duc Pho on a large Romeo Foxtrot inserting a lot of grunts. I was peter pilot to McCall, Mike Rogers was crew chief and Carl Fox was gunner. Wiegand was flying the wing gunship. We had already landed a flight load of grunts on the ground when we started receiving some .50 caliber anti-aircraft fire. All of a sudden, I saw a flash and heard a crashing explosion. The gunship made an abrupt lurch. I immediately assumed we were about to die. It happened so fast, though, I didn't have time to feel any fear. The next thing I knew, I felt a spine-jarring crunch. We were now perched on a rice paddy dike. Frantically, I was fighting to get out of the armored seat and then the door of the chopper. The smell of something burning, especially the smell of burning flesh, made you move mighty fast.

I stepped out on the skid, looked back into the blood-spattered chopper, and gaped at a remarkable, unreal scene. Fox was writhing and moaning with his uniform smoking, blackened, and torn. His boot was blown apart, along with his foot. The only thing I could think of was to grab Fox, put him over my shoulder, and get him away from the chopper. I stepped into the rice paddy and was promptly submerged up to my thighs. I was immobilized.

The gunship was no longer an option, and I was not about to drop Fox into the mud. Just then, Wiegand landed in front of our chopper and waved for me to get my ass over there. Rogers and McCall were injured, too. I stood there staring at them. I finally looked over, and spied a grunt medic scurry out of a tree line toward us. I didn't know if we were being shot at, but the guy was hunkered down and dashed toward us as if he was running for his life. The friendlies were about fifty meters away. The hostiles were about a hundred meters from the gunship. This medic dude was stepping lightly and didn't sink into the rice paddy. He grabbed Fox and loaded him on Wiegand's chopper. Wiegand's gunship immediately took off, because Fox needed quick attention.

The medic asked if I was hurt. I said, yes, I was hit in the arm. He pulled out his knife and cut the sleeve off a brand new set of jungle fatigues I had just gotten. He then curled his lip and took off running to help the others, leaving me stuck in the mud. My arm was numb, and I could not look for fear of it being gone. I gathered my courage and peeked down at my arm. I had shed one drop of blood for my country. One tiny piece of shrapnel had punctured me. The heat of the shrapnel had apparently numbed my arm!

The crash was caused by one of our rockets exploding exactly in front of Fox. The blast blew the landing skid in two and blew out the engine and the transmission cooling systems, and some other parts. A .50 caliber round hit the rocket, making it explode. The fuel cells were in pieces. Why the helicopter didn't explode in flight no one could figure out. The odds were that we should have flamed up like a Molotov Cocktail. I could only attribute my good fortune to clean living!

When the chopper's landing skid was blown in two, Fox caught the same blast with his body. Rogers spent a month in the hospital, recovering from all his puncture wounds. At the hospital, a very strange event happened. The doctor told me he could cut the shrapnel out of my arm, and I would be grounded for five days; or I could let the metal work its way out and continue to fly. One of two things happened. It was either one of my macho days, or I was in shock. Looking back, I'm sure it was shock because I told the doctor, "I want to fly!" McCall and I were given a day off, received a pat on the butt, and told to go "sic 'em."

I learned something else from my harrowing experience in the rice paddy. It was definitely best to "travel light." That day I sank into the muck to my thighs. The grunt medic stepped out on it and did not even sink. He barely even cracked the hard crust. Besides having Fox over my shoulder, I carried an armored chest protector (called a "chickenboard"), a flak jacket, ballistic helmet, bowie knife, two pistols, two big boxes of pistol ammo, a survivor radio, and a survival kit. I had to really tighten my belt up because all the crap I carried almost pulled my pants down. I swore that the next time I was in a rice paddy, I was going to be able to run like that grunt. When I did end up in the muck again, I was traveling much lighter and faster. At least I had learned one lesson!

Twenty-five years later, I talked to Fox on the phone. He kept asking who I was. Besides being blown to heck and being in VA hospitals on and off all these years, he thought everyone else on the helicopter was killed. I finally got up the nerve to ask him if he still had his legs. He said he did; and they still worked!

Parsons and McCall also once survived a .50 cal. anti-aircraft round in the rocket pod. This is Parsons's account:

> *McCall and I were flying at altitude over the Que Son Valley heading west toward Antenna Val-*

ley . . . when some grunt broadcast over the radio, "Attention . . . Be advised! Huey heading west toward LZ Ross . . . you are under fire by a .51 cal. located just to the northwest of Ross!" I turned and gave McCall a wide-eyed look (was this grunt talking about us?). Just as McCall turned to look at me, we took two .51 cal. hits . . . Thwack, Thwack! Rolling right and descending, the crew chief confirmed that we had been hit. One of the rounds caught us in the left pod of the Hog gunship, just missing one of the rocket warheads. The other hit higher up on the fuselage. Talk about luck! That guy must have been shooting from two "clicks" (kilometers) away. Would you believe that, up until that time, I had never thought about taking a round that might set off a bank of HE (high explosive) warheads! You think about getting shot . . . or getting shot down, but never about becoming an AIRBURST!

Joe Bruce recalls how a rocket nearly made an airburst out of his gunship one day. As he fired his M-60 machine gun, some of the links that held the bullets together, plus some brass (the bullet case), blew into the rocket tube. It stuck between the rocket's explosive head and its tube. When the rocket was fired, the rocket motor ignited but the rocket was stuck in the tube! Bruce screamed at the pilot to flip the switch to explode the bolts that held the rocket pods on the gunship. It didn't explode the bolt. Bruce took his machine gun and cut the bolts with machine gun bullets. One of his bullets bounced back and knocked a hole in the gunship. The CO chewed his ass for shooting his own chopper.

At one time, someone got concerned that static electricity would set off the rockets on the gunship, so each day they told us to go use them if we had not fired them on a combat mission. Supposedly, the electrical current from a flashlight battery would launch this type of rocket. A pilot from another helicopter unit in Vietnam was killed when the gunship behind him was struck by lightning, setting off a rocket. The rocket penetrated his armored seat. We even had a Firebird rocket that accidentally went off and blew a hole in the door of the gunship.

Maritime Operations

We used to fly to an area six miles south of Chu Lai where a river emptied into the ocean. We would then take target practice on sharks. I always thought the pilots who got too far out over the ocean were insane because they'd never make it back to shore if their engine failed. I'll bet the sharks would have been plenty happy to see us after they had all the rockets and machine guns shot at them! On one such mission, Parsons saw a Vietnamese guy in a bubble boat who was being trailed by a fourteen-foot shark. The pilots decided they needed to save the guy's life so they dove the gunship at the shark and started shooting. The Vietnamese guy assumed the gunship was going for him so he leapt into the water, joining the wounded shark and its relatives. I asked Parsons, "What happened?" He laughingly said, "Oh, you know . . . the guy jumped back in the boat."

Wiegand tells a story about how the Firebirds used a rocket to disable an oceangoing vessel. This took place on July 15, 1967, before I arrived. It is probably the only such incident involving helicopters and a ship. This ship, a Russian-built trawler, had enough supplies on it to equip two enemy regiments for a year. One interesting fact concerning this story is that two other aviation companies, the navy, and the Korean military all claim credit for this event.

The Firebirds arrived at the scene to witness two navy swift boats shooting at each other. Then they spotted the Russian-built ship under artillery flares apparently fired by the Koreans. After they got the Koreans to cease fire, the Firebirds attacked. They were led by David Ellingsworth. Wiegand was his peter pilot. They flew into the return fire from a quad- .50 caliber antiaircraft gun mounted on the fantail. The other gunships from the other aviation companies were not on station at this time. A Firebird rocket caused a secondary explosion from the .50 cal. ammo stacked on the deck of the ship. This put the antiaircraft gun out of commission. They also were very lucky, in that they punched the ticket of the guy who was supposed to blow the whole thing to kingdom come before it was captured.

Besides all the guns and ammo, the ship had five thousand pounds of TNT and plastic explosives rigged to detonate if necessary. The resulting explosion would have certainly taken a helicopter or two with it. When the Firebirds left the area, the antiaircraft guns were silent, and the wheelhouse was on fire. This fire did not spread to the cargo hold where all the explosives were stored.

The ship was beached by the dinks as the other gunships attacked, and the Koreans hauled off untold numbers of "souvenirs" before the navy could tow it to Chu Lai. There the Americans would get their "souvenirs." By the time Wiegand arrived at the navy docks at Chu Lai, only the big stuff was left, and he came away empty handed. The most interesting thing on the ship, which the Koreans kept but also took pictures of, were wooden fish. The ship was disguised as a Chinese fishing trawler. Its nets were full of intricately carved fish. These fish had been painted and placed in the nets. From a distance, the ship truly gave the appearance of an innocent fishing vessel.

On November 8, Anton got an Article 15 (disciplinary action in lieu of a court-martial) for landing on the beach and sucking sand into the turbine engine on the gunship. He made this emergency landing so he would not miss any of a show being put on by a Filipino band at the Officers' Club. The show certainly was not worth the fine he had to pay! Sand was a constant nuisance at Chu Lai. Everyone thought living on a beach would be great, but sand got everywhere. It was like sandpaper in your bed and impossible to get out. During the day, fine granules would penetrate a blanket and sheet. Each night you took your hand and knocked all of it from your bed before lying down. By morning, it was back again as bad as ever. It really took a toll on the machines.

November 8, 1967

I FLEW BACK DOWN TO DUC PHO AROUND THE VICINITY WHERE WE HAD BEEN SHOT DOWN. NOTHING WAS HAPPENING, SO WE SHOT SOME ENEMY TRUCKS (WATER BUFFALOES).

X-Rated Cookies

I received a package from my fiancée, Kathy. Letters and packages from back home were treasured and savored by all the guys. They were special and mail call was everyone's favorite part of the day. On this occasion,

NOVEMBER 9, 1967

The first Saturn 5 rocket, called Apollo 4, lifted off as the final countdown toward a manned moon mission began.

Kathy had sent me some homemade chocolate chip cookies. While preparing them, she had placed little paper messages in each cookie. Some of the messages were quite intimate and suggestive. I had no idea that the cookies were "loaded" and shared them with some of my buddies. I was not amused when the other pilots and crew members sat around eating the cookies, reading the private messages, and howling with laughter. I censored my mail quite closely from that day forward.

My First Big Battle

November 10–15, 1967

THE FIRST CAVALRY HAD TWELVE HELICOPTERS SHOT DOWN AND OVER TWENTY SHOT FULL OF HOLES. THE CO OF THE CAVALRY HELICOPTERS WAS ALSO SHOT DOWN. THE NVA UNIT DOING THE FIGHTING WAS PART OF THE SECOND NVA DIVISION.

On November 10, we went north of Chu Lai to LZ Baldy on the northern edge of the Que Son Valley. When we stepped out of the gunship at LZ Baldy, we were warned to stay low. A sniper had been taking pot shots across the helipad. I distinctly remember thinking "SSSHHH-HIIIITTTT!"

The First Cavalry Brigade, a part of Task Force Oregon, was there, but was out of gunships because of damage from intense ground fire. They had two gunships shot down on the same attack run on a target site. Some of the gunships hit a huge ammo dump south of Million Dollar Hill causing a tremendous secondary explosion as the rockets impacted.

We went deep into the valley that night searching for sampans on the river west of Heip Duc, but didn't find any. I assume the First Cavalry expected the enemy to either leave the area in sampans that night or move more ammo in after their big ammo dump was blown sky high.

On November 11, we flew numerous missions in support of the First Cavalry and spent the night at LZ Baldy. The grunts and NVA blasted each other all night, and our bunker was hit with ten machine gun rounds.

NOVEMBER 17, 1967

General Westmoreland made his famous statement that there was "light at the end of the tunnel" as far as ending the Vietnam War. What he saw was the light from a freight train being driven by Ho Chi Minh.

All this fighting in the Que Son Valley started over what was called a "snatch" mission. The NVA made some poor fool stand in the middle of a rice paddy and act as if he wanted to surrender. Waiting nearby, hidden by tree lines, was an NVA antiaircraft battalion. A chopper spotted the decoy, attempted to land and "snatch" him, and the antiaircraft guns opened up on the helicopter. After they shot down the first chopper, they continued to fire on any other helicopters trying to come to the rescue. Before long, the NVA helped the First Cavalry establish a regular helicopter junk yard.

I swore then that I would never do a "snatch" mission. However, later in my tour, I did do a few. These missions usually caused nothing but mayhem. A flight school friend from our aviation battalion at Chu Lai had the bones shot out of both his legs trying one.

On November 13, Sutton, a Firebird pilot, said he shot two rockets at a target. This time the target fired two rockets back! He believed they were B-40 rockets. He was flying in support of the First Cavalry.

I had finally figured out this war shit. On the 15th, I wrote home, "They are trying to kill me over here."

Big Game

In this support of the First Cavalry, I was peter pilot, firing the miniguns. We took a bullet through the tail rotor. I was with Anton. Seeing movement in the bushes short of the target, I fired. Then I heard Bruce, the crew chief that day, say, "You just shot the biggest pig I've ever seen!" He said it was eating a dink body. I blew up the bacon on that pig. Anton raised hell with me for wasting bullets on a stupid hog. I told him that I saw a clear violation of the Geneva Convention—mutilation of a dink body—and I stopped it.

November 17, 1967

THE FIRST CAV CAPTURED SOME DOCUMENTS FROM AN NVA HEADQUARTERS THAT CLEARLY STATED THAT A UNIT OF THE SECOND NVA DIVISION WAS INTENDING TO ATTACK ON JANUARY 4, 1968. (THIS DATE TURNED OUT TO BE VERY IMPORTANT FOR MANY OF MY FRIENDS.) WELL AFTER THE FACT, IT WAS LEARNED THAT THE JANUARY 4TH ATTACK WAS TO DRAW ATTENTION AWAY FROM THE MOVEMENT OF MEN, SUPPLIES, AND AMMUNITION NEEDED TO LAUNCH THE TET OFFENSIVE LATER IN JANUARY.

Near the end of my tour, while flying with the special forces, my crew saw tigers and elephants. One pilot (I believe it was Roger Kucera) shot a deer. The special forces guys talked him into landing and getting it so they could eat it. Here, I must also mention the "pink elephants." The special forces guys used to talk about them. At first I assumed they were smoking funny cigarettes; but come to find out, around the Laotian border, the red mud turned the elephants pink!

Around this date, I learned that my friend from flight school, Chase, had been killed. He was the youngest helicopter pilot killed in Vietnam: a little over nineteen years old. He was last seen alive on the ground after being shot down and was apparently executed by Charlie.

Upper Echelon Stuff

The 196th Light Infantry Brigade relieved the 101st Airborne Division Brigade in the Que Son Valley. For the remainder of my tour, the Rattlers and Firebirds supported the 196th Light Infantry Brigade the majority of the time.

It can be said that the 196th was the first, last and part of the biggest. The 196th was the lead unit in Operation Attleboro, which was the first field test of the army's doctrine of "Search and Destroy." The 196th was the last American combat brigade to leave Vietnam. It was also a participant in the biggest continuous battle in Vietnam, which was the Battle of Dai Do (Dong Ha) with the marines against the 320th NVA Infantry Division. The 320th NVA came to fight and brought their lunch because the continuous action lasted nearly two weeks. Luckily, I wasn't there. The 196th had three combat battalions in November, 1967. The 4/31 located on LZ West, the 3/21 located on LZ Center and the 2/1 located on LZ East. The headquarters was located initially between Tam Ky and LZ Baldy at Hill 35 along Highway 1.

November 19, 1967

A UNIT FROM THE 101ST CAPTURED A DOCUMENT WHICH DISCUSSED A PLANNED, NATIONWIDE OFFENSIVE. THIS WAS TO BE THE TET OFFENSIVE LAUNCHED ON JANUARY 30 AND JANUARY 31, 1968. NOBODY TOOK THE DOCUMENT SERIOUSLY.

The 196th was part of the newly formed Americal Division, which became notorious for the My Lai Massacre. A lot of people considered it the worst division in Vietnam at the time of its formation. To get the officers for the division headquarters, the other divisions in Vietnam had to transfer some of their own officers. It was rumored that the other divisions didn't transfer their best officers.

At one time in 1967, there were four hundred and sixty thousand American soldiers in Vietnam. The military considered only fifty thousand available in combat units like the 196th that could conduct offensive operations. If you subtract the sick, lame, lazy, wounded, AWOL, short timers, and soldiers on R&R, some people felt only twenty-five thousand were available to carry a weapon in an offensive operation. If the above numbers are correct, we were considerably outnumbered.

Expensive Rocks

On November 22, we only had two gunships flyable because of combat damage. The gunship I was on took several .30 cal. hits plus a bouncing machine gun round fired by our slicks. Most of the action around Thanksgiving was around Rock Hill (Hill 62) in the Que Son Valley south of the road from the LZ Ross to LZ Baldy. Three different times in one year, I saw many Americans die going up and around that worthless pile of rocks.

On November 23, we had four Rattlers shot up—two of them shot down. One was on fire from taking hits in the fuel cells. Miraculously, everyone made it out alive. Wiegand took a hit in the gear box on his tail rotor.

The next day, the 196th combined with our gunships to kill 123 NVA from the Second NVA Division at the Rock

Hill. John Cervinski, one of the Firebird gunners, was wounded. The official reports said seven Americans were killed and fifty wounded. With my own eyes, I saw American bodies stacked like cord wood outside the medic tent at Hill 35, although I suppose it is possible that there had been other fighting in the Que Son Valley that day.

NOVEMBER 23, 1967

General Westmoreland announced that the retaking of Hill 875 in the South Vietnamese highlands marks "the beginning of a great defeat for the enemy."

To stop the automatic weapons fire at Rock Hill, you had to fire directly into the bunkers that the NVA had built among the rocks. We loaded the gunships with white phosphorous rockets to enable us to burn them out. After witnessing the scene at the medic tent at Hill 35, it didn't bother me that our phosphorous rockets had the Charlies "fryin' in their own fat."

Wiegand was having his own adventures while all this was taking place. He spied a woman emerging from a "spider hole" carrying a box of AK-47 ammo. Because he was out of minigun ammo, rockets, and door gun ammo, he decided it was time to improvise. Wiegand handed the controls to Anton with directions to go low and slow beside the fleeing woman. He fired his .38 pistol six times and missed every shot. Wiegand swore that she turned and laughed at him as she successfully made it to the next spider hole.

All troops in Vietnam were supposed to get turkey and dressing for Thanksgiving. We had C-rations. The C-rations we ate were all dated in the early 1950s from the Korean War. They tasted old. Bruce even recalled a time he was eating some C-rations and was amazed by the date he found. He remembered that the C-rations "tasted like canned crap" and looked on the bottom of the can for the date. He could not believe what he saw and exclaimed, "I'll be damned, this shit is older than me!" It was vintage World War II canned in 1944.

NOVEMBER 26, 1967

Sen. Robert F. Kennedy accused President Johnson of turning away from the Vietnam policy of his brother by escalating the war.

On November 26, the Firebirds were supporting a Romeo Foxtrot. For some reason, we were flying close to the area of the pick up zone (the area where we would pick up the troops, called a PZ). Generally the gunships stayed in the area of the LZ. The NVA had moved up close to the PZ and opened up on the troops and slicks with automatic weapons as the grunts loaded onto the helicopters. We blasted a lot of dinks that day. It was really stupid for the NVA to move into an area where they didn't have bunkers or foxholes to enable them to hide from our rockets and miniguns. We assumed it was an inexperienced unit.

On the 28th, we started stationing two Firebird gunships at Hill 35 each night. This was not exactly "great" duty because most of the night, the artillery was fired directly over our tents. While in a deep sleep with artillery ripping over our heads, the hill shook and shuddered as if it was alive. We had the gunships parked away from everything; so when Charlie attempted to blow them up, it would not hurt anything but the gunships—and of course us.

On the 29th, a helicopter from another aviation company at Chu Lai was shot down with all the crew killed.

The next day, a First Cavalry helicopter crashed near Duc Pho (south of Chu Lai) and a US Army doctor (Kushner) was captured. He was later interned in the same POW camp as Anton. Kushner lived longer than anyone else known in a Viet Cong POW camp.

Tam Ky

On November 30, Anton and I got into a little incident at the Tam Ky "soccer field." The gunships often staged out of a so-called soccer field at Tam Ky, the provincial capital. Tam Ky was closer to the Que Son Valley than was Chu Lai. For a large Romeo Foxtrot, all the slicks and gunships would meet at the soccer field. At other times, we would use it as a refueling station. There was usually a bunch of kids there, looking for handouts. Sometimes, they would climb all over the gunships, helping themselves to all our food. Anton once said we were lucky that they didn't haul the whole helicopter away.

NOVEMBER 30, 1967

Senator McCarthy announced that he would run for president. He said that he would remove the napalm and the flame-throwers out of a country that scarcely knew how to use matches. I supposed he would have taken away our white phosphorus rockets, too. They made a real nice fire.

On this day, as we shut down at the Tam Ky soccer field and kids converged on the gunship, I made the mistake of pitching a handful of candy at them. It was almost a brawl to the death. I could not believe the way they reacted. When we prepared to take off, the kids would not back away from the chopper. They knew I had one roll of candy left and even the rotor blades starting up did not faze them. I told the crew chief to point his M-60 at them to "encourage" them to back away. Then it was like a stampede in the opposite direction. We started laughing because it was obvious they knew what a machine gun was. After I had more experience under my belt, I realized I was lucky I did not have one of those crew chiefs who blasted the little guys and then said he was just following orders!

A Vietnamese drove up on his motor bike to sell hot Coke for a dollar a can. I bought one for Anton and myself. The Vietnamese told me I was a "number one GI." I glanced at him, and there he was licking his lips staring at my crotch. I concluded he had fallen madly in love with Mrs. Carlock's handsome son, so I whipped out my bowie knife and put him and his motor bike on the road. Anton recalls that I cut the seat on his motorbike with my bowie knife, but I'm sure I wouldn't have done something that primitive. As I chased him through the soccer field, he was pushing his motor bike trying to start it. I ran just fast enough to scare him real good.

Another day, there at the field, a young kid asked if he could borrow my pistol so he could shoot the VC that came each night to "boom boom" (have sex) with his sister. I told him to go get that sister because I would protect her from the VC. We had to leave the field before he got back.

Parsons tells another story about the Tam Ky soccer field. In his words:

> I was flying with Latimer, and we were staging/refueling out of the refugee camp on the north side of Tam Ky. We had landed and were approached, as usual, by ten to fifteen kids looking for candy and C-rats (C-rations—or as they called them, chopchop). Three or four of the little buggers were in a huddle and kept looking at me. As I unbuckled and swung out of the aircraft, the group approached me. One kid came forward with his hand behind his back. He yelled, "Hey! GI!" and then pulled what looked like a pistol from behind his back! I ducked behind the gunship's door and went for my .38 pis-

tol. At that instant, I heard a "BANG" and figured that the little prick was a VC assassin, and I was dead meat. The whole group broke out laughing at me. I probably had blanched white as a sheet. Breathing a sigh of relief, I stepped over, took the gun from the little urchin, and was really amazed at its construction. It had a bamboo barrel that was just large enough in the chamber area to accept an empty .30 cal. carbine case inserted with the primer end forward into the barrel. The empty brass case was reloaded after each firing by being filled with match heads. The firing pin was a nail that was imbedded in a piece of dowel and was projected into the match heads by a piece of tire tube. When the nail jammed into the match heads, it ignited them and produced a real loud bang.

I also remember the tiny children lining up with huge grins on their faces while they gave us the finger. Some GIs with a deficient sense of humor had taught them that this was the American way to give a friendly greeting.

We'll All Get Silver Stars

On December 3, our engine blew up in flight. This was the same engine that maintenance had declared fixed a few weeks earlier when it overheated on startup. I was peter pilot with Leopold. We were flying wing to McCall with me on the controls. The helicopter suddenly lurched. At first, I thought the rotor head had flown off. Thank goodness, I had good flight instructors in flight school concerning landing a helicopter with no engine. The complete hot end of the turbine engine had blown out. The next thing I knew was that Leopold and I were hugging and celebrating in front of the grounded helicopter. We were congratulating each other for no other reason than that we were alive! As of that time (and probably for the entire Vietnam War), this was the only fully loaded UH-1C that was put on the ground with no damage after a complete engine failure. Leopold was congratulated by all the commanding officers and written up in the various military newspapers. Twenty-five years later, he walked up to me and asked, "You were the one who landed the helicopter, weren't you?" I always thought I was, but I was so scared I could not swear to it.

As we were jumping around and laughing in the rice paddy, it dawned on us that we hadn't made an emergency radio call. Quickly, we hopped in a Vietnamese grave to hide. In this region, they buried their dead in round mounds with a little dike around each grave. Leopold told me to go make an emergency radio call. I said, "No way!" I was not about to stroll over to the helicopter and sit out in the open to try to contact someone. I swore I could see what was surely Charlie peeking at us from several villages about a quarter mile away. I assumed they were deciding whether to make "bang bang."

Leopold, Bruce, Aker, and I stayed crouching in the grave behind the dike. I was scared to death by then when I heard Aker say, "Smile, I'll take your picture." He then proceeded to snap my picture just like a tourist! Aker always carried a small camera in the pocket of his armored vest. I guess he was the Firebird version of an "on the spot" photographer. Bruce then said, "Sir, I am fixing to shoot up that village!" Bruce claims to this day that Aker said it, but all three of us agree it was Bruce. In the distance, you could see people peering at us. I asked Bruce why he wanted to shoot up the village, and he said, "If we get in a big fight, we'll all get Silver Stars!" I was speechless. All I wanted was to get out alive! I told him not to shoot unless they shot at us. As we squatted down in the grave, I felt like we were in a piss pot, and Charlie was about to take a dump on us. I will never forget the feeling of euphoria when I spotted McCall circling a hundred feet above us. He was grinning and waving.

At the same time that we noticed McCall, we became aware of an unusual sound coming from the area behind the tall elephant grass that grew close to the edge of the grave. Either Leopold or I told one of the crew members to train his M-60 toward the direction of the noise and be ready. We had visions of a horde of VC coming at us in a human wave attack!

We were totally alarmed to witness the rapid advance of a swarm of APCs (armored personnel carriers), plowing through the grass, charging to our rescue. The problem was that they were probably going to run over us instead of save us! Good old McCall had forgotten to tell them to slow down. As the lead APC burst through the elephant grass, the driver frantically slammed on the brakes to keep from mowing us down. The other vehicles careened around on either side because they did not have time to stop. If we had heard a bugle playing, I would have sworn that the Cavalry had just rode in to the rescue. Naturally, I was frightened again. We had lived through the gunship going down only to be nearly smashed by a bunch of APCs. It was times like this that I wished the army would go ahead and fly my mom over to watch over me. This place was a little too dangerous for my liking.

Back at Chu Lai that night, Leopold and I discussed various ways to inflict pain and suffering on the maintenance guys who had signed off that helicopter engine as being safe to fly. This was the same chopper that earlier had the hot start because of a faulty valve. The excess heat had crystallized the engine bearings.

On the day of our engine failure, I saw how Bruce and Aker performed in an emergency situation. They were assisting us pilots out of the armored seats as they were taught—grabbing their M-60s and lots of ammo. I knew these rogues were the guys I wanted with me when I flew.

They did become my crew chief and gunner when I later flew gunships as aircraft commander. If Bruce's gunship was down for maintenance or shot up, then I flew whatever was available. When I got good and scared, I would fly at 1,500 feet. This was when the NVA came out to rumble. As a general rule, we traveled at 1,000 feet in the gunships. Bruce and Aker had songs they sang about seeing an angel sitting on the tail boom because I had them so high. They loved to fly lower. At 1,000 feet, around the Que Son Valley, some fool would generally rip off a shot at any helicopter. Bruce and Aker wanted to get something going with these nuts so they could shoot back. They had another little song about needing oxygen because I had them too high. I think they were trying to tell me something! I was sure it was Bruce whom I told to paint "Kamikaze Carlock" on the helicopter, and he replied, "How about Chicken Liver Carlock?" One day, they were singing their little tunes over the intercom while I cruised at 1,500 feet when some NVA idiot shot a full clip at us. That finally shut "Simon and Garfunkel" up for at least a few minutes.

DECEMBER 5, 1967

Pediatrician Benjamin Spock and poet Allen Ginsberg were among 264 people arrested in an antiwar protest in New York City.

Twenty-five years later, Bruce told me that they really enjoyed flying with me because they knew I would not get them killed doing anything unnecessary. The problem was, I did do stupid stunts sometimes when I was in my "John Wayne" mood!

On December 4, I wrote

home to my fiancée Kathy (now my wife) and asked her to meet me in Hawaii to get married. I was happy to be alive and able to walk away from that grave we landed in the previous day. I was even feeling brave enough to get married!

Sniffers

A sniffer was a slick helicopter with a machine in it that picked up odors and campfires. It had to come in at tree-top level in order to get a reading. Another slick would be flying at around 1,500 feet to guide the lower slick into the areas the grunt commander wanted us to check out. Some gunships would accompany them, and if the sniffer machine got a good reading, the gunships would blast that area.

Close to Laos, the jungle was triple canopy, about 150 feet high. After my December 3rd adventure, I was always concerned about an engine failure over this type of jungle. One ought to remember that Uncle Sam bought his equipment from the lowest bidder. This time out, we fired into the dense foliage at the points of reads from the sniffer machine, but did not draw any return fire.

R. J. Williams describes two sniffer missions very well. I must have flown gunships on these two missions myself, because I remember using the Canberra bombers twice and have never heard any talk about anyone else using them at other times. In Williams's words:

December 6, 1967

McCall and I flew a sniffer mission close to Laos. We were to check out an area along a river that marked the border between Vietnam and Laos.

We used to run a mission called "sniffer," which was a high-tech approach to bombing the piss out of enemy troop concentrations. I use the word piss, because that is what the sensors were set to detect (actually, the ammonia in the urine).

The mission was set up with the sniffer ship flying over double and triple jungle canopy at treetop level, usually out close to the Laotian border. The crew had the job of marking the initial target with smoke grenades and tracer bullets. To the sniffer's rear, also at treetop level, were the Firebird gunships. Their job was to follow the smoke grenades with white phosphorus rockets and miniguns. The third player in our little hunt was an air force "Birddog" spotter plane that would watch for the choppers to mark a target. The spotter plane would then direct an airstrike of B-57 Canberra bombers. These planes carried a fairly substantial load of ordnance. Last, but not least, was a flight of ten slicks flying a waiting orbit at a safe distance from the airstrikes. Their job was to land as close as possible to the target, mop up the area, and come out with a body count (the all-important measure of a successful hunt).

The two sniffer missions I participated in had remarkably different outcomes. On the first mission, the needle on the sensor pegged, indicating a large concentration of ammonia. The special operations people who were monitoring the sensor yelled for a mark. The need for an immediate accurate mark caused the gunner and me to fly with the pins pulled on the smoke grenades. Then we would adjust the grenade's positions by confirming the marks with our door guns and belts of solid tracer ammunition. The smoke grenades would alert the gunship pilots and the door gunners. Spewing a solid red line of tracers would give the Firebirds a chance to adjust the willie petes (white phosphorus rockets) to their targets. As I stood in my gunner's compartment to fire the door gun to the rear, we flew over a break in the jungle canopy. I saw about six people in black pajamas, standing in what was obviously a chow line with plates, their weapons slung over their shoulders. They were all looking up and appeared as surprised as I was to see the enemy in a place where they thought they were absolutely safe. I was firing away by this time, wondering if I had hit any of them when our pilot banked hard right and out of the area. I was still looking back at the puffs of white smoke from the gunships when I saw the first bombers diving toward the target. I know we caught them totally unprepared. That very rarely happened to the bad guys—most of the time they were hard to find.

We then returned to our staging area to refuel, our pilots went to the briefing hootch and found out that we had located and destroyed a North Vietnamese antiaircraft training battalion. I guess that would account for the hole in the canopy. They probably cut it out so they could practice tracking American planes that flew over.

The next day we started out again with the same setup, and I felt like we were going to win the whole war without any help. I may have been a little over-confident. After about an hour of no indications on the sniffer, my hand was starting to go to sleep holding that smoke grenade. Suddenly, we got the call from the special operations guys, "Mark!" I stood in the door again to fire to the rear. I didn't see anything this time; the jungle was too thick. The gun-

> *ships marked again, and the bombers came in right on target.*
>
> *This time there was a notable difference in the pilot's attitudes as they walked toward us from the briefing hootch. They had just been informed by the ground troop commander that we had located and destroyed a herd of elephants! I guess we needed to tune the ammonia discriminator a little more to protect the wildlife.*

Most sniffer missions were not as elaborate as these. They rarely had troop carriers and sometimes didn't even have Firebird gunships. Later on, when I was flying slicks, I'm pretty sure we went into Laos whenever we went without Firebird gunships. I can't be positive, however, since our maps didn't go out that far. The grunts in the back had the maps. On these missions, we were usually accompanied by F-4 Phantom jets.

Fireflies

A firefly mission usually consisted of two gunships and a slick with a large light in the cargo bed, used to shine on rivers and pinpoint enemy supply sampans. One gunship at a time did low level shooting. The other one was higher up waiting its turn to come down and sink the sampans. Any sampan moving after 9:00 P.M. was considered the enemy.

That night (December 6), Parsons flew with McCall in a minigun gunship on a firefly mission. For some reason, that night he used flares instead of the normal lights mounted on the slick. Parsons describes this mission in his own words:

McCall and I hit and sank one "jumbo" sampan east-northeast of Hill 35. It was at least forty-five feet long and loaded with crates of what looked like lettuce and cabbages under the light of the flares. As we rolled in on what we thought was a load of produce, McCall punched a pair of rockets. One hit just short of the stern, sending up a geyser. The second one hit right in the ass-end of the wheel house at the stern. I started at the rear with the miniguns and worked them forward. Shit was flying everywhere, and five or six dinks went off the sides at every point of the compass. Gary's next pair hit amidships and forward, right in the huge pile of produce. The explosion from the rockets sent cabbage crap skyward, and just as we started our break, the whole thing went off in a massive secondary explosion—flaming boards, beams, crates, and "cooked produce." We started hollering and laughing so hard that I thought I was going to piss in my pants! The cabbage was covering up a load of explosives!

Flares

On this particular mission, the flares worked without a hitch. But they could provide some interesting moments! To support the gunships on night missions, a slick helicopter was kept on flare standby. On these missions, the aircraft was loaded with about thirty-five magnesium flares. These flares were about three feet long and about six inches in diameter. The flares had a two-stage firing system which was preset as they were loaded. A small wire cable extended from the firing system and was at-

tached via a D-ring to the floor of the aircraft. To ignite
the flare, a person would pull the safety pin and toss the
flare out the cargo door. As the attached cable jerked
free, the first stage would be activated. The flare parachute would blow and suspend the flare. Stage two
would actually ignite the flare. The crew preset the
stages at five and ten seconds. This procedure was extremely dangerous. Magnesium burns at several thousand degrees. If accidentally set off in the aircraft, the
flare would burn through the aluminum airframe in seconds. A blackout curtain was placed between the pilots'
seats and the cargo area to prevent the pilots from losing
their night vision.

Ron Seabolt, a slick crew chief, remembers a scare he
and his crew had one night while out on flare duty:

> Knapp and Cervinski were the gunners and were
> sharing flare-throwing duty. Because the flares
> were being dropped from the left side of the aircraft,
> for this mission only, I was riding in the gunner's
> normal position behind the M-60 on the right side.
>
> We received a call to fly to an area and drop
> flares to try and locate a missing H-23 helicopter
> with two men aboard. We cleared Chu Lai and
> headed north, accompanied by a team of Firebird
> gunships. The gunships were close to the deck,
> while we were at about 2,000 feet traveling in
> straight and level flight. Suddenly, our aircraft
> lurched upward violently. My first thought was that
> we had a flight control tube break, and we were
> "goners." At the same time, I heard the aircraft
> commander shriek, "Damn, did you see that?"
> Knapp, who was on the other side, yelled back,
> "See it, I could count the rivets on that SOB!" I
> could not tell what they were talking about, so I

asked what happened. The pilot answered that we had just missed a head-on collision with an F-4 Phantom jet. At the last second, he had spotted the lights of the F-4 and jerked as hard as he could on the controls to avoid the crash.

We continued on to the search area and started our flare drops. After several drops, I heard a pop. I glanced around to the cargo area and observed Cervinski lying on the floor in a fetal position. Instantly, the entire ship was filled with a flare parachute. Knapp jumped to push all the flares out the door. I was swinging out from the gunner's position to help them.

A flare had prematurely blown a cap off, hitting Cervinski in the balls. He went down like lead. Here we were, seconds from death, and all Cervinski could think about was the family jewels. I gathered the parachute and severed the shroud lines with my survival knife. We began to breathe a sigh of relief, but then the chopper was illuminated by a flare that was way too close. All the flares but one had been released from their cables. This one was dangling below the cargo area near the skids and blazing. The pilot, who could not see what was happening, cut the engine and put us into autorotation, free fall. We headed east toward the coastline with the aircraft commander sending a Mayday. He thought we were on fire and going down.

Knapp grabbed a pair of wire-cutting pliers; and, as I held onto his belt, he hung out the cargo bay cutting through the large bundle of cables. He finally located the correct one, which immediately solved our problem. Again, we caught our breath, and poor old Cervinski was still holding himself!

Flying into the mountains west of Chu Lai at night without being able to see the horizon was a terrifying experience. Once the first rocket was fired, and you no longer had night vision, it was nearly suicidal. When the clouds were high enough, we would take out the slick loaded with flares to light up the attack area. Some infantry units didn't like the light because they preferred to fight in the dark. The most memorable missions to me were the ones called in the mountains at night while it was raining. Putting in a gunship attack, while in the rain and under the flares, made for a "psychedelic" fantasy-like scene. As the flare floated down under the parachute, the elongated shadows moved before your eyes. It was like a vision from hell. Then, when the last flare sputtered and burned out, it was pitch black and scary. Home was in your heart in times like that.

Another Day at the Office

During daylight hours on December 9, the First Cavalry killed one hundred and two NVA southwest of Hoi An, northeast of LZ Baldy, with our assistance. I assume they had all their gunships shot up or shot down. Besides being a moving target all day for Charlie, that night they had us looking for an AWOL soldier. We could not believe that someone in a real combat area would go AWOL. But there he was, strutting down Highway One at night. The two gunships had a long discussion over the radios about whether we should keep our landing lights on him (the NVA might see him) or try to land and retrieve him. Each time we turned the landing light on him, he would start dancing. The grunt commander wanted us to land and pick him up, but we had a full load of ammo and fuel and figured the idiot would run from us anyway. I remember that a crew member, probably Bruce, suggested he could stop the soldier from running by nipping him in the leg. We followed him for a long time before we could get a slick to give him a ride. By now, he had traveled several miles from the closest American base. He was either crazy or doped up; no one could ever get that drunk!

At noon on December 10, we only had one gunship flyable because of combat damage. By the afternoon, we got another up and ready. After two months in Nam, this routine was like another day at the office. We shot at them; they shot at us. They hit us and tore up the helicopter, and we got to go take a break. Truthfully, I was nearly always terrified, but you sort of went numb after a time. That night, we flew a firefly mission in the same area where the one hundred and two NVA were killed the day before. We only sank two sampans.

On December 11, a truck rolled into one of the three gunships we had flyable and put it out of commission.

Memorable Dink Shots

On December 12, Leopold swaggered in from a flight as the entire crew was bragging about his great rocket-shooting ability. They swore he blasted a running dink. The 2.75 rocket blew the dink's head smooth off while he was in full stride. The crew then watched as the dink kept running with no head. I informed them that they couldn't count it as a kill if the hapless fellow was still moving. Leopold's gunship also took some hits in the action.

We always sat around sharing tales about memorable "dink shots." Some seemed rather incredible but were witnessed on a regular basis.

Anton and Wiegand were flying along as Wiegand ate a can of C-rations. At about 1,200 feet, a dink ripped a lucky shot at them that hit the helicopter. Wiegand sat the C-ration can on the console and calmly relayed, "I've got the controls." As he turned, he spotted this stupid dink with a rifle darting for a tree line down a dike. As the chopper dove downward, Wiegand felt a strange urge come over him to run the guy down. He was positively going to smash the VC with the nose of the helicopter. The idea, as far as he was concerned, was to make the dink into "roadkill." About fifty yards from his target at a hundred knots, Anton opened up with the miniguns and proceeded to blast the offender to little bitty pieces. Wiegand was really pissed at Anton because he was going to give the VC the ultimate payback for interrupting his lunch.

Bruce spoke of one time he blasted a dink into a "red haze." The last thing the Charlie did was to reach for his hat and place it on his head as tracers passed through him. Bruce was surprised the man's last thought was making sure he had his hat.

One bizarre account told about "blasting a dink" happened later in my tour, when I was aircraft commander flying wing to Leopold. East of LZ Baldy, on the flat ground, the grunts were advancing down both sides of a river. The grunts on the east side were ahead of the ones on the west. All of a sudden, a VC hit the water and was doing a good job of freestyle swimming. He did not notice the soldiers on the opposite side of the river and headed in that direction. Everyone on both sides opened up on him at once. We were flying north and heard the grunt commanders scream over the radio to cease fire. The bullets the grunts were shooting were bouncing off the water and skimming straight over the heads of the troops on either side. Approximately fifteen to twenty grunts on both sides of the river were trying to peg the terrified dink. Tracers were bouncing off the water and going in every direction. The guy was swimming in frantic circles. This dink had about as much of a chance as Hillary Clinton would have had trying to win the "best legs" contest back at the Rustler's Rest in Fort Worth, Texas. Leopold, in a Hog with all the rockets, flew over and said something over the radio like, "Well, would you look at this." The soldiers had not even grazed the moving target. I told Leopold, "Get out of the way." I had a minigun ship; and being so low, I did not want a ricocheting round to hit Leopold's chopper. I had my peter pilot fire a burst of the guns. Miniguns shot into the water looked like an underwater explosion because of the way the spray erupted from all the bullets popping it at once. The peter pilot hit right on the dink from around a hundred feet in the air. The water exploded all around him. Leopold, as he turned his gunship, started laughing over the radio. We missed the joker, too! How we missed this guy, we never knew. He was like a cat that had just used up eight of his nine lives. Leopold came around in his gunship one more time. This time all the rockets were trained on the one lone target. It was then "Good-bye, dink." Leopold was later mouthing off that I was going to give the Firebirds a rotten reputation for missing anything from that height with the miniguns.

Ron Seabolt, the national director of our reunion association, gave an account of being in a flight of ten slicks when he spotted a VC dashing out of some bushes next to the LZ. Seabolt started shooting at the runner toward the front of the helicopter and continued to fire until the guy was behind the chopper as it took off. All ten machine guns from the slicks on that side of the flight were firing at the guy. Tracers were going under his arms and between his legs. All this did was make the guy run a hell of a lot faster! Seabolt personally fired six hundred rounds. Everybody missed. He said his aircraft commander, O'Quinn, yelled over the intercom, "That is the damnedest example of marksmanship I have ever seen!"

On December 13, one of the helicopters in our battalion was shot down, and everyone aboard was killed.

Up Close and Personal

One of our missions on December 16 was a blocking mission. Four armed VC broke from the village and ran across a rice paddy to a shallow creek bed. I was flying right seat in the Hog (with forty-eight rockets) which was the seat that has the sight for aiming the rockets. McCall had two pieces of tape on the left seat windshield forming an "X" in case he wanted to shoot a rocket using the tape as his sight target. He was training me to become an aircraft commander. From probably 1,000 feet, I dove at the four VC and started shooting the rockets in pairs. After two or three pairs, McCall hit the cyclic with his hand and fired several more from the left seat. I fired again. The dinks continued to scoot toward the dry creek bed and some adjacent trees. McCall shot some more. With all the uproar, I thought he was flying, and he thought I was flying. One rocket had hit dead center between the shoulder blades of a VC, and as it exploded, his commie soul was left in a geyser of mud, blood, and human debris. The others were all hit by shrapnel. At the last second, both of us realized the other was not in control and jerked the cyclic

December 16, 1967

McCALL AND I FLEW ELEVEN HOURS AND THIRTY MINUTES OUT OF A TWENTY-FOUR-HOUR PERIOD. THAT WILL VIBRATE YOUR BRAIN LOOSE.

back to the stops. We barely missed crashing as we pulled
the gunship up through our rocket blasts. We pulled back
on the main control, and you could feel the gunship vibrate hard as the blades slapped the air trying to stop our
nose-down descent into the rice paddy. Later, after my
nerves calmed down, I knew I had nearly lived up to my
flight school nickname. If I had crashed directly on the enemy in a flaming fireball of splattered debris, I would
have certainly earned the name "Kamikaze Carlock."

After all the shooting, I remember looking around at
our crew chief, Rogers. In a Hog gunship, many of the
crew members stood outside the helicopter on a gun run
so they could shoot their M-60 machine guns straight
ahead at the target. They would put one foot on the rocket
pod and step out. When I glanced at Rogers after flying
through the rocket blast, he had mud all over him—on his
clear helmet visor and on his face. I started laughing.
Mild-mannered Rogers said he would gladly kick my ass
if I would kindly land the gunship! By the time we got to
Tam Ky to rearm, he was finally laughing, too. At least I
was giving him good targets for his M-60 machine gun.
They were up close and personal!

The day he looked like a mud ball, we reloaded and
shot VC from morning till night. That afternoon, we were
escorting a sniffer mission. As we zipped along low level,
I saw an open-sided hootch with NVA soldiers looking at
me. Whether or not it was the information the sniffer machine turned up (plus my sighting), I don't know, but a
B-52 strike hit the area the next morning. That night we
flew firefly missions all night and only sank six or seven
sampans.

Bob Hope came to Chu Lai on December 20 to entertain the troops for Christmas. All gunships were put on
five-minute standby.

We fired our hootch maid for stealing. She said she did

not make enough money to feed her children. The interpreter said she made more than an ARVN major, but based on the prices of food in our area, she was having financial trouble. It helped me understand why the Vietnamese military was so corrupt. A lot of them were apparently merely trying to feed their families.

It was also on December 20 that I heard some news about our military using jets to drop CS bombs on the dinks. Supposedly, after the tear gas ran them into the open, B-52s were brought in to bomb the hell out of them. It sounded like a good idea to me.

We sank thirty-eight sampans on a firefly mission on December 22. The next day, Charlie mortared Chu Lai but was unable to shoot the mortars far enough to hit the company area.

On the 24th, Anton was out flying a gunship and spotted four or five NVA marching along. He radioed for permission to blast them and was denied because we were in the midst of a Christmas truce. Needless to say, he got into big-time trouble for disobeying that order!

The truce ended at one minute past midnight on the 25th, and B-52 bombers bombed west of Chu Lai.

I remember December 29, because of an odd incident. We flew numerous combat missions for the 196th Light Infantry Brigade, and I spent the night at Hill 35 next to the medical tent. They were hauling in NVA wounded—for interrogation, I assumed. I saw one NVA who was badly wounded, but still had creases in his pants and shined boots. The bodies of American GIs were stacked beside the tent. Among all the NVA soldiers, dead Americans, and chaos was a VC

JANUARY 1, 1968

O. J. Simpson rushed for two touchdowns as top-ranked Southern California defeated Indiana in the Rose Bowl to win the national championship.

about eighteen years old lying beside a sewing machine. I have no idea why that machine was brought in with the wounded, but I do remember scrutinizing the VC boy. He observed me with eyes that bulged with fear, and for some reason, I reached down and took his belt buckle— the only war souvenir I still have.

Body Counts

On January 1, the Firebirds, along with other gunships from our battalion, were credited with ninety confirmed kills in the area of My Lai. This was not the famous My Lai massacre, which took place on March 16, 1968 and is discussed later in this book. My Lai was an area of continual VC activity. For us, this was just another day in support of the infantry. The Firebirds were generally credited with several kills per day when the infantry was in contact with the enemy. However, I know for a fact that many of the "kills" were estimates. The number of confirmed kills actually became a joke among the pilots. One day I was flying wing behind Leopold, and we shot up some triple canopy jungle northwest of the Que Son Valley. The grunt commander, who never moved his position, asked if we could confirm six killed. Leopold, in his typical fashion, came back over the radio, "Yeah, six monkeys." I cannot remember but I hope he said this over VHF radio, which only I could hear in the wing gunship. I have no doubt that the report showed us with six KIAs for the day.

On January 1, the infantry boxed in a VC unit and left it to the gunships to give the commies a good send-off. We took several hits in the rotor blade and tail boom. The VC were dug in hedge rows, not tree lines. With them located in hedge rows (like bushes), we proceeded to make each gun run lower and lower. Before too much longer, we could have turned the gunships into hedge clippers! It was a lot better being on the side that has the other out-gunned about forty to one. We were chunking metal at them at the rate of about forty times what they were chunking back.

A sniper was shooting at a grunt company from a tree line. We flew over and dropped several CS gas grenades over the tree line and flushed the guy out. As he took off running in the open, I zapped him with the miniguns. That VC would be eating his rice from the roots up.

The ARVN

To put it mildly, I cannot say that I was overly impressed by our so-called allies. I watched the US marines in action in Happy Valley. They attacked just like the military did in the Civil War, except instead of being shoulder to shoulder, they spread about six feet between each marine. They would sweep on a straight line. Many times I saw the ARVN sweep large valleys spaced at three feet apart. The problem was they were following each other. They looked like a trail of ants going through a valley. I saw grunt officers roll their eyes when they observed this. I also saw an ARVN commander screaming and raising hell with his troops over the radio; but he never ordered me to land, so he could force them to spread out. I never saw him go down and lead them personally. We used to say that the US did "search and destroy" missions, while the ARVN did "search and avoid" missions.

There was something seriously wrong between the officers and the enlisted men in the ARVN, and I picked up on this fact early in my tour. To be an ARVN officer, a Vietnamese man had to have at least twelve years of education. This one requirement eliminated nearly all of the troops from ever becoming officers. It also effectively ensured that only the rich could obtain officer status in their army. In the NVA, a man was made an officer based on leadership and bravery. In the US Army, it was a big honor to get a combat command, while in the ARVN it meant that a guy didn't know the right people to get him out of it.

January 2, 1968

WE ESCORTED A FLIGHT OF SLICKS DOWN TO QUANG NGAI NEAR MY LAI, TO PICK UP SOME FOUR HUNDRED ARVN SOLDIERS TO INSERT IN THE AREA WHERE WE PREVIOUSLY ZAPPED THE NINETY VC. ONLY TWO HUNDRED ARVN SOLDIERS SHOWED UP FOR WORK THIS TIME.

Through 1967, the marines had lost over six times as many majors and light colonels as the ARVN army had lost, and the ARVN army was substantially larger than the number of marines based in Vietnam. A major mistake concerned the military chain of command. In Korea, they had a unified command that let the US generals determine the commanders of the Korean military units. Our military leaders could throw out any incompetent Korean generals. This problem was considered many times during the Vietnam War, and for some reason, the method successfully used in Korea was never implemented. Some people blamed General Westmoreland. In one incident, an ARVN general was relieved of command for corruption and then was promptly made ARVN inspector general. His new job description included rooting out corruption in his military. The ARVN never had a chance with the system it had of selecting and promoting officers.

Corruption and black marketeering were rife in the

ARVN. The Americal Division had a program called VIP (Volunteer Informant Program) which paid for information or weapons turned over to them. I was told that the ARVN soldiers routinely stole the grenades we had given them and handed them over to their kids or relatives, who then sold the pilfered supplies back to us. This was a good way to make a little salary supplement. One time the Americal Division paid $423 to get back a 105 Howitzer that had been stolen from the ARVN.

The ARVN once pressured our army into helping them clear the road to the Tra Bong Special Forces Camp, southeast of Chu Lai. It was a major effort, because the road had been closed for years by the VC. After the Americans suffered numerous casualties in both men and machines, they successfully opened the road. The rumor later on was that a rich Vietnamese businessman wanted to open the way so he could truck out his cinnamon crop. Large amounts of cinnamon bark were hauled out by truck. Once the operation was completed, the road was again taken over by the Viet Cong.

Another problem was that there was no love lost between the different groups of the country. Most of the ARVN were from the cities and considered all the villagers hicks and VC sympathizers. When I would fly a group of ARVN, after they had been through an area, it was incredible what they brought aboard the chopper—pigs, chickens, baskets, pots, pans, furniture, and anything else that was not nailed down. Some people considered it a war crime to allow the ARVN to pillage and loot the villages. No one in our area bothered to stop the practice, though. I can honestly say I made those guys drop a lot of their ill-gotten gains because I could not get enough of them on the helicopter when they were loaded down with all their loot.

The result of all this was a military force that was inefficient, had low morale, and (because of lack of leadership) was not known for its courage. In 1975, when South Vietnam fell to the Communists, the enemy started the ensuing panic by cutting the country into two pieces with a tank assault on Tam Ky. The same ARVN unit that I flew for in 1968 performed its most familiar military tactics in 1975 when they launched an "aggressive retrograde." In other words, they ran like hell!

When supporting the ARVN, it always took some extra time to get the locations of all the friendly troops. Foley shared that one day west of Tam Ky, the ARVN advisors were telling the helicopters to hold their fire. Foley saw a tall dink in black pajamas carrying a Browning (BAR) machine gun run directly under the helicopter. They followed him and kept asking for permission to fire. The location of the friendlies was being sorted out by the ARVNs and advisors. After the guy hit the tree line, jumped in a tunnel, and made his escape, the advisors to the ARVNs said a guy in black pajamas with a BAR had just shot the ARVN commander.

Quang Ngai had so many ARVN units around screwing things up for the rest of us that it was always a zoo to work there. They certainly didn't enhance security, either. The ARVN knew where the Americans were going and what their plans were. Our guys may as well have set up a billboard announcing their intentions to the enemy. The only difference in the outcome would have been the amount of time it took for the ARVN to relay the information to the enemy!

Many of the ARVN soldiers were reluctant to enter combat and extraordinarily anxious to leave it. In June, I was actually attacked by a small group of ARVN who wanted me to extract them, though I was already overloaded. They tried to hold on to the helo skids as I lifted off. Many of the flight crews who regularly worked with the ARVN used to grease their skids to stop them from hanging on and overloading the helicopter. Once, we escorted seven slicks into an LZ west of Tam Ky. The ARVN refused to get off the choppers!

The ARVNs were notorious for shooting each other by accident. One time, when our slicks were moving some ARVN, one of them tripped getting off the helicopter and shot an entire clip into his own guys. When I flew slicks, I always told the crew chief and gunner to make them take their clips out upon getting on the chopper. They could still have one in the chamber, but they would generally clear the bolt also. One day an ARVN soldier refused to remove his clip. It was possible he didn't understand. I did not see the soldier myself, but I told the crew to "get the clips out." As we took off, the next thing I heard was a "gong" sound. I couldn't imagine what had caused the strange noise. I thought the helicopter was coming apart. The gunner had smacked the ARVN over the helmet with an M-60 barrel. The ARVN was laid back against a buddy and seemed to be knocked cold. I looked around, and the gunner said, "Just following orders, Sir." I told the dumb-ass gunner to keep an eye on all the ARVN; because if I were one of them, I would shoot the crap out of him. Luckily, nothing happened that time.

While flying slicks, I did have a gunner nearly killed for pulling a similar stunt. I was picking up a load of ARVN at Quang Ngai. I ordered the gunner to allow only eight or nine to board. The load depended on the strength of the chopper's engine. As the soldiers approached a helicopter on a dirt helipad, they generally had their heads down to keep the dust out of their eyes. When they carried a loaded M-79 grenade launcher, like a single shot shotgun that fired the 40 mm grenade, they kept the barrel broken open. Something about the safeties didn't work properly. The gunner counted the ARVN soldiers, and instead of grabbing the extra men and telling them we were full, he kicked the extra guy on the helmet and knocked him down. The problem this time was he kicked the wrong soldier.

I had only seen two ARVN soldiers like this one in Vietnam. He was an old senior sergeant who wore his combat ribbons into the field. He had more combat ribbons than a South American dictator. These guys had fought wars their whole lives.

Anyway, this ARVN instantly snapped his loaded M-79 closed. Then and there, the gunner and I both knew that he was a split second away from dying. I start yelling and waving at the ARVN sergeant, and he lowered the M-79. I hopped off the helicopter and apologized. I also made the gunner apologize in front of the troops. The gunner did not hesitate.

January 2 was also the day Leopold was wounded for the first time. A .30 caliber round came through his side window and blew shrapnel and pieces of Plexiglas into his face. Most gunship pilots flew with a clear visor down on their flight helmets with sun shades underneath to keep shrapnel out of the eyes. The very next day, Leopold was back flying. We had two gunships shot up, and Leopold got the crap shot out of his chopper. Again, a bullet came through the cockpit and blew shrapnel into his face. He told me, "I am tired of this shit, I quit!" The next day he was out flying again.

A Major Battle in the Que Son Valley

Two regiments of the Second NVA Infantry Division were getting set up for a big fight. On the south edge of the Que Son Valley, a recoilless rifle of some type shot at our gunship on January 3. It made an airburst up and to the side of us. There were no Americans around the location, so we practiced our "lookback tactics." We "looked back" at the area the airburst was fired from as we got the hell out. The battalion had twelve helicopters shot up this day alone.

The next day, the NVA drove down into the Que Son Valley from the hills with their better units. A friend from flight school, Beck, who was flying with one of the other aviation companies in our battalion was hit in the knee and the wrist. Sutton, with the Firebirds, was hit in the leg by shrapnel caused by a tracer round which hit his chopper that night. Hannah was with Sutton on this flight, and said that it was the only time he saw a bullet coming at him and knew it was going to hit. He ducked down. Fortunately for Hannah, he was small enough to hide fairly well in the armored seat and chickenboard.

The NVA warmed up with an attack on a company of the 196th Light Infantry Brigade. This must have been D Company 4/31 Infantry Battalion, north of LZ West. The weather was really rough with heavy clouds down on the deck. We weren't able to arrive on station to drive the NVA back until about 3:00 A.M. on the next day.

The First Cavalry pulled all their companies back into their fire support bases on the north side of Que Son Valley and slaughtered the NVA units that attacked that night. The NVA was only able to penetrate the wire on one firebase of the First Cavalry. The 196th, however, left infantry companies in the valley.

Anton was in the Officers' Club, ragging our barmaid, Mary, about her VC boyfriend. She told Anton that the VC were going to get him. Sure enough, they did get him the very next day!

At first, we probably regarded January 5 as another one of those routine days, albeit a busy one. We were flying numerous combat assaults, and I was with Latimer. The clouds continued to drop during the day to about 800 feet. We were making attack runs against antiaircraft guns under the cloud cover. As we came in to attack our targets, we were consistently fired on from numerous other locations. It felt like the NVA was everywhere. I spent most of the day in the right seat as acting aircraft commander. Latimer was the boss.

A gunship from our battalion was shot down in the Que Son Valley. Taylor, from our company, rescued the crew in a Rattler slick.

Later in the day we landed at Hill 35. As I started to get out, Latimer asked, "What are you doing?" Being scheduled to go and fly with Anton that night, I was going to free up Carson, Anton's peter pilot, to go on back to Chu Lai (Hannah said the written schedule showed him being Carson's replacement. Anton had only been back from R&R two days and that may have caused the confusion over the schedule). Latimer told me to tell Anton that I had been flying all day and most of the previous night, so I was going back with him. Foley was with us serving as crew chief. While at Hill 35, we traded over to McCall's helicopter and left Foley and his gunship there (apparently for maintenance). Anton and Carson were to fly with Lewis as crew chief and Pfister as gunner. Foley handed over his extra M-60 to Pfister. (This simple action almost got Foley put in military prison later.) As Latimer and I left, we had no premonition, no indication whatsoever, that something disastrous was about to take place. Five long

January 5, 1968

THIS WAS ONE HELL OF A DAY! I AM NOT SURE HOW MANY GUARDIAN ANGELS I USED UP THAT DAY OR HOW FAR I PUSHED LADY LUCK, BUT I KNOW I WAS MUCH MORE FORTUNATE THAN SEVERAL OF MY CLOSE BUDDIES BY THE TIME IT ALL ENDED.

years would pass before I laid eyes on Anton again. He, Lewis, and Pfister were about to spend those years in various Vietnamese prisoner of war camps.

The Firebirds, with McCall flying lead and Anton flying wing, scrambled off Hill 35 to support an infantry company in heavy combat. The grunts were located north of LZ West in the Que Son Valley. The infantry company was C Company 2/1 Battalion, 196th Light Infantry Brigade. We were told a slick had landed mail for the troops which included large quantities of late Christmas presents. Apparently, as our guys opened their Christmas presents, six NVA companies closed in for the attack. The 196th combat journal reads:

1800 (hours)	C/2/1 company commander and a platoon leader wounded and medevaced
1935	C/2/1 Needs help ASAP!!!
2025	Gunship shot down (Anton said he was shot down forty minutes earlier than this.)
2036	C/2/1 Surrounded ... fire from all sides
2040	NVA inside company perimeter
2400	(12:00 a.m.) acting company commander killed, replacement acting company commander killed, radio operator in control of survivors
0044	Company A 4/31 Infantry Battalion links up with survivors of C/2/1

The company was hit with three human wave attacks, and only eight men survived uninjured. The brigade had sixty-six men killed in the southwestern part of the Que Son Valley close to LZ West during this action. In the overall engagement with the NVA, US infantry counted 892 NVA bodies killed on January 5.

Anton and Carson got into immediate trouble by having both sets of hydraulics shot out on their C-model Gunship. In a D- or H-model slick, you could still fly the helicopter to a certain extent if you lost the hydraulics. A C-model had two sets of hydraulics, and when they both went out, it was time to "turn out the lights." Anton's gunship hit the ground hard and flipped on its side. Bley, who was flying a Rattler slick in the area, then had his chopper shot to pieces trying to pick up Anton's crew. The enemy shot holes in his chopper's fuel cells. Still another slick was shot up trying to get to them.

McCall, who was flying the other gunship, told me that for twenty-five years he had worried about whether he did enough trying to get Anton's crew out. (McCall was killed in a medevac rescue in Colorado while I was writing this book.) During my last conversation with him, I could tell he was very relieved because he had just talked to Foley, who was his crew chief that fateful night. McCall had blotted from his memory much of what happened. Foley shared with McCall that they had turned on the landing light of the gunship, searching around Anton's crashed helicopter from a high hover. Foley had never seen so many tracers flying. Anton said that McCall's helicopter lurched as it approached to rescue Anton and the crew. This was caused when a pedal was shot off under McCall's foot with an antiaircraft round. The fuel cells were also shot out. Carson, the peter pilot with Anton, counted at least sixteen different antiaircraft guns zeroing in on McCall.

Carson, seeing the antiaircraft fire and judging that rescue was impossible, jumped in the river next to the helicopter and was swept downstream with the current. The problem was that this river ran in the wrong direction. It ran west instead of east toward the coast. Carson was also hit by artillery shrapnel during his escape. He was picked up the following day, dressed as a VC. He never did talk about where or how he got those clothes. The written account of his escape that follows later does not mention the way he was dressed. The military has changed some parts of his account.

The grunts, because the infantry company was being overrun, would not shut the artillery off to allow us to land a flight of helicopters with troops to rescue Anton and his crew. By the time the two infantry companies were linked up during the night, the clouds had dropped to ground level. At daylight, a flight of helicopters was inbound, but this was when the NVA found Anton, Lewis, and Pfister.

Our commanding officers wouldn't entertain the idea of trying to land troops at night with all the heavy cloud cover. The weather stayed bad for several more days. The low clouds made the helicopters easy targets. Because the weather limited the amount of helicopter support, the infantry had trouble getting their wounded out from the two companies that had joined together. Four medevac helicopters attempted to reach the area, but only one made it successfully. Warrant Officer Brady left LZ West four different times. He hovered sideways down the hill at treetop level through the valley north to the location of the wounded. The sideways hovering allowed the rotor blades to blow the fog away so that he could see under the clouds. His chopper alone brought out thirty-nine wounded. Brady received the Congressional Medal of Honor for his actions and later became a general. Anton and his crew were further north, away from where the wounded were.

The combat records of the 196th implied that Firebird gunships arrived at daylight to make airstrikes around the infantry companies before the wounded were hauled out. We were really on station above the clouds but couldn't get into the area until later. Anton said he could hear us coming in as he was captured. He also recalled how they had only been crashed into the rice paddy about ten minutes when some villagers showed up at the site. They came crawling out of the darkness, in the midst of heavy artillery and gunfire, to strip any removable parts from the gunship—C-rations, cameras, personal items, etc.

After being located and taken prisoner by the NVA, Anton, Lewis, and Pfister spent about three years in a camp in South Vietnam. For approximately two years, they were held in North Vietnam. The camp in South Vietnam, if you exclude prisoners released, had nearly fifty percent of the prisoners die. This was a higher death rate than any known for American prisoners in any war. The *Pacific Stars & Stripes*, April 27, 1973, quoted an American doctor, Major Floyd H. Kushner, who was a POW with Anton. Kushner said there were twenty-seven Americans in his POW camp in South Vietnam. Five were released, and only twelve made it to Hanoi. Two died because it was too hard to live. Dr. Kushner said they told him they couldn't hack it anymore and just laid down and died. The POWs often suffered from dysentery, malaria, scurvy, gingivitis, furunculosis, and hepatitis. They were also starved and worked nearly to death. He stated that they were happy to get to Hanoi. As bad as it was, the conditions there were far better than in the southern camps.

When we finally met in 1973, Anton related his experiences with the military after he was released. They gave them a test at the hospital in the Philippines. The doctors handed him cards with different questions on it. He was to put the cards in either a "yes" or "no" slot in a box. I curiously asked, "What kind of questions?" Anton said, "Oh, questions like—do you feel you have spiders crawling around in your head?" As we sat drinking beer and laughing, I asked "How did you answer?" Anton laughed and said he put it in the "yes" slot.

He then asked if I knew he had signed some statements against the war during his imprisonment. They starved him, whipped his knees with bamboo, and knocked him around before he relented and signed. I could tell he was worried about what I thought about him signing the statements. I quickly told him there was a huge difference between him and me. All I would say to the SOBs was "What line do I sign on?" I believe that many helicopter pilots who dealt with our allies (the ARVN) and risked their lives on a daily basis, felt the same way I did. The NVA would not have had to lay a glove on me to sign. I still remember the rage I felt after Anton was shot down when the peace talks were delayed just because they could not agree on where to have them. Later, it became even more ridiculous when they argued over the shape of the table used at the meetings.

Even at my young age, I was smart enough to know you did not cause so many American boys to be needlessly killed fighting for the same worthless pile of rocks three times in the same year. I knew you didn't use American boys as cannon fodder like the US marines did when they lined up in a long line and marched across the rice paddies as if they were on a bird hunt. When our marines swept an area, they were two arms' lengths apart. At least they had learned something over the years. In the Civil War, they would sweep an area shoulder to shoulder. These senseless maneuvers were ridiculous. I knew it. My buddies also knew it.

Carson, the "lucky" man on the fallen gunship, vividly

remembered the night they were shot down and he made his escape. This account was written during the war and published in the *U.S. Army Aviation Digest*, February, 1970. This is in his own words, but the military has changed some of the facts:

> *I was almost upside down, suspended from my seat belt, when the grinding of tearing metal ceased. A fantasy land of orange streaks played before my eyes, and I was shocked into reality. The clapping concussions of machine gun fire were everywhere; tracers illuminated the blackness.*
>
> *Looking back, and to the right, I could see a cargo door. Then I was on the ground diving for the safety of a rice paddy dike. Like me, the rest of the UH-1C crew found momentary shelter in scattered locations against the dikes.*
>
> *A momentary silence afforded time for a self-examination. My left arm felt numb, and, as I straightened it with my right, the shoulder popped into place. On further examination, I determined the cuts on my arms and face to be minor. I had no broken bones to restrict mobility. I was in good shape!*
>
> *Suddenly, the tree line to the immediate front was illuminated in a white blinking rhythm by erupting muzzles; the mud and water around me came alive with zapping bullets.*
>
> *I thought, "My rifle, my pistol!" They were in the aircraft along with a rescue radio and a survival kit. They all might as well be a million miles away.*
>
> *Take heed, army aviators, what the old-timers said was true, "If it is not on your person when you crash, then it won't be with you when you exit the aircraft." My pistol belt, I remembered, was hanging on the seat; my survival radio was on the floor.*

I was in a completely helpless position with no avenue of escape. It would have ended there for me had not the second gunship commenced pounding the tree line with seventeen-pound warhead rockets. As the gunship drew the hostile fire to itself, I scrambled to some adjacent brush, and for a while, observed the heroic rescue efforts being attempted by my gallant companions. However, it soon was obvious that an escape by air was out of the question. The enemy troops were no longer assaulting the aircraft openly, because of air cover and flares, but were managing to infiltrate the area. When seven of them glided past my location, I resolved to move as far away from the aircraft as possible. Otherwise, it would only be a matter of time before I would be discovered.

Eventually, only the flare ship remained overhead. Its murmuring sound, with the recurring pop of an igniting flare, became a hypnotic rhythm in the still night. One could sense the enemies' silence, listening for a voice, a sound, a movement, anything that would betray their prey.

Then I became aware of the sound of water . . . the steady gurgle and tinkle of a stream or river. If I could just get to that river, I could swim well. It should flow eastward to the ocean. That could be my avenue of escape.

The flare ship was not orbiting directly overhead; and, consequently, with each igniting flare, the rice paddy dikes were casting shadows. These inky shadows became my camouflage. I eased myself out of the brush and into the black water alongside one rice paddy dike. Remaining in the shadow, I began the painfully slow progress toward the sound of moving water.

As I eased forward on my belly, I prayed I would not ripple the water. I reached each intersecting dike, and I waited until the aerial flare died. Then, I slipped up and over the top before the next flare ignited. After an interminable time, I had covered only several yards. Yet, the sound of water was louder.

Suddenly, a loud whistle and whine broke the night air. It had begun with a high pitch and wound down to a low whine with a resounding thud. The artillery shell impacted, and the ground trembled.

There was another more distant impact. Then a closer one; another impacted behind me and another in front. The American artillery, coming from LZ West, was impacting artillery all around our downed ship in the desperate attempt to stay the enemy until morning. How could they know that the enemy was inside the bracket with us? (I learned later that during this time LZ West also was under heavy ground assault, yet continued to provide artillery support for the lost aircraft down in the valley. They even tried to locate the ship all night with a huge spotlight.)

I finally reached the river bank, and in my ungraceful effort to slide over the top, I was spotted. The slime on my fatigue shirt must have shone like a mirror in the flare light, giving my position away. I splashed into the water with the sounds of shouting and shooting behind me. With the snapping of bullets above, I went under the surface and swam with the current, coming up occasionally for air.

I began to feel truly trapped again. Artillery was pounding on one bank, and enemy shouts were getting louder on the other. I chose the artillery side

*and scrambling onto the bank I began a fast, low
crawl. Belly to the ground, my only thought was to
keep going. One impact followed another until my
senses became dulled. My ears filled with a low
ringing. (Later a doctor would show me that the
concussions had driven tiny pieces of shrapnel and
particles of dirt into my chest and side.)*

*Emerging from my concentration, it occurred to
me that the concussions were no longer close. The
artillery was behind me. I realized that by some
miracle or quirk of fate, and against fantastic odds,
I was now beyond the immediate aircraft area and
beyond the artillery bracket. No longer was the
downed aircraft a marker to the enemy for my location. No longer was I a target. The danger of the enemy had diminished.*

*Dawn could not be far away, and I felt mentally
and physically exhausted. I decided that traveling
during the day would be too risky, so I looked for a
place of concealment in which I could sleep until
the next night. The sound of gunfire and impacting
shells assumed a distant and far away place, leaving only a ringing in my brain.*

*Thankfully, I slid down an incline into a sunken
area beside a clay embankment. I grabbed an arm-
ful of fronds, dead branches, and leaves as I went. I
let my body sink below the black ooze, and with the
collected debris, I covered my head and chest.
Dimly, I was aware of movement, but it was not the
sound of man. Before my eyes closed, I attempted to
analyze my future activities toward rescue. I tried to
recall the aerial map but could only come up with
generalities.*

*To the southeast, an American infantry company
was in contact with the enemy. I would avoid this*

area. The idea of creeping up on a besieged company didn't agree with me at all. To the north was LZ West. It was common knowledge that the slopes of fire support bases were heavily mined. That area was also to be avoided.

I realized that there should be nothing to restrict my movement directly down the valley, due east. Once on the coastal plain I could contact friendly forces more easily . . . EAST! I sat up. Where was east? Above me, through a clearing, I could see the constellation Cassiopeia, which is north of the zodiac. I drew an arrow facing east in some elevated dirt, then leaned back and closed my eyes.

What caused me to awaken some hours later I do not know; subconsciously, however, I knew something was wrong. The air was heavy with fog, yet the light above me indicated it was morning.

Something was blocking the vision above my eye. I removed the brush from over my head and tried to remove the object from my face but could not. My hand was in view, and completely enveloping my fingers and hands, were leeches. In a frenzy, I pulled at them. They only slipped through my fingers or broke in half. I finally gathered my composure and, crawling from the water, I sat for a long time just pulling leeches from my body. They had gone up my sleeves, up my fatigue trousers, and covered my hands and face. Some were six inches or longer.

After I had removed the leeches, I stood up. That was the last thing I remembered until I awoke from a prone position. Obviously, I had fainted.

Suddenly, I wanted to laugh; the universe was playing games with me, plucking me from hell only to watch me flounder, too weak to walk. Angrily, I rose to my feet. I knew I must move before I weakened further.

As I reflect back, I realize I did a crazy thing. I made an insane decision which, comical or not, very possibly saved my life. To travel, I would have to take an easy path and avoid the rough undergrowth of jungle. In order to achieve this, I decided to go native-style; off came the clothing, including everything except the dirty, soiled (once white) boxer underwear.

I was dark complected, as are the natives, even though my six-foot-two-inch frame was stretching the idea a bit. Rubbing a little additional mud around my ankles, I brazenly walked out into the morning fog lacking only my water buffalo. My buried clothes behind me, I went into the middle of the valley, striding with toes pointed outward and shoulders sloped as do the natives of the Republic of Vietnam. Onward I went, paralleling a major trail which led east, taking care not to go near the main trail nor pass close enough to any object which might afford a perspective on which to compare my height.

Eventually, the sun beat through the thinning fog and onto my face. Being successful thus far, my body began to relax as I shuffled along. I then heard helicopters followed by the sound of gunfire. Passing by an embankment, I spied, beneath an overhang, a stack of assorted enemy weapons. Again, the adrenaline flowed. I looked neither right nor left and continued my shuffling walk. After a while I came to the mouth of Que Son Valley long after the sun had devoured the fog, long after my walking became mechanical.

It was now afternoon. The sun was on my back

when a profusion of natives, men and women on the main trail carrying goods to the marketplace, gave me hope that I was in friendly territory. I apprehensively turned to intersect the main trail.

Immediately, several nearby and very surprised natives looked at my height, then my face in astonishment. Shortly, I collected a crowd of no less than twenty children, laughing and shuffling along with me.

A Popular Forces (South Vietnamese) soldier, who witnessed the comedy, approached and attempted to communicate a question. Over and over, I talked on an imaginary phone until he finally got the idea and led me, followed by an impossible assortment of natives, to the outpost of Nuic Loc Son. Here, a bewildered American sergeant radioed for a medevac helicopter. Within the hour, I was in the American infirmary on Hill 35. Now, I could relax, contemplate my ordeal, and thank my friends for my life.

Sometime after Anton was shot down, the MPs showed up at LZ Baldy, arrested Foley, and took him to Chu Lai. He did not know which one of his many sins had come back to haunt him, and the MPs did nothing to enlighten him. Once he arrived in Chu Lai, he was grilled about selling a machine gun on the black market. Apparently, the grunts later recovered the machine gun which Foley lent Pfister. The company records showed the gun to be his with Pfister's M-60 being lost on Anton's gunship. Luckily, Foley had told a sergeant in the company armory what he had done the day Anton's gunship went down. The sergeant admitted that he had been told, but forgot to turn in the proper paperwork.

On January 5th, we also had a battalion chopper on a

mission in Laos shot down with all the crew killed. It was
hit at 4,000 feet altitude by 37 mm antiaircraft fire. Another slick, on the same mission, was hit at 300 feet with
all aboard killed as the chopper fell to the earth in flames.
Three Green Berets were killed when these aircraft
crashed. One of the pilots on one of these choppers was
married to his high school sweetheart just three months
prior to his death. In 1971 Wiegand married her (Donna)
and has been happily married since.

When I finally wrote home about Anton and the others,
we really never expected to see them alive again. Some
marines, fighting in the same region, told us about one of
their choppers that went down. Eight guys were on board,
and all eight were executed. Luckily for our friends, and
unknown to us at the time, the NVA and VC in our area
had just begun to take prisoners.

Everyone was in a deep funk for days after Anton was
shot down. The worst part was not actually knowing anything. There was also the realization, in the back of our
minds, that next time it might be one of us. It was de-
pressing and frustrating. One minute, Anton, Lewis, and
Pfister were a visible part of our lives. The next minute,
we knew nothing about what happened to them and knew
no way to help them. Even though we had all these emotions, the war went on, and we had no choice but to go on
ourselves.

January 6, 1968

I MADE AIRCRAFT
COMMANDER. WE
HAD A RECOILLESS
RIFLE SHOT AT US AND
A BATTALION
HELICOPTER WAS
SHOT DOWN AT LZ
CENTER.

I was nearly killed on January
6 because I followed the lead of
my heroic gunner and crew chief
(Aker and Bruce). That night we
stayed at Hill 35. The tent we
slept in was fortified with sandbags stacked around it about
three feet high. As I laid there in
an exhausted sleep, I jerked

awake as I heard a WHOOSH followed by a loud CRUMP! I jumped about three feet out of my cot. Fortunately, my reactions were delayed. Shrapnel knocked holes in the sandbags in front of our tent and in the tent itself. Had I been standing, I would have been pierced immediately. We were told later these were the big mortar rounds (82 mm). Bruce and Aker quickly tore ass to the chopper, along with the crew from the other gunship. I trotted behind rather slowly and watched as mortar rounds hit on either side of the helicopters. Shrapnel fragments whistled overhead. With the choppers bracketed by the rounds, I assumed that the next would hit dead center. I vividly recall sitting in the gunship, starting the turbine engine, and waiting for a mortar round to snuff out my life. Bruce says I didn't have my helmet on and he sat in the back of the gunship screaming "Crank this SOB, crank this SOB." Apparently, the enemy was out of ammo because the rounds suddenly stopped. I never ran to a helicopter under fire again.

On January 7, all the gunships were damaged except two. The 196th was still in heavy contact with the NVA division. We were attempting to put in attacks under about a 300-foot cloud ceiling. This type of close contact with VC farmers wouldn't have been too bad, but against well-trained NVA antiaircraft units, it was suicide. I was terrified. When an enemy unit was pinpointed, or their location fixed, the helicopter gunships could deal murder and mayhem in our normal indiscriminate manner. However, when fighting large NVA units, which was common in the Que Son Valley on a monthly basis, one location would be under attack and intense fire would come from three or four other locations simultaneously. Being a helicopter pilot at times like these was not the healthiest profession. Heavy cloud cover made the operation even riskier.

Even the jet jockeys did not relish maneuvering in some of our areas of operation. Because of the narrow valleys leading into and adjacent to the Que Son Valley, the jets had to make bombing runs down the very narrow gorge. As the jets came in for a second bombing run, the NVA antiaircraft units knew they were coming and would fire in front of the jet and let it fly through a warped version of a fireworks display.

The CO came up to me and asked me if I wanted to work in the motor pool. I immediately told him no, thanks. I was puzzled. Maybe I was about to have a nervous breakdown and did not even know it. Realizing that someone else might think you couldn't hack the pressure was very disconcerting, especially at that early invincible age.

On January 8, there were so many wounded soldiers at Hill 35 that they were placed on cots out in the open. They had run out of tent space. Apparently, the hospitals at Chu Lai and Da Nang were also full of the wounded and could not take on any more themselves.

While out flying, I glanced down and noticed a frail old Vietnamese man with a water buffalo and a cart hauling bodies from the combat area. Most of the fighting was in the southwest portion of the Que Son Valley to the south of LZ Ross. I often wondered if he was hauling his son and other village boys home to be buried. It took a brave man to be in that area.

On January 9, we had a Rattler slick shot down around where Anton's luck ran out. The helicopter burned, but the crew made it off without anyone getting hurt. That same day, Carson's wife had a nine-pound, four-ounce baby boy. One little baby boy being born and so many young men dying—all at the same time.

Somewhere around this time, Collins was flying slicks in a formation with Burroughs as peter pilot. They were picking up grunts from a PZ while under fire. A slick from our battalion hovered past them as they waited for their troops to load. This helicopter took Collins's place in the flight. On takeoff, it was hit by a recoilless rifle or a B-40 rocket. The helicopter exploded in flight and all aboard were killed.

Another Rattler slick was hit with a mortar round while sitting on LZ West. Our division had a small observation chopper (loach) and a gunship shot down in the same location where Anton was shot down. All crew members died as the gunship exploded. I was given credit for seven kills on NVA soldiers attempting to get to the crew on the observation chopper. I stayed in a perpetual state of fear. Most of the time, I was so scared that I walked around in a fog!

On January 10, some Fourth Infantry grunts were moved up to the Que Son Valley. One of the company commanders was killed by a sniper as he stepped out of the helicopter. The 196th was quickly running out of troops.

Carson and I were airborne in separate aircraft as A/Cs. Each of us took .50 caliber hits—Carson's was right through the fuel cells. We were in the process of escorting a medevac into a company of the 4/31 Battalion. This was Carson's first time to fly after his escape from his ill-fated mission with Anton. If that .50 caliber round had been a tracer, the fuel would have exploded and Carson's name would be on the Vietnam Memorial.

We flew air strikes all night long. The NVA division had worked us hard for nearly a week.

A Bullet in the Pecker

It was around this time that a very unusual incident took place. A loach (observation helicopter) landed one day at Hill 35, and a guy was carted out of it into the medic tent. Taylor and I walked out to look at the damaged loach and saw blood splattered all over the interior. We noticed that .30 cal. holes in the chopper seemed to indicate that the bullet had changed its trajectory passing through the helo. The angle of the hole in the floor did not line up with the one through the top of the chopper. As we were trying to figure out what caused this, the doctor stuck his head out of the tent and said, "Come here, you are not going to believe this!" We went over and stuck our heads in the tent. This poor guy was stretched out on the bed with his eyes rolled back in his head. The doctor pulled up the wounded man's pecker and showed it to anyone that wanted to look. I swear Taylor walked in for a close-up.

Come to find out, the round that did all the damage hit the guy's pistol. Most guys flew with some kind of pistol "between their legs." The bullet hit his pecker, then the pistol, and was deflected through the roof of the helicopter. If it had not been deflected by the pistol, it would have struck the guy under his chin. The doctor summarized the consequences of the injury succinctly: "This guy will have a built-in French tickler."

An Angel on the Tail Boom

I was scared to death after all the .50 caliber shooting on the previous days. In the dark, a .50 caliber tracer looked like a flaming foot locker heading toward you. At night, a tracer, even if headed ninety degrees away from you, looked for an instant as if it was about to explode squarely between your eyes.

Around this time, I stopped preflighting my aircraft. I was not sure if other aircraft commanders did this or not, but I would have the peter pilot check

January 11, 1968

BRUCE AND AKER SWORE THAT I WAS FLYING SO HIGH AN ANGEL WAS SITTING ON THE TAIL BOOM.

everything out and then would ask the crew chief if it was ready to go. Superstitiously, I always kicked the toe of the skid before I boarded. By the time I made aircraft commander, I figured if my chopper was going to fall apart in the air, I was not going to catch the defective part. On January 12, I wrote home, "As for the war, it is still going like hell. I could hardly sleep last night. I feel like a coward. I flew all day with the jet traffic. It is not dangerous to fly low; it is plain murder."

A Turtle in the Cockpit

On January 12, the Firebirds sank ninety sampans on a night firefly mission. On that mission, Parsons was in the right seat, and I was shooting the miniguns when Charlie opened up out of a village with some tracers. We wore armored plates on our chest which we called chickenboards. Not being very large, it did not cover the shoulders or up around the neck. Being regular army issue, naturally, one size fit all. We were flying low and tracers were coming in fast. Parsons thought it was the damnedest thing when all he could see was my eyes peaking over the chickenboard. For a guy my size that was a pretty good trick. I resembled a turtle going into his shell to hide when the tracers lit up the night.

A Dummy on the Radio

January 16 was my day of infamy. We were on a firefly
mission along the river, east of LZ Baldy. Col. Buck Nelson, an infantry commander, was flying as door gunner.
He flew with us on numerous firefly missions. As the
light ship spotted the sampans, we received automatic
weapons fire from ten or so weapons about 100 feet below us. We flew away from the light with no lights on, so
on a dark or moonless night, the dinks had to guess at our
location. We shot up the village, but this time the old VC
were looking for a fight because they really poured it on
us.

We always laughed at the dumb VC who could not resist shooting at the sound of the gunship as they flew over
at night. Because of the muzzle flashes from their
weapons, we could usually dispose of the stupid, gun-
crazy bastards very quickly.

On this occasion, Col. Nelson, our high-ranking door
gunner, tried to radio out from the back of the gunship to
call in artillery. The radio box in the back would not let
him transmit, so he told us to call it in because we were
running out of ammo. Leopold had the controls. Our conversation went something like this: Leopold ordered,
"Call in the artillery." I responded, "I do not know how, I
slept through that class!" He retorted, "You went to flight
school after me, call it in, and besides that, I outrank you
and I am the boss." So I pulled out my trusty map and, using a red light so as to not lose night vision, I attempted to
find our coordinates. I changed the radio to the artillery
frequency and called in a spotter round. The artillery people would say "shot out" then "shot in." They said "shot
in," and this was when they timed the artillery shell to hit
the ground. I glanced down at the village and saw a large
flash exactly where the VC had been blasting at us. So I

radioed, "Fire for effect." I was really amazed that the artillery was that accurate and completely astonished that my map reading had been so precise. Apparently, the artillery guys knew the colonel was on the helicopter because I heard later they had fired every tube within range.

Once again, they said "shots out" then "shots in." I then stared down at the village and saw nothing. Suddenly, the colonel reached up, banged me on the helmet, and pointed miles down the river at a huge explosion. Apparently, under Leopold's command, I had given the coordinates for the wrong bend in the river. The flash on the ground below us, which I thought to be the artillery round impact, must have been an old muzzle loader rifle or something similar. Leopold asked the colonel what he wanted to do, and he disgustedly said, "Let's just call it a night." We all agreed.

Taking Hits

After taking hits for four days in a row, I took January 21 off. During some free time, I sat around and contemplated my mortality, concluding that I was destined to die a violent death in the flaming debris of a helicopter. I also drank a "little" nerve tonic that day. I remember mentioning the reason I took a break to several other pilots. They showed as much concern as they would have if I had told them I had a hangnail. One even told me I shouldn't be such a "Magnet Ass."

JANUARY 18, 1968

Singer Eartha Kitt stunned her hosts at a White House luncheon when she told first lady, Lady Bird Johnson, to her face that US policy in Vietnam was entirely wrong.

January 20, 1968

THE NVA LAID SIEGE TO THE MARINES AT KHE SANH. THIS REGION WAS NEAR THE DMZ. IT EVENTUALLY BECAME CLEAR THAT THE MAIN PURPOSE OF THIS SIEGE WAS TO DRAW ATTENTION AWAY FROM THE NVA AND VC PREPARATIONS FOR THE UPCOMING TET OFFENSIVE.

Bruce said one of the hits occurred during a low-level flight along Highway 1. At the time, I told him we had just taken a hit, but no one else on the helicopter heard it. We were hurrying to another destination, or I would have taken time out to do a little "hunting." Afterward, Bruce checked out the gunship and found no damage. I insisted that a bullet had hit the helicopter and told him to take a closer look. He went back, inspected the thing closer, and found the place where the bullet struck. The round hit the windshield wiper arm right in front of where I sat. I began to seriously consider the motor pool job!

I always considered there to be a big difference between being in a shoot-up and taking a hit. A "shoot-up" was when they kept pouring on the rounds with numerous automatic weapons fire. I have taken hits when we only heard a single shot fired. Unfortunately, a slick pilot in our company, named Cotton, was killed by a single round on what was scheduled to be his last flight in Vietnam. Some people still feel that a grunt in the back of the helicopter shot him by accident with an M-16 rifle.

M-16s

The M-16 rifle could lead to accidents. I have had experience with rifles since I was about eight years old and always considered myself safe. One day, while walking down the flight line at Chu Lai after a flight, I pulled the clip out of an M-16, pulled the bolt back, looked in the chamber, and noted it empty. I released the bolt, pulled the trigger and nearly shot off Collins's foot. The round in the chamber wasn't extracted off the bolt; and when I released the bolt, the round went back into the chamber. I missed Collins's foot by mere inches! Needless to say, he was mad as a hornet!

The M-16 rifle was a piece of crap back then. It was said that if the NVA stripped a dead American body, they would take everything but the poor guy's M-16. The NVA didn't waste their time picking up junk. I very rarely carried one—only during the periods when we couldn't get away with carrying non-issue weapons.

JANUARY 23, 1968

The North Koreans captured the intelligence ship USS Pueblo *in international waters.*

I once talked to an LRRP (long range reconnaisance patrol) team member at LZ Baldy who said that his M-16 had jammed on him four times in critical situations. He had threatened to quit if they refused to let him take his AK-47 on missions.

The Calm Before the Storm

On January 24, we were on a firefly mission. For some reason, the light that we normally used was not working. In order to run the mission, we decided to have a slick drop flares to light up the area, which they did nearly as well as sunlight. In about two and a half miles of river, we were shot at from ten different locations. Needless to say, we found an excuse to terminate the mission early. Otherwise, things were fairly quiet. No one in Vietnam (at least on our side) realized that the enemy was resting up to try to kick our ass big time on January 31.

On January 27, we escorted an insertion of grunts in the Que Son Valley and did not have a shot fired at us.

JANUARY 29, 1968

President Johnson asked for a tax increase to finance the continuation of the war.

That afternoon, just before dark, we extracted an LRRP team under fire. They reported seeing a hundred dinks marching along in a column. Naturally, nobody believed them. The enemy was closing in for the Tet Offensive.

Tet I

The Tet Offensive started on January 30 in our area by accident. Eight locations in South Vietnam were attacked a day before the offensive was actually supposed to begin. Hoi An, between Tam Ky and Da Nang, was one of the towns that was attacked on January 30. I guess the NVA and VC military was like ours in that there was always someone who never received the correct word.

I was flying wing gunship behind Latimer and Taylor on a firefly mission south of Hoi An late at night after it was attacked. Apparently, the brass figured the attacking forces would retreat south down the river. But we only sank five sampans that night.

Flying back early on the morning of January 31, I saw an incredible sight. It looked like Chu Lai had been hit by a nuke, and we were flying straight toward the inferno. An NVA 122 mm rocket had hit the ammunition dump and also blew up thirteen aircraft. The initial explosion was huge, and the ammo continued exploding for hours. Everything was blown up or under attack. LZ Baldy, LZ Ross, Hill 35, Tam Ky, and Chu Lai were all being hit by rockets and mortars. The time was somewhere around two or three o'clock in the morning.

Since we still had ammo and fuel, we were directed to Tam Ky, and flew into the war without even landing. Latimer's flight helmet was acting up, so Taylor had to talk to the American commander on the ground at Tam Ky. The grunt told him they would fire a string of .50 cal. tracer rounds, and we were to attack several hundred meters from this location. I was aircraft commander of the wing gunship and listened to the directions.

Shortly, Taylor saw a string of orange tracers. The grunt commander started screaming, "Don't fire! Don't fire!" The enemy had been monitoring the transmission on the radio and had fired tracers at the Americans.

From 3:00 A.M. until daylight I remember two things. I remember sitting on the ground at Hill 35 with mortar rounds hitting around the gunship and I remember being in a panic about running out of fuel. Bruce, Taylor, and Aker remember those events better, and between us we pieced together this account of the frantic actions that took place that morning.

After expending all ordnance at Tam Ky, we were forced to land at Hill 35 to refuel and rearm. It appeared that every base was under attack. I knew I wasn't brave enough to sit on the ground during a mortar attack and rearm the miniguns because it took a while to lay the ammo in the trays. Bruce says even he wasn't that brave. As the mortar rounds got closer, he and my peter pilot loaded rockets in the tubes, Aker pumped fuel in the gunship and Bruce threw ammo cans into the back of the chopper. Bruce and Aker loaded the minigun ammo trays in flight and threw the large empty ammo cans out the door. Bruce says they pumped just enough fuel into the gunship to make the low fuel warning light go off. We went back to Tam Ky and expended all our ordnance one more time. I remember being terrified that I would run out of fuel. Bruce says I screamed at Taylor and Latimer that I was out of fuel but we continued to attack the enemy positions. Once we expended the ammo, we took an informal poll and decided I didn't have enough fuel to make it back to Chu Lai. They said I had "dicked around too long." We landed at Tam Ky in the middle of an attack by enemy soldiers. Bruce says he and Aker stood next to the gunship with their M-60 machine guns as he pumped enough fuel in to get back to Chu Lai. He said he was amazed the refueling pump still worked. As we left the refueling point all hell broke loose and we took a hit through the minigun control box. At Chu Lai they made us land to the north end of the runway because shrapnel was still falling from the exploding ammo dump. Bruce says the Seventy-First was out of control boxes for the miniguns and Aker jumped in the Firebird jeep, drove to another aviation company area, and stole a control box while they were hiding in their bunkers. While Aker was stealing the control box, I jumped in another gunship flying wing to McCall and flew back to Tam Ky.

I was my normal self—scared shitless. The feeling was unreal! At times like that I was concerned about a court-martial for destroying government property, putting skid marks in Uncle Sam's underwear!

Already, an NVA regiment and the Main Force VC unit had penetrated Tam Ky. They had plenty of VC help on the inside of the town and, consequently, expected to overrun the place easily.

Because of the attack the previous day on Hoi An, our desk jockeys had actually done something right. They had moved a US Cavalry APC unit inside the town of Tam Ky.

The dinks were not expecting the Americans and were surprised.

At daylight, the NVA started their retreat. They were pulling back to the north-northwest out in the open, pulling their dead and wounded along with them. Over the radio, there was the most confused and dangerous madhouse atmosphere I ever heard in Vietnam. Marine jets, air force jets, South Vietnamese A-1Es, air force A-1Es (propeller driven bombers), a C-130 Spectre (large plane with miniguns on it), plus all kinds of artillery units (Vietnamese and army) were trying to get permission to shoot at the same instant. An air force FAC (forward air controller) was attempting to control the bedlam. One problem he encountered was that McCall and I were already on the deck chasing after the NVA like ducks going after June bugs. To add to the NVA's woes, the men fleeing could not run fast enough because each was dragging or carrying wounded or dead.

I had heard that NVA soldiers were trained to follow orders so well that they never gave a thought to doing anything different. I am absolutely convinced that the dink commanding officer told them to save all the wounded and drag out their dead, and that was exactly what they attempted to do without deviation. AK-47s were perched on their shoulders; and in the open, we came in 100 feet above them. They never attempted to fire back at us or protect themselves. We mowed them down without mercy. While engrossed in our mission, a FAC and a Spectre gunship kept screaming over the radio, on the emergency frequency, "Army helicopters north of Tam Ky, we are going to shoot you down if you don't leave the area!" I radioed McCall asking, "What do we do?" He just stated, "Keep shooting!" Although dawn had finally come, it was still technically dark. However, you could now see the retreating soldiers clearly. I am positive the air force guys were hopping mad at us because this was one of the few times they would ever actually see so many of the enemy, and we were in the way. I had never even dreamed of seeing that many NVA in the open.

My crew had their machine guns chattering viciously, shooting down every commie who even thought about moving. During this battle, one could clearly see the difference between a normal VC unit and an NVA unit. The VC unit would totally panic. They scattered like cockroaches under a light. You could usually dispose of them quickly and callously if they didn't make it to their holes first.

The NVA survivors made it to a tree line next to a creek, and apparently an officer rallied the troops. They decided to fight back. We were still down under 100 feet, firing furiously. The man in the FAC aircraft was still screaming over the emergency radio channel that he was going to shoot down the army helicopters if we did not leave the area, pronto!

When the NVA hit that tree line, the gunfire that immediately came out was amazing. There must have been thirty or forty AK-47s shooting on full automatic. A barrage of tracer tracks burst from the tree line; and in the early morning darkness, all the light looked like a laser show. My gunship was dealing out death and destruction away from the tree line while McCall flew close to it. Suddenly, the AK-47s zeroed in on him. He yelled over the radio, "Receiving fire!" I jerked my gunship around to fire some rockets under him. At that moment, I had several rockets left. All the minigun ammo was spent. One door gunner was out of machine gun ammo and was firing a rifle and a pistol. We would have thrown rocks if we had any. I started the rocket run from about 100 feet up. My gunship became a sitting duck for all the communists' automatic weapons. I screamed, "Receiving fire," and attempted to fly away from the tree line as bullets and scrap metal ricocheted all over the inside of my gunship. McCall circled back in his Hog gunship, angling further from the tree line than I was. He still had enough rockets to make them duck while we once again engaged in our "look back" tactics. (We looked back at them while we got the hell out of the area!)

My gunner, Palazzo, and crew chief were yelling that both of them had been hit. McCall had saved our lives, because I could not avoid the fire from the automatic weapons at my altitude and airspeed. There was little doubt in my mind that, at that height and distance, thirty or forty automatic weapons could down a gunship in seconds. We left the remaining NVA for the Spectra and headed out of there.

The 196th Light Infantry credited the helicopter gunships and the Spectra with six hundred NVA and VC killed at Tam Ky on January 31, 1968. That was our personal initiation to the start of the Tet Offensive.

The Americal Division recorded 486 killed in a report ending on January 31, 1968. It is possible they had not counted all the bodies on that date and also on February 1. I truly did not believe we killed that many. I always believed some of the dinks were attempting to drag up to two bodies each. Many NVA had been killed by the Americans and ARVN in Tam Ky. The bodies had just been dragged out in the open when we pounced on them. Palazzo, on the other hand, thought that six hundred was a fair number.

As that crazy crew member had told me when I first arrived in the Nam, "Death was our business and business was good." McCall's gunship was shot up, my gunner and crew chief were wounded, my helicopter filled up with an acrid burning smell, and I thought I was about to die. As our choppers limped from the combat scene, my chest was heaving frantically. We were not taking prisoners; therefore, the enemy would have loved to help us to a slow death for shooting them with their wounded. Luckily, I was not destined for such a messy fate.

Sometimes, during fierce fighting, bullet hits caused an electrical short that would smoke the wires until the circuit breaker popped. When numerous hits came through the floor of the helicopter, the heat of the bullets, mixed with the heat of the aluminum shrapnel (pieces of the floor) and some hydraulic fluid on the aluminum shrapnel, gave off a burning smell. This burning smell always alarmed me. On this date alone, I smelled it four different times. Palazzo, my gunner, had a .30 cal. round hit on the chickenboard where he was sitting. This was the second time that happened to one of my crew members in Vietnam. Palazzo limped around the flight line for several days just as the other gunner had done. It seemed that a .30 cal. round did put a pretty good bruise on the rear end when it hit one of those chickenboards.

The gunner and crew chief were struck with shrapnel from the rounds that hit. These were either pieces of the copper jackets from the bullets or shrapnel from the helicopter. I flew back to Chu Lai, and Bruce's helicopter was waiting there. They had replaced the minigun control box. I jumped in, with Hannah as peter pilot, and told someone to take the other crew members to the hospital. Off I went again!

To this day, I still wonder about my own reactions to the events in Vietnam. One thing I still cannot understand was how some days I would be so scared I could not move my finger to say something over the radio. Days later, I would volunteer to go out and be a target. With combat raging unabated for hours, I had been up all night and was sure I could have refused to go back out. Refusal never entered my mind. Hannah and I went back to Tam Ky in a single gunship. The others were all shot full of holes.

Rattler Operations ordered me to join up with a single Musket gunship from our battalion. I then made radio contact with the Musket and was surprised to hear a guy I went to flight school with, Gaither. I told him to go ahead and fly lead. He declined, so I ended up as lead. En route, I contacted the American advisors on the ground. A man came up over the radio stating that he had a thousand VC in the open. My immediate reaction was, "Yeah, I sure believe that." This guy was at an observation post west of Tam Ky on a rock hill and was crying and sobbing over the radio. He was completely freaked out!

Twenty-five years later, at our reunion, I related a strange "vision" that I witnessed on the first day of Tet I. As I recalled my strange vision, everyone just looked at me. My old buddy McCall even raised his eyebrow, and I could tell he thought I just had a screw come loose. My story was about looking down while flying and seeing a huge parade of Vietnamese marching down the road out in the boondocks. This was a very unusual spectacle, to say the least. The parade was around a thousand people with some carrying huge banners that stretched completely across the road. As I flew over low level, some of the marchers proceeded to shoot my gunship to pieces. Even the craziest helicopter pilots in the group had a very hard time swallowing this tale. They thought I definitely had a severe memory problem.

The only support for my story at that time was from the slick pilot, Jim Miller, who asked, "Was that out by the rock hill west of Tam Ky?" I answered yes. He then told us the day after the Tet Offensive started, he flew over and watched bulldozers burying many bodies. Since our reunion, I have found my peter pilot that day, Hannah, my crew chief, Bruce, and my gunner, Aker. Each one vouched for this unlikely story.

When the American advisor finally calmed enough to direct us to his thousand VC, I came up on a scene that was surrealistic. It was a parade! Sure enough, about a thousand people—women, kids, and old men—were carrying signs and banners. The banners stretched across the road. Hannah remembered the parade going away from Tam Ky. I remembered the people being in the process of turning around when we first saw them. Supposedly, the NVA told all the villagers they were going to capture Tam Ky and wanted to have a big parade to celebrate the victory.

Our first pass was at about 1,000 feet. The American was in a frenzy telling us to shoot them up because the NVA had begun dragging their wounded into the parade. Between the NVA and their wounded and the gunships, the people in the parade began to panic. I consulted with Gaither about what he wanted to do, and he merely said, "You're the lead." Hannah said I lined up and went hot, turning on the electricity to the miniguns. I told him to fire, and then saw the kids. Immediately, I yelled, "Don't fire!" By then, we were not more than 100 feet above the parade. From the ground, they shot the living shit out of us!

(In 1993, I was talking to Bruce and told him I had not allowed them to fire on the parade. He thought my memory was faulty because he and Aker really let the marchers have it.)

The helicopter began filling up with the burning smell from all the rounds hitting it. I then told them to suppress the muzzle flashes. Gaither's helicopter called saying Gaither was shot in the foot.

We flew back to Chu Lai, and upon arrival, maintenance had another helicopter flyable. Hannah and I climbed in and went back to Tam Ky. My bravery and gung-ho attitude possibly was a direct result of my lack of sleep. It may have also been the consequence of shock, resulting from everything we had seen and done that day! Maybe, I was just out for revenge over what I assumed had happened to Anton.

For the fourth time that day, we flew back to Tam Ky. Once there, I went hunting for dinks in the area where we sighted the parade. I was angry at myself because flying over the parade at such a low level could have gotten my crew killed, not to mention the crew on the wing helicopter. Who would have thought there would be hostile parades in Vietnam! As we arrived over the place where the people had been, I was astonished. Some fixed wing aircraft had dropped antipersonnel bombs on the road. The blood and gore were unbelievable. Mounds of bloody flesh were strewn along the road. (That was what Miller saw them burying with dozers the next day.) As I flew along, I was startled to see a black flash pass in front of the helicopter. It was a bomb falling right in front of me. I got the hell out of there!

From the ground, American advisors then had us shoot into a tree line where some uniformed dinks were hiding. I cannot remember if I had a wing aircraft, or had joined up with a gunship from our company, or was just out hunting solo. Anyway, we were shot up again.

For twenty-five years I told the story about actually seeing a bullet fly past my head that day. I remember looking straight at Hannah as the bullet went between our heads. While reminiscing with Hannah, he laughed and commented, "That wasn't a bullet, it was a piece of the floor that pinwheeled past your head. It went in slow motion." I started laughing because I had always wondered how I could have seen a moving bullet! Whatever it was, it took care of my brave feelings for the rest of the day.

After we left Bruce and his shot-up gunship at Chu Lai, troops from division headquarters drove up and arrested everyone. A large truck took them to the headquarters area. Apparently, word had gotten back to Chu Lai about the parade and helicopter gunships in the vicinity. By the time they got to headquarters, the men from Chu Lai found out some fixed-winged plane had dropped antipersonnel bombs. Once dropped from a plane, this type of bomb detonated above the ground and released hundreds of "bomblets" which exploded at different intervals.

With this information on hand, the troops loaded everyone up again and took them back to the Firebird flight line. Later, I heard the massacre was blamed on South Vietnamese planes.

On February 2, Miller flew me to Da Nang. I was to leave from there for R&R in Hawaii and my marriage to Kathy. On the way to Da Nang, we stopped at Tam Ky and picked up a load of prisoners who just happened to be kids around ten years old and younger. Their guard told me they had been rigged with explosives and were expected to crawl into the perimeter wire and bunkers and blow themselves up to launch the Tet Offensive. The kids got scared, or smart, and would not pull the pins to detonate. They would not choose to die a hero's death for Uncle Ho.

I thought to myself, "What kind of men would use kids to fight a war?" Then, I thought about some of the crap I had seen from our side.

February 1, 1968

THE MILITARY DISCUSSED USING TACTICAL NUCLEAR WEAPONS ON THE NVA. I SLEPT ALL DAY.

These kids were not large enough to shoot a gun, but apparently were large enough to be taught to be human bombs. I sat and stared at them, and they stared back at me all the way to Da Nang.

In Da Nang that night, the VC

mortared the R&R center. There were huge bunkers for everyone, and the dinks shot mortars at us for hours. There must have been a hundred people in the bunker where I spent the night. While sitting there, I was concerned about satchel charges being thrown into the bunker or else having some other ten-year-old kid walk into the bunker with the bombs hung all over him.

The next morning I walked out to take a look at the perimeter and couldn't believe my eyes. The perimeter was just a little wire with a small mine field and a little more wire. I thought surely that must be an internal perimeter. Chu Lai had internal perimeters set up, and surely Da Nang did too at certain places. However, I could not locate any more defense lines! I vowed that if I had to spend another night there, I would not go back in that bunker! The defenses did not look very convincing to me.

Parsons relates some of the continuing Tet Offensive action that went on while I was on R&R.

> *We flew a night mission out of Hill 35 and found a large number, maybe even a battalion, of NVA. They were out in the open in a region west of Tam Ky. We worked them over good. A Spooky (C-47) came on station to relieve us. Then, someone reported that they had picked up the NVA's frequency. Naturally, we tuned in and listened. They were screaming and yelling big time.*

While in Hawaii, I read an article by a syndicated columnist about the Tet Offensive. He quoted General Custer at the Battle of Little Big Horn, "the battle has turned the corner and we have the Indians on the run." Apparently, he did not know that the rumors of our demise were premature.

February 3–10, 1968

I WAS MARRIED AT
THE CENTRAL UNION
CHURCH IN
HONOLULU, HAWAII
ON FEBRUARY 5,
1968. ABOUT ALL I
REMEMBER OF MY
R&R WAS EATING A
LOT OF STRAWBERRY
SHORTCAKE AND
NEEDING TO GET BACK
TO VIETNAM FOR A
REST!

On February 7, 1968, the NVA
used tanks to overrun a Green
Beret camp. Four days later, I
was back in Vietnam.

On the 13th and 14th, we flew
support for units in the area of
My Lai. During the night of the
13th, Chu Lai was attacked with
rockets. There were as many rumors flying around Chu Lai as
there were rockets. One rumor
was that the Russian tanks that
overran the special forces camp
had poison gas shells aboard. I
don't believe this, however.
Even at the time, I doubted that one; but it was hard in the
midst of heavy combat not to be affected by such rumors.
Even if you could reject them intellectually, they worked
on the emotions by adding to the environment of fear.

People Call Me Forrest Gump

In Happy Valley, the Firebirds tangled with the "Forrest
Gump" of the NVA. Unfortunately for him, his story
didn't turn out as well as the movie did. We scrambled out

FEBRUARY 8, 1968

*Sen. Robert F.
Kennedy of New York
says that the United
States cannot win the
Vietnam War.*

of LZ Baldy. I was flying lead
helicopter in a Hog gunship. The
grunt commander told me over
the radio that Charlie had a light
machine gun set up at a little
crossroads. In reality, it was a
path that crossed a dirt road. The
grunt warned us to watch out for

this guy because he had plenty of ammo. He said the machine gun was dug in several feet from the road. Now, I really did not believe this grunt because the man or men would have no cover.

Even as I was expressing my doubts over the radio, the machine gun began to fire at us. The shooting was coming from a place that was completely in the open. Since we had never flown in the area before, I was flying at 1,500 feet. I planned to dive to about 500 feet, which would allow me to shoot twenty or so rockets from my Hog gunship if needed. I started my gun run from 1,500 feet coming in at an angle that was straight at the firing site. As I began to let the

February 15, 1968

GEN. WESTMORELAND, CONCERNED ABOUT THE ENEMY UNITS LOCATED AROUND DA NANG, ORDERED A BATTALION OF THE 196TH AND A BATTALION OF THE 198TH INFANTRY MOVED NORTH TO BAIL OUT THE MARINES AT HAPPY VALLEY. THE MARINES CALLED THEIR LOCATION HAPPY VALLEY, BECAUSE THEY WERE EXTREMELY HAPPY WHEN THEY GOT OUT OF THE PLACE ALIVE.

machine gun nest have it with rockets, my door gunners were also furiously peppering the area with their gunfire. The little pukebag in the hole started a steady stream of .30 caliber tracers coming back at me. For some strange reason, this action pissed me off, and I just kept pouring on the rockets. Out of the dust and smoke from those rockets came a steady stream of tracers. At least the guy's vision was impaired by the smoke and dust so that he could not see my gunship. However, the muzzle flashes of his machine gun could be spotted quite clearly. The minigun ship flying my wing finally extinguished the return fire on its gun run.

During my tour in Vietnam, I never witnessed another

situation similar to this incident. It was completely suicidal to be dug in out in the open. What was even crazier was the guy taking his stand against a gunship that was zeroed in on him. I suspect that some NVA officer told the most gullible, gung-ho soldier he had to guard the crossroads and stop anyone from passing. I assume the officer did not actually order him to dig in only two feet away from an open road. After we shot up the machine gun nest, the grunt radioed that he had counted "six confirmed dead." This probably meant there were actually two dead.

FEBRUARY 16, 1968

President Johnson abolished draft deferments for graduate students. This order should have supplied the army with all the long-haired, dope-smoking, bearded hippies hiding out in England at Oxford University.

We were fighting a unit of the Second NVA Division, and by this time, we were down to three flyable gunships. On a firefly mission that night, we had six confirmed kills and sank twenty-four sampans. My gunship took two hits. We must have wrecked and flamed a village because the official reports credited us with eighteen structures destroyed and twenty-five damaged. As my companions and I flew off into the treacherous night, I suppose we should have given thanks for the great opportunity we had to put up some nice stats for the brass and the folks back home!

A Routine Couple of Weeks

February 18: A unit of the Eighty-Second Airborne was moving into the area. A slick helicopter based at Chu Lai was shot down, and all crew members were killed.

February 19: We flew a firefly mission and had five confirmed VC kills along with twenty-one sampans and forty structures destroyed. Charlie baited a trap for us and had a crossfire of machine guns set up over some empty sampans. We taught them not to try that again.

February 20: The NVA crawled out of their holes and back out into the Que Son Valley. A battalion helicopter was shot down, and the 196th Light Infantry was engaged in heavy combat. Somewhere around this date, I witnessed a US Army unit completely mow down a village. They knocked down every hootch, tree, and bush. Nothing was left standing. A sniper kept firing at the grunts, killing them, and then hiding in tunnels under the village. After the village was leveled, the sniper could not possibly attack them again from that particular vantage point. Someone suggested we make a parking lot out of the whole place. The enemy would then have no place to hide.

February 23: Chu Lai was mortared, but the dinks could not shoot them far enough to hit our company area. They had to use rockets to reach us in bed at Chu Lai, because it was such a large base. The NVA had a company of US grunts caught in the jungle. We flew all day shooting around the jungle area attempting to drive the enemy back. That night we rearmed the gunships three times and escorted six medevacs into the unit of the 196th. We safely brought out six helicopter loads of wounded. Once again, one of the grunt commanders promised us big medals, but as usual, we never saw or heard any more about it.

February 24: Our military finally mopped up the action against the NVA at Hue. This ended the last fight of the Tet Offensive. Rumors were flying that the Firebirds might be sent to Hue to help in the fighting. I personally felt we were getting all the action we could handle in our own area without going somewhere else and looking for more trouble.

February 25: The grunts attacked in an area where the My Lai massacre would take place several weeks later. The VC Main Force unit ambushed them, and the grunts were caught in several mine fields. When the units went back on March 16, it was said they were out for revenge.

February 29: I had flown five days in a row. I landed at LZ Baldy and saw that the First Cavalry had flattened the villages around it for five miles. I guess you could say they were practicing President Johnson's "urban renewal" policies.

March 2: The NVA were certainly out to fight. We had a slick pilot shot in the foot and another slick shot down. Taylor and I spent the day flying out of LZ Baldy. That night, Taylor and I crawled to the perimeter to shoot some unauthorized guns we had procured. One of us accidentally hit a trip flare, and World War III erupted! The grunts fired the entire night. For some peculiar reason, we did not get any sleep at all!

On March 4, my friend Parsons was shot down. Parsons describes the harrowing events of that day in his own words:

My last day with the Seventy-First (March 4) . . . (Lt. Litchfield was peter pilot, Reynolds was crew chief, and Smith was gunner). I believe it was Saturday (March 3) evening when Latimer and I flew a mission to cover a convoy that was heading to LZ Baldy. We were to refuel and then report to Baldy to be the first crew to start standby at that place instead of at Hill 35. We landed there late that afternoon and started asking all the important questions . . . Where can we get fed? . . . Where can we sleep? As usual, we couldn't find anyone who knew what the hell was going on. We found some engineers with a small dozer and they dug us a deep bunker, covered it with

MARCH 2, 1968

The American Civil Liberties Union announced that it would help represent Benjamin Spock and Yale University chaplain William Sloane Coffin, who were indicted on January 5 on charges of advising young men to avoid the military draft.

PSP (metal planking used to make airport runways) and our new palace was ready.

Early the next morning, we were scrambled to escort a medevac to pick up some wounded from a mountaintop on the northwestern end of the Que Son Valley. I remember going about as far out on that mountain chain as I could ever recall going before. We were told the unit was made up of some special forces and LRRPs that had been looking for a POW camp. (I kept thinking that maybe Anton, Lewis, and Pfister might be there.) The team had been hit hard during the night and suffered high casualties. We headed west, met the medevac ship, and then turned north up a valley that was a "deadend" due to the low ceiling. The mountaintop was to our left, the valley floor climbed to the north up into the mountains and clouds. The ridge line to our right (east) was just barely under the clouds.

We escorted the medevac back up the valley until he slowed and started hovering up the mountainside to get to the top of the mountain that was socked in. We set up a right-hand pattern, and the first lap went fine. The second lap also went smoothly. I was thinking we should move back down the valley or at least away from the area where we lost sight of the Huey that was "at the top in the clouds." I figured that we were sitting ducks for a mid-air if he took fire or came out without advising us.

Latimer broke right on lap three, and I was inbound. Just as I started my break, I saw Latimer still outbound, not having started a turn to the base leg of the pattern. All hell broke loose! Reynolds was screaming "We're taking .50 cal. fire." The noise became deafening. I felt a few hits. My visor was up and small "crap shrapnel" peppered my face and right leg. Every light on the caution panel, including ones I was sure I had never seen before, went on at one time. The turbine took a deep "death breath," and then it was "glider time." Falling like an anvil lubricated with grease, I continued my break to the right, down and out of the valley. I let the rotor rpm build to the redline. I pulled in pitch and called Latimer. I was so rattled by now; I didn't call "Mayday! Mayday!" I just radioed "97, this is 95 going down, 97, this is 95 going down!" Latimer didn't even see me!

I had to make a quick choice. I could continue away from the .50 cal. and put the chopper down in the valley. This valley was all double and triple canopy jungle. Or, I could stretch the glide and try to maintain some altitude to get us across the valley to a pinnacle-finger on the ridge which had a clear area. I headed for this finger, and I could have sworn it was impossible for a fully loaded C-model to travel horizontally that far without power. Too bad I never got a chance to practice horizontal/pinnacle autorotations in flight school! Litchfield and the guys stayed on their weapons the whole way. Litchfield picked up on where I was taking that "dead bird" and hosed the area thoroughly with the miniguns. He stayed cool and got the switches turned off. I ran out of airspeed and altitude. I probably pulled the collective through the greenhouse. I also ran out of ideas at about ten to fifteen feet, just short of the top of the ridge.

We hit hard, but the C-model was so heavily loaded, it stuck like a chunk of pancake dropped in Aunt Jemima syrup. If we had been empty, we probably would have bounced over the ridge line. The

resulting injuries were mainly from rectovocal
trauma, better described as "four tight assholes being jammed vertically up to our vocal cords." My
chickenboard had slammed under my chin and almost broke my neck. It felt like Muhammed Ali had
given me an uppercut. My lower back felt as though
someone had cut me open and wrapped some of
that German razor wire around my lower spine and
tailbone and was yanking on it! Litchfield remained
on the minigun flex sight up until impact. It looked
like he had been force fed the reticle and pistol grip
assembly! He was bleeding profusely.

The adrenaline took over and I tried twice, unsuc-
cessfully, to get out of the bird without unfastening
my harness. Releasing my harness, I wedged my left
foot up against the console and proceeded to launch
myself through the slide chicken plate on the armored seat and out the door. I always did hate
the thought of "crashing and burning!" Outside, the
first thing I heard and saw was Reynolds. He was
writhing on the cargo floor holding his back. The
next thing was the sound of less than friendly small
arms fire mixed with a background of that same old
.50 cal. and some Vietnamese shouting in the distance. I then heard the beautiful shriek and explosion of 2.75s being put in down the ridge by Latimer
and saw a slick on final to the top of the ridge.

I picked up Reynolds and slung him over my
shoulder. (Boy, did he let out a holler. It was definitely not the best way to treat a back injury.) I
grabbed his M-60 and some ammo, and ran up to
the top of the hill. I believe Litchfield and Smith
passed me on the way. Kretchmer had been flying
some colonel from the 196th around the AO (area of
operations). He came in to get us. I hefted Reynolds

up to the door gunner and noticed that the colonel, with eyes as big as moon pies, was reaching and motioning for me to hand him Reynold's M-60. I turned it horizontal thinking he would grab it by the foregrip and not the red-hot barrel. Wrong! He grabbed the barrel, and his immediate facial expression was one of the greatest representations of pain that I have ever witnessed. I heard later that the colonel got a Distiguished Flying Cross for "ordering" the rescue. (Could you believe that anyone ever ordered Kretchmer to do anything, or that he wouldn't have come in to get any Firebird that went down with or without some colonel ordering him to do it?)

Like a dummy, I did not get in the slick but ran back down the mountain to get the SOI, maps, survival radio, miniguns, and maybe pull some radios. I was confused, but clearly remembered the importance of not leaving those items behind. At the slick, I found that Litchfield had brought out the SOI, maps, and radio. As I went to the nose to get some radios, the crew chief from Kretchmer's slick caught up with me, grabbed me by the arm, and pointedly said, "Leave that shit . . . let's get the hell out of here!" It seemed like a reasonable idea to me, so we adiosed the AO.

Kretchmer later told me that we were still taking fire when he was hovering on the top of the ridge and while we were loading the ship to evacuate. Being in the left seat, his side was turned to my gunship, he noticed rounds impacting under the chin bubble. He turned to his copilot and said, "You got it." Then he drew himself up into a little ball in the armored seat. They sped first to the MASH unit at Baldy as I was still in a daze. Kretchmer related that I looked glassy-eyed. All I could say over and over apologetically was, "I sure am sorry about losing that aircraft." At first, enough adrenaline was in my system that I didn't feel too much pain. I was walking around. In short order, they medevaced us to Da Nang. As we flew there, I began to hurt big time! When we got to the hospital at Da Nang, the medics came running out with litters. Smith, Reynolds, and Litchfield were placed on the stretchers. I was asked, "Chief, can you walk?" I replied, with my best Mr. Macho, John Wayne imitation, "Sure guys," and promptly slipped out of the cargo bay. The last thing I remembered was my feet hitting the pad and a pain that was probably similar to someone setting off a claymore behind my back shooting through my body. I blacked out and collapsed in a neat little pile around my boots.

When I woke up some time later, I was in a hangar with what must have been a hundred other wounded. Next to me was a little surgery area with white shower curtain–like walls. They were parted, and the surgeons were operating on some GI who was missing a large portion of his skull! I rolled over, and a few minutes later, a medic came by and cut off my boots and started cutting off my clothes. I asked if I could keep my sweater. (It was difficult to get one of those three-button wool pull-overs that were so warm during the cold season.) He merely laughed as he stripped me completely. I laid there for a long time feeling somewhat like naked exposed whale meat. Finally, some nurse came by and asked me if I needed anything for pain. I popped back, "I'll take a triple dose of whatever you are serving." Blessedly, I was then introduced to the wonder and beauty of Demerol! For the next day or so, in that hangar, they would come by every few hours with a cart filled with "Magic Medical Mixtures." They would ask if I needed anything for pain, and I would smile and immediately, and painfully, roll over so they could stick me in the ass with more Demerol. I later learned to mix 500 mg Darvon tabs with the Demerol injections and found it to be a most relaxing combination . . . just lay in a drug daze for days!

To wrap up the shoot-down story. They X-rayed my back and didn't find anything the first time. I was diagnosed with a sprained back. (OK, if you say so, Doc!) Hell, I didn't know what a sprained back or broken back should feel like, so I took their expert word for it! If enough Demerol and Darvon were consumed, it really did not matter. Because of an acute shortage of hospital beds all over the country, the USS Hope and Repose were also full, they were shipping out the recently wounded to Japan. Once I arrived in Japan, I was put on an exercise program! (No one knew that I had two vertebrae with compression fractures!) It hurt like hell, but I was in a ward with guys who had lost arms and legs or had suffered severe burns. They were all going through extreme pain during rehab exercises, so who was I to complain about a little "sprained back." The other factor that helped immensely was that I gave my liquor ration card to an old NCO at the hospital. He made sure that I got plenty of Johnnie Walker Red to mix with my Demerol and Darvon. This helped keep the pain under control during my twice-a-day rehabilitation exercise routines for my broken back. Finally, I was X-rayed again and found to have fractured vertebrae. I was sent to Fort Rucker, where I became a classroom instructor of

Aircraft Armament Systems and M-22 (SS-11) wire guided missiles.

I was sent back for a second tour in September of 1969, and was transitioned as an instructor pilot. Once again, I was sent to the American at Chu Lai. I joined D Troop, First Squadron, First Cavalry flying scouts and guns (Cobras). I was blown out of the sky three more times. One of these times, I took an AK round in the back of the helmet. Luckily, it didn't penetrate, but a small metal sliver lodged in my skull. Several years later this sliver formed a bone tumor that had to be removed. I now have a nice hole in the back of my head a little larger than the size of a quarter. The CO was overly generous, and consequently, I received a DFC and Silver Star during that tour. I did manage to get more than even with the NVA around Chu Lai for shooting me down the first time in '68.

Parsons was shot in the head while flying around the area of My Lai. The group that Parsons was supporting on March 4 included special forces soldiers. One of their primary functions in Vietnam was to locate POW camps. Apparently, they were searching for Anton. On that particular mission, whatever they found on those steep slopes must have been important. Shortly after Parsons was shot down, they bombed the mountains with B-52 bombers.

The gunship that Parson crash-landed on March 4 had to be destroyed. There was too much gunfire in the area to attempt to salvage it. Other Firebird gunships shot it up and set it on fire the day it went down.

Liz Trotta

On March 6, a slick door gunner was shot in the neck. A slick pilot, Robinson, came to show me his flight helmet. The radio cord was shot off the back of it.

Robinson was the only black pilot in the Rattlers during my tour. He now lives in Saudi Arabia, and I recently wrote to him to let him know that he'd been on TV. The show was a documentary about news reporters during the Vietnam War, and had a segment featuring Liz Trotta, currently with the *Washington Times* newspaper. The footage included a shot of her in Vietnam running to a helicopter with a Rattlesnake on the front. Running behind her was Jerry Ericsson, a pilot from the Seventy-First. Ericsson recalls that the incident occurred at the Thoung Duc special forces camp in September 1968, where his helicopter was hit with a mortar round on takeoff. It crashed over the side of the hill below the helipad, and he ran back up the hill where Robinson landed under mortar fire to pick them up. Ericsson and I both have talked to Liz Trotta since then. She was under the impression that Ericsson and his crew were all dead, having been so informed by someone on the scene and having seen the chopper crash over the side of the hill.

Lieutenant David Zbozien

On March 11, a company of the 196th really tangled with the NVA. Seventeen helicopters in our division took hits, three were shot down. I had never seen the NVA so aggressive. Parsons was in the hospital in Japan after being shot down and injured. He received a letter from Latimer, dated March 13, 1968, describing the action, part of which follows:

> *Killer-Whale, [Parson's nickname]*
>
> *You don't know how good it was to hear from you and find out you're all right. You did the most outstanding job of getting an airplane down that has ever been done in this company. You made the only spot you could have possibly made and still save all your crew! I was damn proud of you—you should be proud, too. I guess you heard that Carson and I had to destroy the gunship with rockets. The recovery crews couldn't get in to it because of the .50 cal. fire.*
>
> *Day before yesterday, Buzzell and I really got into a fight. That Third NVA regiment that was in Carson's valley hit a company just west of Hill 62, in the flatlands. It was one of their typical "U" shaped ambushes and they were really tearing those guys up. Well, Buzzell and I got there before anyone else and the poor bastards on the ground didn't have any smoke to mark with—it took us almost forty minutes to finally locate them, and in the meantime I took two .50 hits and Buzzell took one. When we did get our strike in, we caught about the worst fire I ever heard—but no more hits. We learned later that there were eight known .50 cals. there. In the course of the day, seventeen ships were shot up and two shot down. Buzzell and I took gunship 611 into that area that evening to extract one wounded grunt and the crew from a 123rd gunship that was lost that afternoon. I took one more hit (ceiling was 800 ft. and we were just lucky).*

A flight of UH-1D "Rattler" slicks over Vietnam.

The author—in my best John Wayne pose. Note the pistol carried between the legs to protect this vital area from shrapnel and stray bullets.

Crew Chief Joe Bruce—one bad dude. Maybe the baddest dude in Vietnam, until his luck ran out and he was badly burned by hot oil as he was pinned under the wreckage of his chopper. But he lived to brag about it.

Frank Anton. I flew my first combat mission as his copilot. He wasn't impressed. Behind him is the chopper he was flying when he was later shot down and captured (January 5, 1968). He spent five years as a POW.

Crew Chief Ray Foley—in his best John Wayne pose. He was flying with McCall in a futile attempt to rescue Anton and his crew, who were shot down January 5. McCall's chopper nearly became the second Firebird casualty of the day because of the intense fire encountered in that daring rescue attempt. One of the pedals was actually shot off from under McCall's feet. On another occasion, Foley was hit in the leg by a VC bullet and then almost court-martialed for damaging government property (himself) because he hadn't bothered to have the wound treated and it became infected.

What would you do if you'd just been shot down? Why, pose for a picture, of course! From left to right: Murphy, Foley, and Engle. This happened in June 1968. Not long after this photo was taken, the gunship was totaled when a Chinook helicopter tried to pull it out of the mud.

Could this be the guy Parsons attempted to save by shooting at a large shark following the boat? The boatman misunderstood Parson's intentions and jumped in with the shark!

Three guys without a care in the world. Parsons is in front, Anton is behind him, and I'm on the right. It looks like Parsons might have had a beer or two.

The gruesome reality of war. These are the bodies of Viet Cong killed during Tet I, south of Da Nang. Many times I saw bodies—both American and enemy—stacked like cordwood.

Thanksgiving dinner. From left to right: Rogers, me (in back), McCall, Cervinski. Rogers had just gotten out of the hospital after being wounded. Cervinski was wounded later that same day when a bullet came up through the floor of this chopper. There is a good view of the miniguns on the side of the chopper in this picture.

Wiegand, standing in front of the burned-out hulk of a Russian-built North Vietnamese trawler that was set on fire by Firebirds on July 15, 1967—possibly the first time in history that a surface combatant was destroyed by helicopter attack.

This is the soccer field at Tam Ky that we used for staging and refueling. There were always kids around it. Note the four small, light-colored squares on the side of the chopper—they're patched bullet holes. I'm in front, talking with a couple of kids. Rogers is in back to the right.

Latimer at the Tam Ky soccer field examining a home-made cap pistol, which the young kid on the right pointed at Parsons and fired. Parsons thought he was a goner.

Here's a picture you don't see every day! This is a Musket gun-ship that has just been shot down. Note the broken tail boom. The crew is just getting out of the chopper immediately following the crash. This picture was taken from a Rattler slick by Taylor on his way in to rescue the downed crew. This action was part of the big battle that started on January 4, in which Anton was shot down and captured just a half mile from this spot.

Firebird gunner Ned Flecke, showing how that hole got put in his chopper—a wayward 2.75 rocket fired from his own bird. This incident happened before my tour. The story is not included in this book, but the photo is graphic evidence that anything could happen when you had rockets on board.

This medevac chopper was shot down and bent double when it crashed. Note the prominent red cross on the side—a great target for NVA gunners! Parsons saw the actual crash and says that wounded were thrown everywhere. Amazingly, no one was killed.

If you look closely, you can trace the bullet's flight path. The entry hole is centered in the lower third of the side window. Behind and above, you can see where it ricocheted off the side armor of the pilot's seat. Above, you can see the large exit hole through the Plexiglas. Leopold was flying without his helmet visor down, and was wounded in the face by flying Plexiglas (January 3, 1968). The next day, Leopold was back flying again.

Two "wake-up calls." The bullets entered through the floor and exited through the window and the door. This was one of the choppers I was flying on January 31, 1968, in the Tet Offensive. Palazzo was shot in the rump on this mission.

Hannah is on the right, Carson on the left. Between them you can see the entry hole of a bullet that went through the windshield, hit the rocket sight, and ricocheted off of Carson's helmet. This was on May 2, 1968. Three days later, Hannah was shot down in flames in this same gunship, but survived. Besides hurting his back, Hannah nearly broke his neck when he hung himself on his helmet cord trying to exit the wreckage.

Taylor and I were flying this one on May 10, 1968. An antiaircraft round went past my feet, clipping the nose of the gunship— Taylor only grinned after we were safely on the ground.

This is the only fully loaded gunship in Vietnam that was put down undamaged after a complete engine failure. Leopold and I were the pilots (December 3, 1967). Here we're walking around with some maintenance guys. The graveyard where we hid until we were rescued would be off to the right, outside the frame of the picture.

This photo is understandably blurry. It was taken an hour or so before the one above, just after our forced landing. That's me, hiding near a grave, worried about whether or not the VC we could see a quarter mile away were going to attack. Only Aker would have thought of taking a picture under such circumstances.

A heavily armed Crew Chief Williams, the only guy in Nam who carried a Bowie knife bigger than mine. Behind and left of Williams is a body rolled in a poncho liner, which they had just unloaded from their chopper. Malek is on the far right.

Can you believe it? This pile of rubble I'm standing in is part of the remains of a bunker that I was running to when we heard an NVA 122 mm rocket inbound. I dove into the concrete portion just as the rocket hit! This was on June 15, 1968.

This is McCall (left) and me in front of our Hog on December 16, 1967. We were both so intent on shooting VC that neither of us noticed that the other wasn't flying the chopper, and we almost crashed. You can still see the spattered mud and Viet Cong on the front of the chopper in this shot.

This is a Frog gunship with twenty-seven bullet holes, two of them in the windshield. The 40 mm cannon has been opened up and you can see the internal feed mechanism. This wasn't a Firebird chopper, but it was flown by my friend, Lively, who was in another company in our division. Lively talked me into becoming a helicopter pilot in the first place.

That's me, pointing at another "wake-up call." The bullet just missed my leg and harmlessly impacted the bottom of my armored seat.

This is the infamous "Rock Hill" as it looked in 1993. Three different times during my one-year tour in Nam, American soldiers died capturing it all over again. Doesn't look all that valuable, does it? You can see from the graveyard that it was also expensive real estate for the VC and NVA.

At our reunion. Left to right: Leopold, Carlock, Anton, McCall, and Wiegand.

Also at our reunion. Left to right: Leopold, Carson, Anton, Collins, London, Carlock, Igoe. These were all Firebird pilots, but Terry Igoe and Bill London were there the year following my tour.

This is the scene of Anton's crash as it appeared on January 7, two mornings after the crash. The crew is no longer here. Carson is in the process of making his escape, and Anton, Pfister, and Lewis have already completed the first day of their five years as POWs. Legend: **A**—Anton's chopper, barely identifiable from this distance. **B**—the "river" (really just a creek) that Carson crawled into to escape. **C**—Sixteen NVA antiaircraft guns were hidden in these trees. They shot Anton down and, with the help of bad weather, prevented his rescue in spite of daring attempts. **D**—In this area, an infantry unit had been overrun. Anton was shot down trying to help them. Four different medevac helicopters attempted to haul out wounded the morning of January 6, but only one made it. The pilot, Warrant Officer Brady, was awarded the Congressional Medal of Honor for flying four trips into the antiaircraft fire and hauling out thirty-nine wounded.

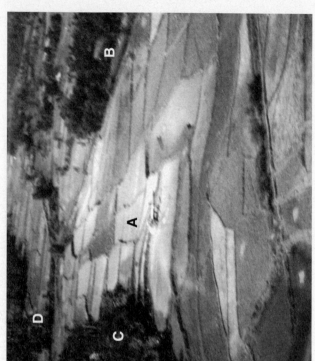

Latimer's count on the helicopters did not include a Rattler slick that "died" from combat damage, as it limped back in and landed at LZ Center. Both a colonel, who was riding in the back of the chopper, and one of the door gunners were wounded by intense enemy fire. The Rattler was attempting to dump some ammo into Lt. Zbozien's platoon when it was hit by at least twenty AK-47 rounds. These rounds were shot at the aircraft by an NVA soldier perched in a tree close to the landing site. For years, Zbozien wondered why the slick unceremoniously unloaded the much-needed ammo about a hundred yards from his location, while his men were under siege. He later learned that the ammo itself had taken a hit and was beginning to burn. The helicopter crew frantically ditched the boxes before the whole thing exploded in flames.

As Latimer retreated from the area of fighting to rearm, he radioed me on my way into the fight. Latimer said that he had been in radio communication with the grunt commander, when the commander was shot two times. This grunt commander was Lieutenant David Zbozien.

Zbozien gave me the following story of the events of our mission in support of B Company 3/21:

First Platoon had been out on ambush the night before. As the First Platoon moved back into the company perimeter, Second and Third Platoons moved out on patrol in different directions. The Third Platoon came up on some hootches as they searched the surrounding terrain. Food was cooking, but the entire village was devoid of any humans. The residents had plainly disappeared in a hurry. Lt. Zbozien felt his skin crawl; something was "going down."

At the same moment, Second Platoon fell into the ambush mentioned in Latimer's letter. Third Platoon dashed to the aid of the other men. As the men arrived at the clearing, Zbozien spied numerous muzzle flashes firing from the enemy positions. Almost immediately, he also spotted what appeared to be about two enemy platoons stealthily jogging toward the rear of the Second Platoon's position. At first, he did not comprehend who he was watching. Then he noticed a trademark feature used by both the VC and NVA. The uniforms were adorned with branches, leaves, and other pieces of underbrush for camouflage. His men were in extreme danger; this was the enemy!

Zbozien quickly positioned his two M-60 machine guns and began a "turkey shoot," as they riddled the flank of the enemy formation with intense fire. Rapidly, the tide turned as the dinks returned fire, encircled his platoon, and bombarded them with mortar rounds. It became increasingly clear that the enemy unit engaged was substantially larger than B Company.

Third Platoon was buffeted with two human wave assaults. The second human onslaught was stunted by the impact of an LAW rocket that exploded in the middle of the marauders. One NVA soldier was vaporized. During the peak of the heavy fighting, Zbozien was shot twice and hit by a mortar round. His radio call sign was "Viking." He came to, after a momentary blackout, only to hear his frantic radio operator screaming into the radio, "Viking is dead, Viking is dead!" As the severely wounded lieutenant lay motionless and mute on the ground, he stared at the bushes moving toward him and his surrounded men. The final assault was about to begin.

The survivors of Third Platoon had only minimal ammo left by this time. They merely had several rounds of M-16 ammo and two LAW rockets to hold off the ever-increasing wave of enemy soldiers. This was the instant mentioned in the prologue to this book, when Zbozien looked up over his left shoulder and observed Firebird 94,

my gunship, zeroing in for the kill. When I asked where
he wanted us to shoot, he responded "Everywhere, shoot
everywhere, they are everywhere!" I finished off my attack run with Aker and Bruce blasting away with their
M-60s. Bruce said that the NVA were racing like rats in
all directions trying to evade our guns.

When Third Platoon attempted to move from the tor-
turous ambush the first time, Zbozien ordered his men to
check the downed soldiers to ensure that no living were
left behind. By the time the platoons tried to move a second time, the lieutenant himself was covered in blood.
Whoever checked the men this time left the lieutenant for
dead in the chaos that ensued. Three Americans were captured during the battle, and luckily for Zbozien, a platoon
sergeant discovered him alive on a later sweep of the site.
He was finally evacuated.

For his rescue of one of the crews of a downed slick
that day, James Malek earned a Distinguished Flying
Cross. Initially, he was told to go in and try to pick up the
crew of a gunship that had been shot down. As he concentrated on clearing his helicopter blades from the jungle around the helicopter crash site, he did not pay any
attention to the Americans he was trying to rescue. He assumed that there would be four men, a standard crew for
the gunship. After successfully setting down his chopper,
he looked up and saw some movement from the jungle.
All of a sudden seven or eight guys, with boomsticks
blazing, were running pell-mell for his slick. It took
everyone aboard the chopper several long seconds to determine that these men were Americans. They were all
looking back over their shoulders, as they fired in the direction they were running away from. A colonel, who was
aboard Malek's helicopter, did not recognize the approaching soldiers as ours and began to fire his M-16 into
the running men. Thank goodness the colonel was a lousy

MARCH 16, 1968

Robert Kennedy announced that he was running for the Democratic nomination for the presidency of the US.

shot; no one was hit! They took off with the lucky men. Latimer flew in somewhat later and rescued the crew of the gunship that had crashed.

We were one of the seventeen helicopters shot up that day and took hits in the sync elevator and the tail boom. Other than the accounts in my letter home, Latimer's letter, and the statements by Zbozien and Bruce, I have no personal recollection of this engagement. My nerves were totally frayed by then, and most things had become a blur.

That night at LZ Baldy, I suffered a panic attack. Because of the stifling heat, I had moved my cot outside the standby tent. These fire bases routinely fired artillery and mortar rounds intermittently all through the night. As I lay in my cot, I heard one of our mortar rounds as it ascended. It then made a strange sound, and I heard it begin to come back down. Even though I was nearly asleep, I vaulted at least three feet off the bed. I rolled over and hit the ground on my knees and elbows. I managed to tear all the skin off my elbows digging with them trying to accelerate to the bunker. The short mortar round hit in the perimeter wire. My elbows were torn up, and I was so excited that I actually forgot to stand and run. Afterward, I was too tired to walk down to the medic tent to get patched up, so I just laid back on my cot and bled. I now felt like a zombie. I wasn't sleeping because artillery and mortars were always going off nearby. I also wasn't eating and wasn't even drinking. I just wanted to get the hell out. I wrote home that we must be losing the war, because the NVA just kept coming at us with fresh troops.

My Lai

"I gave the army a good boy and they sent me back a murderer." This is what one mother said about what happened on March 16, 1968, the date of the infamous My Lai massacre. The famous picture of the helicopters landing the troops that day has a Rattler slick in the number two position in the flight. Four Rattler slicks were landing troops along with other choppers from our battalion. Castle was flying one slick, and Jeffcoat was crew chief on another. Later in my tour, Castle became my platoon leader.

Eventually, Lt. William L. Calley was convicted of killing over one hundred women, kids, and old men on this day. Many men in Calley's platoon participated in the slaughter. Calley's infantry company had come to Vietnam as one unit, and had already suffered twenty-eight killed or wounded in a short period of time without any actual combat. These casualties were from booby traps and snipers. On March 14, one of the most popular men in the company was killed when he stepped on a booby trap. The grunts swore that the kids at My Lai knew where the booby traps were and would watch from a safe distance to see the Americans blow themselves up. On March 15, they had a memorial service for their buddy, and then were briefed on the next day's mission. Many of Calley's men swore under oath that the company commander, "Mad Dog" Medina, told them to kill everything alive.

After Calley was convicted and released, he said that he killed the babies because they would grow up to kill Americans. It's amazing to me what a human mind can rationalize. I had nearly gotten two gunship crews killed by not shooting at the women and children in the parade at Tam Ky on January 31. On the other hand, I had seen the human bombs on Miller's slick helicopter, and I had heard a grunt tell about a small girl about eight years old running at them down a rice dike wearing a gown when one of the soldiers screamed at her in Vietnamese to halt, then fired his M-16 at her. She exploded from the explosives underneath the gown she wore. I suppose it's possible that we had done the same thing as Calley's men when we attacked villages with our miniguns and rockets. But I was told that the villagers dived into bunkers when the shooting started. (On blocking missions, pamphlets were dropped telling the people not to run.) In my mind, there's a difference between shooting in the heat of combat as opposed to shooting in cold blood children being held by their mothers.

Most Americans don't realize how brutalizing war is and can't believe that good American boys would execute women and children in cold blood. But Americans did it at the turn of the century in the Filipino guerrilla war. They did it to the Indians shortly after the Civil War— General Sherman even advocated in writing the slaughter of women and children. In World War II, it was common to send your girlfriend a letter opener made of Japanese bone. A guerrilla war strips away the thin veneer of civilization. When this is combined with a war of attrition (the magic use of "body counts"), the whole thing becomes a huge meat grinder.

My Lai was always a stronghold of resistance against both the French and the Americans. The story around the military was that they had fired-up the troops to expect a big fight. Then they landed them in the wrong place. My Lai consisted of four connected villages; the VC unit was at another one. The Americans finally found who they were looking for on March 17.

Lieutenant Calley was part of the Eleventh Infantry Brigade, which after this was known as the "Butcher Brigade." Also, at the trial, it came out that President

Johnson had ordered the Eleventh Infantry to Vietnam before they had finished their training, and Lt. Calley was not qualified to have graduated from Officer's Candidate School in normal times. The chain of command on the 16th was a Task Force command instead of normal Brigade command, and the troops had no combat briefing on handling of prisoners. (The Nazis used this argument to justify executing Americans at the Battle of the Bulge in WW II. These guys stated that the higher ranking officers expected the execution of prisoners because they didn't tell the combat soldiers what to do with them.)

I find it ironic and interesting that this was probably the only time in history that two Americans, a pilot and a gunner, received medals for rescuing people from getting killed by other Americans! The door gunner was awarded one medal, which he received posthumously, having been killed in another action before receiving it. The pilot received a Distinguished Flying Cross for rescuing kids caught in the "intense crossfire" of the Americans.

The most amazing aspect of the My Lai massacre is that after Calley executed the babies, many of the war protesters came to his defense, as if all American soldiers were ordered to do what he did. Even the future president, Jimmy Carter, came to his defense.

On March 17, we flew several attacks in the area of My Lai. I wrote home that I blew up a clothesline full of clothes at Pinkville. This was our nickname for My Lai. I hit it with four or five rockets. I actually remember shooting at that clothesline several different times. It must have been a VC laundromat. We also flew all night putting in airstrikes for the 196th in the Que Son Valley.

We went back to My Lai again on March 18. There, the battalion commander waived his 1,000 foot ceiling rule, and we had another low-level shoot-out. The clouds were down to about 300 feet. I took several hits. My letter home indicated that I was flying lead, and we burnt a village. We went through that village like General Sherman went through Georgia.

Another pilot, whom I will leave unnamed, said he was at My Lai one day, and two Firebird gunships were circling, waiting their turn to put in an airstrike. Another set of gunships was ahead of them. He spotted three women running with poles over their shoulders with baskets on each end. He noted that at each step the pole would flex, and he could tell they had a lot of weight in the baskets. As the gunships circled, it dawned on him that these women were running to the fight, not away from it. He told the door gunners to shoot them. As they fell, the baskets spilled. They were full of mortar rounds that were being taken to the skirmish.

The stories involving firing upon women shocks most Americans. In Vietnam, many women took an active role in terrorist actions upon our troops. Also, grunts sometimes found VC wearing long wigs. The enemy knew most Americans hesitated to shoot women and used the fact against us. Unfortunately, for these female VC, the Firebirds did not have such qualms.

The Walker Spy Ring

March 19, 1968

TWO CAPTURED NVA SOLDIERS STATED THAT THEY HAD FORTY-EIGHT HOURS NOTICE BEFORE ANY B-52 AIRSTRIKE.

Not a few people noticed that flying into Laos was inordinately risky. Beginning in early 1968, the marines simply refused to fly into the region. They were sustaining heavy losses in helicopters. Prior to May 1968, one special forces team refused to go on a mission, and the soldiers that did eventually go in suffered an 80 percent casualty rate. The word was that they had to watch out for enemy choppers. In 1969, a Vietnamese-piloted Russian helicopter was supposedly shot down in Laos.

It was not until 1985 that our government finally figured out what was happening. The Walker spy ring was selling our cryptographic code books to the enemy—the same codes used by the special forces. Walker was a navy warrant officer who sold out his fellow countrymen by selling secrets to the Russians. He began his treason in late 1967, and by 1968 the NVA was regularly reading the special forces mail.

On one occasion, a team of soldiers was dropped at the LZ only to discover a welcome sign waiting. The welcome sign was adorned with their specific radio call sign. Because of the limited number of places available for landing in Laos, it was extremely dangerous, even when the enemy did not realize the choppers were coming. With Walker's help, the NVA made these missions almost suicidal.

MARCH 20, 1968

Bill Clinton, future President of the United States, was classified as 1-A draft status.

A Major Geezer

McCall had gone home and had to be replaced as instructor pilot. So, the brass brought in an old geezer to give me a checkride. He was a major and had to have been at least thirty-five. He certainly did not

March 21, 1968

I WAS MADE PLATOON INSTRUCTOR PILOT.

have good eyesight. Instead of doing autorotations (engine-off landings) at Chu Lai, he flew me up to Tam Ky to the dirt landing strip. At 1,000 feet, I looked down and could see large potholes everywhere. All of a sudden, gramps cut the engine and in he went. He didn't control his forward motion, and I almost jerked the controls away from him. He also didn't stop his forward airspeed, and touched down still doing about thirty knots. I was surprised that he didn't knock the skids off the gunship. Fortunately, the rocket pods had already been removed.

Gramps asked if I could do better, so I grabbed the controls, went up to 500 feet, and lined up to do the autorotation from the opposite direction. (This major's eyesight was so bad he couldn't see the windsock, and he had landed downwind instead of into the wind.) Going into the wind, I sat the gunship down on a specific spot.

I passed my checkride.

MARCH 22, 1968

After the Tet fiasco, it was announced that General Westmoreland was being "promoted" out of Vietnam. He didn't actually leave until summer, though.

Flying Blind

On the night of March 27, I felt more helpless than I ever had in Vietnam. It was the first time I had been out at night flying fireteam lead in such terrible weather. A Musket gunship was on my wing, and believe it or not, it was my old friend Gaither, who had been hit in the toe while flying behind me during the Tet Offensive of January 31. An LRRP team was in heavy contact on the side of a hill southwest of the Que Son Valley. The clouds

were very low with intermittent drizzle. At least, I could
see the tops of the mountains on occasion. The LRRPs
had three or four out of five wounded, and the guy on the
radio was too scared to mark his location. He was positive he could hear the NVA searching for them. The valley on the end was narrow, so I was concerned about
crashing into my wingman, who had no lights on. I was
concentrating on not hitting the mountains, and at the
same time, trying to calm the guy down enough to get
him to mark his location. He kept pleading, "Help us,"
over the radio. I knew I was not qualified or confident
enough to be flying fireteam lead and make the decisions
involved in such poor conditions.

First, the guy fired one tracer round and told me to
shoot around it. I had seen McCall fire around a position
where a guy fired three tracers up, but I wasn't about to
try it for fear of hitting the LRRP team. The LRRP on the
radio finally agreed to turn a strobe light on for a second
or two. I was too scared to fire rockets, because when the
strobe light went off, I was in the mist under the clouds
just slightly above their position on the side of the hill.
We had orbited for quite a while getting the guy to turn
on the strobe light, and the wing gunship said the clouds
were getting lower. I finally decided to line up and fly
parallel to the ridgeline, overfly the LRRP position, and
let the door guns work out both sides. I had a minigun
ship. As I lined up, I was getting real close to the mountain ridge to fly down along it under the clouds. The rotating beacon in the mist and reflection off the clouds
immediately above the gunship confused everything. The
LRRP heard us coming. He flashed on the strobe light.
The gunners opened up, and I let the peter pilot rip the
miniguns past the strobe light.

The LRRP screamed over the radio that we were
killing them. I told the wingman to hold fire. My heart

stopped! The LRRP screamed, "Bullets hit all around me!" Apparently, this LRRP was a new guy (the team leader who normally would have been talking on the radio had been wounded). One of the wounded finally informed him that it was just our bullet cases and ammo belt links falling around them as we fired at the enemy.

We made several gun runs waiting for a slick to arrive, and the clouds got so low the slick could not see the strobe light. One NVA light machine gun shot a string of tracer rounds straight at me, but my door gunner hit right on the enemy location. After that, we did not receive any more fire. Apparently the NVA decided they did not enjoy our company and withdrew. After the NVA pulled back, the artillery kept them back until first light, so a medevac could hover up the mountain through the clouds to get the LRRP team out.

On leaving the valley, the clouds were so low I nearly had to do what I saw McCall do once. The helicopter was put in the fastest climb possible into the clouds. Then, rockets were fired. If there was no explosion, you knew that the rocket had cleared the mountain ahead (so presumably you would, too). Wiegand called this the "swoosh-boom" method of navigation. The rocket went "swoosh" and you hoped you didn't hear a boom. Once I flew lower, I found the way out of the valley. When I climbed out of the mountains, I gave the controls to the peter pilot. My hands finally quit shaking by the time we arrived at LZ Baldy.

On March 28, I nearly killed myself and my crew again. I was the fireteam's lead, and the fireteam was landing at LZ Ross to refuel. A Musket gunship was at my wing. (The Firebirds were apparently out of gunships again.) This place was always dusty, even though it was sprayed with oil all the time to keep it down. My wingman had less fuel than I did, so I let him land ahead of me at the refueling point. I was going to wait until the dust settled and then shoot an approach to the ground next to his gunship. If you were not hovering, the dust wasn't too bad.

As I came in on approach, the wingman had the bright idea of moving over at the refueling station to give me more room to land. This kicked up a storm of dust. He had clearly never been into LZ Ross at night. I must have been flying with Bruce and Aker, because I remember screaming at them, "Get out and tell me where the ground is!" The dust was so thick, you couldn't tell up from down. I was probably at thirty or forty feet off the ground and could not see a thing. The helicopter had lost translational lift, which meant it was technically at a hover. The problem with this was that a gunship didn't have enough power to hover at thirty feet. I did not attempt to take off because I couldn't see the fuel bladders and radio antennas in the direction I was facing. The ground and the other helicopter were invisible in the dust. I ran out of airspeed and experience all at the same time. When I told the crew to get out, they knew that meant to get out on the skids. There they could tell me if I was moving forward or not, and how far I was above the ground. From the Plexiglas windshield, the view was still totally obscured. By luck, I never changed my glide in, and the crew was able to slow me down enough so I could slam into the ground in a semi-controlled, bone-shaking crash. I was so rattled that I couldn't get out and threaten to shoot the guy on the other gunship. At least, the gunship wasn't damaged. The other pilot should have had a piece of Plexiglas put in his navel so he could see when he had his head stuck up his ass.

Superfly

On March 29, we flew all night on a firefly mission. Colonel Nelson was flying as gunner on Leopold's gunship. At first, we came upon twenty sampans in one cove. We weren't taking fire, so I got very low and slow and eased the gunship over the sampans. This way the gunners could shoot straight down on them. I believe I actually eased the gunship into the light beams being shined from the slick light ship. I was excited about finding that many sampans together. Apparently, Charlie was moving supplies and had abandoned them when they saw us working up the river. I saw a bright flash, heard a "BOOM" and thought we had been hit with an RPG or recoilless rifle. But it was one of the sampans exploding. A piece of shrapnel blew into Bruce's hand. He agreed to keep going, so we reloaded and rearmed all night long.

When we called it quits, around an hour before daylight, we went to the grunt battalion headquarters. Colonel Nelson told us to fill out a report on how many sampans we sank. We told the guy taking the report that we didn't keep count. He said to give him our best estimate. My call sign was Firebird 94, and Leopold's was Firebird 93. I told the guy we sank ninety-four sampans. Leopold said he outranked me, and the number was ninety-three. The division newsletter reported that ninety-three sampans were sunk. We hit a lot of them and could have actually gotten that many or more.

Hannah's Temporary Purple Heart

Hannah was hit by a rocket and got a Purple Heart. Twenty-five years later, he and I were talking, and he asked if I remembered him getting caught in the bunker naked. He decided he wanted to die with his clothes on, so he left the bunker to get dressed and was hit. I laughed and said, "My friend, I hate to tell you this, but your memory is screwed. You didn't go for clothes. You went for the booze—it was your turn!" When the commanding officer found out about this, he was so mad he took Hannah's Purple Heart away. Shortly after that, he got a real Purple Heart.

Somewhere around this time, Hannah and I were flying together and took a round through the floor. It drove a piece of aluminum into my shirtsleeve. The aluminum piece was shaped like a triangle and had a nice point on it. I gave Hannah the controls and was checking the instruments, as we had taken several hits. I didn't say a word, just reached around and positioned the aluminum, which was still stuck in my shirt, so I could push it into my arm. Another Purple Heart! Hannah saw my hand reach around and proclaimed, "Don't do it, Carlock. I will turn you in." I thought to myself, "What kind of friends do I have?" He was still sore because they took away his Purple Heart.

"The War Is Over!"

When I heard about President Johnson's declaration, that night or the next, I ran through the company area at Chu Lai telling everyone the war was over. God, I was young and naive. Never did I dream that General Westmoreland would issue the order the next day to close with the enemy and put maximum pressure on them in order to demoralize them during peace talks. The problem was that the NVA army commanders issued the same order to their troops.

MARCH 31, 1968

President Johnson, stung by McCarthy's strong showing in the New Hampshire primary and by Robert Kennedy's entry into the presidential race, announced that he would neither seek, nor accept his party's nomination. He also announced a wide-scale slowdown of US military operations in Vietnam, saying that he would cease bombing North Vietnam if they would start peace talks. He said the US would meet anywhere to discuss peace. The government then argued for thirty-four days about the location.

Our battalion had a slick helicopter shot down. I wrote home that some people were now flying into Laos, and flatly stated that I would take a court-martial before I flew into a neutral country. In May, I was flying into Laos.

I also mentioned in my letter how much money I was making. I have since computed my hourly wage as if I were covered by the Fair Labor Standards Act. If someone asked me why I was fighting in Vietnam, I can now say, "For $1.08 per hour." We warrant officers were so poor that we had to fart to have a (s)cent in our pockets!

On April 2, I expended the gunship five times—a lot of flight hours! From the 2nd through about the 9th of April, the NVA pulled out of the Que Son Valley. With that pull-out, our area became relatively passive. Because the rear echelon knotheads-in-charge could not get us killed there, they sent us north to get killed with the marines and the South Koreans. We flew for several days around Happy Valley just southwest of Da Nang. The next day, I wrote home that I was supporting Robert Kennedy for president because he would end the war.

One day during this time period, Carson and I (in separate gunships) were out on a blocking mission around Hoi An (south of Da Nang). The NVA and VC bailed out of the target village like rats from a sinking ship. Our job was to shoot anybody that ran. We positioned ourselves down at low level, and I headed up the river. I told Carson that I saw some men who had made it across the river and were now going around a small hill. Carson flew around the hill low level and came face to helicopter with a fully uniformed NVA. The soldier obviously short circuited, so he snapped to attention. Carson stared the guy right in the eyes and was unable to give the order to kill him.

This little event would probably have stayed a secret except that Carson's peter pilot finked on him at the Officers' Club. He caught a lot of crap for that episode, maybe even more than I caught for my first mission with Anton. We were the judge, jury, and executioner; and in this case, Judge Carson waived that guy's death sentence.

Rocket Science

On a memorable mission, we were supporting some Koreans and US marines who had encircled a village and had been ordered to shoot anyone who attempted to flee by jumping into the river. Pretty soon, about five dinks jumped into a sampan and were paddling furiously to escape. I dropped down to about 400 feet and told the gunners to hold their fire. I was going to impress the crew with my mastery of the rockets. I punched off two, but the fins did not open correctly on one of them, causing it to go out of control. As I watched, the impaired rocket looped around and struck exactly under a marine vehicle. Instantly, the marines screamed, "Incoming," over the radio and proceeded to shoot the crap out of everything around, including the village. They thought that the enemy had shot a mortar round or rocket at them, never dreaming that it was a friendly rocket. My wing man greased the guys in the sampan while all hell broke loose on the ground. My peter pilot asked, "What are you going to do?" I did not hesitate. My reply was, "Let's go refuel."

We were told that the 2.75 rocket was originally designed to be fired from jets, and for that reason, wasn't very accurate when being fired from a helicopter at lower speeds. Gunship pilots loved to talk about their memorable rocket shots. Parsons related this story about an accurate shot:

He and McCall were chasing an armed VC down a dike. Apparently, the VC figured he was not going to make it to safety, so he threw down his gun, stopped, turned, and threw up his hands. McCall fired a pair of rockets, and one hit dead center in the VC's chest. The rockets had to travel a certain distance to arm themselves and engage the warhead to explode. This one didn't travel far enough to detonate; it simply "speared" the Charlie, who apparently did not understand that we couldn't land the heavily loaded gunships and take prisoners.

My best rocket shot was on April 17. I shot a rocket from 1,000 feet altitude that hit within four feet of an NVA soldier. That dude had to at least have been injured from all the shrapnel.

Taylor shares a story about a rocket whose warhead had become unscrewed from its motor. When Taylor fired it, the blazing rocket motor flew up into the gunship—certainly enough to increase anyone's pucker factor. He also recalled firing two rockets one day that traveled out from the gunship, hit each other, and ricocheted off in opposite directions. One unnamed pilot fired one that looped and a piece of the rocket hit a Rattler crew chief. The crew chief's injury was serious enough that he got a ticket back home.

Burroughs once fired one of these rockets that just went off course and smacked into the bottom of a slick. From there, it went on out and landed right in the LZ.

Collins also related a great story about a rocket shot. This incident occurred on August 17, 1968 and was written up in the Americal Division newspaper. He was on a mission west of the Que Son Valley, past the next valley (Antenna Valley). During the night, they were extracting a marine LRRP team. A slick pilot from our company, Schoenborn, received a Silver Star for the action that night. The marines were in a precarious position and too frightened to turn on their strobe light to mark their position. Finally, they flipped it on momentarily to enable the choppers to pinpoint their location. They were totally surrounded by NVA, and muzzle flashes lit up the entire hillside. It took awhile, but Collins was finally able to distinguish the muzzle flashes from the strobe light. He circled back from the mountain, lined up, and sighted the rockets forty to fifty feet to the side of the strobe light. As he fired the rockets, one completely blocked the strobe light from his view. It headed straight for the intense light. He held his breath. He was so far back that, as the rocket

APRIL 4, 1968

The Rev. Martin Luther King, Jr. was assassinated in Memphis, Tennessee. During the next three days, at least twenty-eight people were killed in riots across the US.

motor died off (burned out), it dropped and hit about fifteen feet below the marines. They came on the radio and said, "Great shot! Great shot! You just blew an arm and a leg up on us!" Because of these events and many more like them, when I was flying slicks, I did not appreciate gunships shooting rockets too close around me.

Routine Operations

During the day on April 5, we ran a sniffer mission very close to Laos. That night, the commies mortared the fire support bases in the Que Son Valley. We flew most of the night searching for mortar tubes. We were either successful in blowing them up with our rockets, or they ran out of mortar rounds (probably the latter). Unless one of us actually saw the flash from the tube as it fired, it was almost impossible to locate them. Naturally, only a few of them were dumb enough to fire one with us circling the area. Longevity was not much of an option when we spotted one.

April 5, 1968

THE 196TH CAPTURED TWENTY-SEVEN ANTIAIRCRAFT GUNS. THESE GUNS HAD BEEN USED EXTENSIVELY AGAINST US THE FIRST SEVERAL WEEKS OF MARCH. ONE OF THEM WAS PROBABLY THE ONE THAT NAILED PARSONS.

On April 8, a helicopter stationed at Chu Lai was shot down with two crew members killed. They were flying in the Que Son Valley.

On April 10, the NVA moved back into the Que Son Valley for a little action, and we got all the gunships shot up. None was flyable until that night. A South Vietnamese helicopter from the Kingbees was shot down close to the Que Son Valley. The chopper was en route from Da Nang to the special forces camp at Kham Duc. Four special forces team leaders were killed.

On April 12, I gathered Parsons's personal effects and turned them over to the officials so they could send them home to him. Later that day, I took a hit in the rotor blade. Another gunship from the Firebirds was also damaged. One of our slicks was shot down when it took a hit in the transmission.

On April 13, a platoon from the 196th was overrun and thirteen were killed. We flew all night, putting in air strikes to support the survivors. The word was that they had gone into a village at night to take a nap. That decision proved fatal.

On April 14, we flew all night and only sank three sampans.

Snake Doctors, Hangar Queens, and Frogs

It was during this time period that I had two run-ins with maintenance. One night, I was on standby at Chu Lai. The cloud cover was heavy, and the rain was really coming down. The Firebirds had been called out into the mountains southwest of Tam Ky two nights in a row by a grunt unit which heard "noises."

We concluded that the company which kept calling in was very skittish and afraid of monkeys—they had not been shot at yet. Because of the low clouds and rain, I told the crew chief that if that particular unit called again, I wanted the helicopter grounded due to maintenance problems. Only two choppers were there, so if one went down, we would not have to fly. Sure enough, the grunt unit called for their babysitters again late at night and the crew chief grounded the chopper.

I walked out to the helicopter and looked at the cable running through the tail boom to the tail rotor. As it passed through a pulley, the cable resembled a bird's nest with all the broken strands fraying out in every direction. I concluded that the helo really should be grounded for maintenance! But amazingly, only a few minutes had passed when a maintenance sergeant walked into the Firebird hooch and declared the helicopter flyable. Come to find out, the maintenance manual said a certain number of strands in the cable could be broken without jeopardizing the safe operation of the chopper. This sergeant counted the broken strands in the cable and pronounced the aircraft flyable. After nearly being killed by maintenance once already (making me fly the gunship with the burned-up engine), I did not necessarily take the maintenance men at their word. I quickly let the sergeant know I wasn't going to fly the damn thing in the mountains at night in the rain. A few moments later, a company officer drove up in a jeep. He told me the gunship was flyable, and I was going to have to fly it. As we looked at the aircraft, I said I would fly it if he would go with me. After closer inspection, he agreed the worn cable looked plenty dangerous to him also. We subsequently stayed grounded for the night. If the grunts were actually receiving fire, we would never have refused the mission.

Another day, they pronounced the "hangar queen" ready to fly. Most of the time, we had eight gunships. Sometimes, one or two would be cannibalized for parts in order to keep more of the gunships flying. These hangar queens were little more than shells perched next to the runway.

We must have received a shipload of parts, because they decided to get the queen flyable. This hangar queen happened to be a Frog (with the 40 mm grenade launcher on the nose). I got in the thing and ran it up to maximum rpm's. As I moved the cyclic (main control) around, it made a grinding sound and had a grinding feeling to the stick. I told the crew chief to ground it. Not long afterward, the maintenance sergeant came up and again pronounced the Frog flyable. He had determined that the sound and the rough grinding feel to the controls were caused by a small amount of rust that had formed on the magnets under the floorboards that set the trim (alleviate pressure) on the cyclic. I had no problem with that—I just told him to clean off the rust. The sergeant balked, complaining at the time that it was too much trouble. In a few minutes, the same company officer once again showed up in his jeep. We revved up the engine while he listened. Having obtained immediate results the last time I questioned maintenance, I told him the same thing, "I'll fly it if you go with me." The man then gave the order for maintenance to clean the rust off the controls. Funny how a person's perspective changed when it might be his own butt that was on the line! I always believed that I would rather be on the ground wishing I was in the air, than be in the air wishing I was on the ground.

The Frog was a dangerous machine to fly in any circumstance. The grenade launcher mounted on the nose changed the center of gravity. Then, more capacity was added so the chopper could hold 400 grenades instead of the normal 250 grenades. This altered the center of gravity even more. I was the company instructor pilot in the C-models and supposedly knew how to fly them. Yet, I nearly crashed in these things several times. We parked the helicopters in revetments to protect them from mortar and rocket attacks. The revetments were fifty-five gallon drums full of sand. They were arranged in an L shape which, if the wind was from the wrong direction, forced you to hover or slide the gunship in downwind. Several times I entered the revetment in a Frog with the cyclic pulled all the way back to the stop. The damn thing still wandered forward until it nearly crashed into the barrels. The gunners and crew chiefs would laugh at you if you slid it into the revetment. The manly thing to do was to fly it in to position. Those guys did not realize all the pieces that could fly up around you if the gunship crashed or flipped in the revetment. I finally wised up and decided I would come into the area using the slide method. I didn't give a rip if they laughed or not.

On April 20, we had a slick shot down and our mainte-nance helicopter "Snake Doctor" (doctor for the Rattlers) went out to try to work his magic. I was told the slick crew had been picked up by another slick. Supposedly, the crew walked around the area prior to being picked up by another chopper. However, a member of Snake Doc-tor's crew, who came to work on the downed slick, stepped on a bouncing betty land mine. These mines popped up three feet or so from the ground and exploded. In this case, the mine blew up and killed two of the crew. It also tore up the arm on another man. I knew one of the guys that was killed fairly well.

Back in 1965, when different factions of the ARVN were fighting with each other, some VC in Da Nang hauled off thousands of these type of mines. They had free reign for a while during one of the many changes of government that went on periodically. No one was "mind-ing the store," so the VC came in and helped themselves to a few supplies. They spent the next several years using these mines on the Americans.

Lipstick on a Pig

This is also around the time that my career as a gunship pilot was coming to an end. We had a new CO, who apparently had little first-hand knowledge about what a gunship pilot really did. While on five minute standby on the artillery fire bases, it was

APRIL 26, 1968

Students around the world, in an organized effort, cut classes to protest the war.

impossible for most men to sleep. The CO assumed that if he saw us in the company area in the daytime on fifteen minute standby, or on a day off, we were just goofing around wasting time. The brass then came to the brilliant conclusion that "an idle mind is the devil's workshop." So, they devised cute little projects to keep us out of trouble.

We were required to wash and wax helicopters after being on five minute standby without regard to whether we flew all night or not. The temperature on most of the days exceeded one hundred degrees. If we had no wax, we were instructed to wipe the helicopter down with hydraulic fluid to make it shine. It did not take an Oxford graduate to realize this just might have caused a fire hazard. Also, it was easier to target the gunship if it was all bright and shiny. In my opinion, shining a gunship helicopter in Vietnam was the equivalent of putting lipstick on a pig. It just didn't help much. Later, someone at battalion told them to stop putting hydraulic fluid on the gunships. Hannah said that the day before he was shot down, he was out in the heat (over one hundred degrees) painting the skid toes on his helicopter red. I told him that gave the NVA antiaircraft gunner a good target to sight on as they successfully shot down his chopper.

Needless to say, I was not a happy camper.

On May 1, my days as an official gunship pilot came
to an abrupt halt. I had been up all night. I was ordered to
go wash and polish a helicopter, and this made about as
much sense to me as trying to milk a Texas bull.

While I was scrubbing my gunship less than enthusi-
astically, the platoon leader and CO arrived and stood
me at attention. They proceeded to give me one royal ass
chewing in front of the enlisted men. I was raked over
the coals for not following proper procedure while cleaning the miniguns. Each minigun on a gunship had six
barrels that revolved. In order to fire a minigun, all one
had to do was spin the barrel by hand, and they would
fire. Subsequently, the gunner and crew chief always
placed a metal rod with a red flag on it through the barrels so the guns could not accidentally be turned whenever the gunship was on the ground. The metal rods had
not been placed through the barrels of the miniguns on
the helicopter I was washing. It didn't take a rocket scientist to figure out the miniguns had just been cleaned,
and no ammo had been rolled into the guns. Neverthe-
less, my ass was grass.

This display of the enforcement of procedure would
not have been carried out on an enlisted man in the same
way it was done to me. An over-zealous CO ran a very
real risk of getting fragged in Vietnam when he made a
show of enforcing procedure with enlisted men. Fragging
was achieved with a grenade or a "misplaced" shot similar to the round through the door pole that the gunner
from Tennessee had aimed at or near me. Our company
first sergeant had a grenade tied under his jeep one day.
Luckily, he noticed it and avoided injury or death.

After that episode, Leopold and I promptly applied for
a transfer out of the company. I applied to a company
where a friend of mine flew. Latimer was either with us
or else he quit the next day, because he followed us out

shortly afterward. Hannah remembered Latimer flying gunships at least until May 2.

I told the CO or XO that I wanted out of the platoon and moved that day or the next day out of the Firebird hootch to the First Platoon slicks. I still wonder if the company commander was chewing my ass because he had a thing for shiny helicopters or if he realized I was the one who had surreptitiously decked him during a volley-ball game several days earlier.

Tet II (Hannah Shot Down)

On May 2, Carson, flying a gunship, took a hit through the windshield, and shattered Plexiglas flew into his eyes. (He still has problems from this injury.) The round came through the windshield, hit the rocket targeting site, ricocheted off the top of his brain bucket, and deflected through the roof of the gunship. The action took place in another fight at the Rock Hill in the Que Son Valley. It was a totally worthless pile of rocks that the Americans kept dying for. This time, Charlie had dug machine guns in among the rocks. Hannah was Carson's copilot. While Carson was punching rockets all over, Hannah leaned out the open doors, firing his M-16 toward the NVA bunkers. When he felt a tug on his arm, he swiveled around and saw Carson's face covered with blood. Assuming Carson had taken a direct hit with a bullet, he grabbed the controls. Hannah was sure the shot had killed Carson.

I was in my bunk writing home when I was suddenly ordered to take a gunship to LZ Baldy to replace Carson. Even though I was now officially a slick pilot, they were short of gunship pilots, and I had to switch over. My letter stated, "Have to go to Baldy . . . Carson took a round through his windshield and got Plexiglas in his eyes. All this stuff is getting to me. I can't sleep at night!"

On May 3 and 4, I flew slicks. On May 5, I was again in the air in a slick when Rattler operations called and told me to return ASAP to Chu Lai in order to pilot a gunship. For the first time, the NVA was firing rockets at Chu Lai during the daytime and Buzzell and Hannah had been shot down in flames.

Hannah was one of the many casualties incurred by our side during the start of the big spring offensive of 1968, otherwise known as Tet II. It coincided with the anniversary of the 150th birthday of the father of all Communists, Karl Marx. Saigon and 119 other cities and towns were attacked that day. We were told to spend that night in the bunkers. I slept in my bed, and was fortunate we weren't hit. LZ Center, however, was hit with ten rockets and a ground attack. Because of a shortage of gunship pilots, I flew gunships nearly every day from the 5th through the 16th. I can guarantee that I did not wash any helicopters during that period of time. What were they going to do . . . send me to Vietnam?

Earlier, a slick from our battalion had been shot down, and ten people aboard were killed. This precipitated the gunship team being scrambled to the location. Taylor was flying Firebird fire team lead that day. This is his description of the action:

> Following normal procedures, the fire team of Firebird 91 and Firebird 92 flew from Chu Lai to our standby location, LZ Baldy, without incident and settled in for our twenty-four hour standby period. At around 0900, we received a scramble call via "land-line" from the Tactical Operations Center. As fire team lead, I wrote down the mission order while

my copilot and the wing crew ran out to crank the gunships. The order went something like this:

"Scramble your fire team to grid coordinates ***. There is an aircraft down and you are to provide cover for their extraction. Contact ****?"

By this time, both aircraft were running; and as I strapped into my seat, Burroughs hovered out for takeoff. Buzzell and Hannah were in the wing aircraft. Burroughs headed due south in a slow climb to maintain maximum airspeed, while I plotted the coordinates. We were also having to fly on a course to keep us east of LZ East to steer clear of the artillery they were laying down to cover the downed bird. I took control of the aircraft, and Burroughs coordinated the lifting of the artillery, so we could get into the valley.

When we crossed the ridge line, east of LZ East, I gazed out to the west and spotted smoke rising. This was the burning slick helicopter. I turned to the west: and as I did, I heard a crescendo of small arms fire from the south side of the ridge line. Our altitude was about 1,200 to 1,300 feet. I keyed my mike and called, "92, this is 91. Taking fire from three o'clock. Just put down some suppressive fire, I have the downed bird in sight."

As soon as I released my mike, I heard the end of Buzzell's transmission, "—day, Mayday. Firebird 92 going down."

I pulled hard right 180 degrees and saw Firebird 92 heading toward me with smoke trailing behind. I pulled my speed back to about sixty knots and waited for him to fly past me. When he passed, I again pulled hard right and dumped my nose to reach about 110 knots to get close on his wing. I called, "92, get it on the ground quick, you are on fire!" His rocket pods were on fire, and the view was similar to a WW II airplane gun camera. At this point, he tried to transmit something, but his radio went dead. I followed his flight to the ground. On impact, the aircraft had very little flare and hit so hard there must have been very little collective accumulator left. Basically, the controls were not operating. The helicopter rolled over on its nose, throwing rotor blades, dust, smoke, and flame. It finally came to rest on its right side.

While we watched the scene unfold, I rolled my helicopter into a tight right hand turn, so I could see if anyone got out of the downed chopper. I saw Buzzell climb out of the right greenhouse and start to run. He sprinted about ten feet, stopped, and circled back to the aircraft to help a crew member out of the same greenhouse. We later learned that Buzzell was doing all this running with two broken legs.

I began firing rockets as I made the tight turn, and we were hit by six to eight .30 cal. rounds starting front to rear. One round entered just aft of my pedal adjusting knob and smashed into the bottom of my armored seat. The impact threw all the sand and grit from the armored seat pan up through the nylon mesh and hit my butt. (Naturally, this stung like hell, and I was sure I was wounded. Sometime during all the mayhem, a trickle of sweat dribbled down between my legs, and I just knew I was in serious trouble. During our first rearm/refuel I surreptitiously unbuckled everything and stuck my hands down to see if I had any privates left. I found no blood or major damage. Man, was I relieved!)

Still up in a tight turn, I fired six to eight pairs of

rockets to give the men on the ground time to get to cover. Then, Burroughs eased up on the controls with me and stated, "We are down to twenty knots, we've got to get out of here." I rolled wings level and began gaining altitude and airspeed. After that, I began a slow right climbing turn to the right, trying to keep the downed helicopter in sight. As we made the first turn, I saw the downed bird we were to originally cover. It was completely charred. All on board the slick were killed.

Burroughs got back on the controls and said, "Let me fly, you're taking us back over the area of fire." I gave him the controls and came up on the emergency radio channel and began transmitting a "Mayday." My voice was noticeably shrill, and my transmission nonsensical. A Musket gunship, Musket 39, I believe, answered back, "Firebird, this is Musket, calm down, and give me your location. I have a pair of guns and will come help." I did calm down and gave him my grid. Burroughs had flown us clear of the area and over near LZ Center.

My next communication came from Colonel Kelly, commander of the 1/6 Infantry, the unit being moved. (He was the same man who later became famous during the Gulf War for his daily Pentagon briefings.) He advised me he had an LRRP team, Rosie, that he could insert if I would cover his Command and Control aircraft. The Muskets and I teamed up just off of LZ Center, picked up a close wing position on the C&C, and went in.

When we approached Buzzell's and Hannah's crash site, I spied a freshly dug foxhole on the side of the ridge line. I also observed muzzle flashes coming from the foxhole. I rolled left, went wings level, kicked pedal, and checked the ball. I looked *through the sight and was dead on target. It only took one pair of rockets to take care of the problem.*

The C&C put down, and before I could complete one race track pattern; he was out. We returned to LZ Center.

While all this was going on, Colonel Kelly was contacting division and ordering aviation assets for a combat assault. We were waiting for the slicks to arrive, and I was contacted by an air force FAC who had a couple of braces of fighters if we wanted them. We did. I adjusted them with rockets and made a couple of passes doing this. About this time, we were joined by two more gunships. I believe they were also Firebirds. We left to rearm/refuel at LZ Ross.

We were sitting at LZ Ross when Colonel Kelly walked up to my helicopter, pulled my chicken plate away from my chest, and peered at my name tag. He merely said, "I just wanted to know who Firebird 91 is." He then turned and walked away. A couple of days later he sent me his handwritten recommendation for an award.

Back at the crash site, we initiated a two-infantry-company assault. The assault lasted about two hours. The men had to fight their way back up toward LZ East to get joined with LRRP Team Rosie and our guys.

I was on the ground at LZ Ross when we got word that they had reached the LRRP team and 92's crew. We returned to the area to help complete the insertion, and then coordinated with "Snake Doctor," our maintenance helicopter, to meet us at LZ Ross to check out our bird. We located numerous bullet holes in the bottom of the gunship. One hole was found in the door jamb behind the pilot's seat. We

*had been ordered by our ops to return to Chu Lai,
and maintenance assured us that the aircraft was
safe to fly; so we cranked it up and launched for
Chu Lai. As we began to ascend, I glanced down at
the gauges, and everything read "Zero"! I quickly
radioed Snake Doctor and informed him I was turning back. He answered and asked us, "Taylor, did
you turn your inverter on?" I reached up, flicked on
the inverter, and returned to Chu Lai without ever
responding!*

*When we finally arrived at the company area, I
collapsed on my bunk and fell fast asleep. I had
never before, nor have I since, been so completely
wrung out.*

*That night, we went to the hospital to check on
Buzzell and Hannah. They were both in pretty bad
shape. They were in so much pain, they were not
very talkative. Hannah did tell me that LRRP Team
Rosie had a "Kit Carson" scout (an ex-NVA soldier) with them. When he appeared around the bend
in the trail, they almost shot him. If he had not been
yelling, "Firebird, Firebird," as he came into sight,
he would have been history. The day after we saw
them, Buzzell and Hannah were medevaced out to
another hospital.*

*After a couple of weeks had passed, the 1/6 dis-
played some captured weapons they had taken during this period. One was a .51 cal. antiaircraft
weapon. On this particular weapon's sight, there
was pictured a miniature helicopter. It was to help
the shooter hit a helicopter at up to 80 knots, 1,500
ft. The gunners had supposedly been trained to take
the wing helicopter first, which would cause the
lead to turn back to cover. They would then take the
lead chopper under fire. It was while hearing this*

*that I realized how lucky I was to have varied my
airspeed to pick up coverage on the damaged Firebird. By going from 60 knots to 110 knots, I just
plain lucked out!*

Three crew members crawled out of Buzzell's helo before
it exploded. The fourth was blown out by the force of the
explosion, miraculously suffering only superficial burns.

I arrived in the area of the burning aircraft in a single
gunship. Taylor was apparently at LZ Ross refueling. En
route to the location, I was advised that the NVA was operating in the vicinity with at least nine antiaircraft guns.
There were also hundreds of their soldiers running
around armed with AK-47s. Bruce and Aker were my
crew members. As I circled west of the smoldering choppers, a medevac helicopter radioed and asked, "Has anyone tried to get them out?" I answered, "I don't know."
The slicks above us were loaded with field grade officers.
They kept repeating, "Don't go in there . . . Don't go in
there!" The three slicks they were in were flying so high,
they could not have possibly heard any shots fired in
anger at them. They were skittish about being around the
antiaircraft guns of the Second NVA Division.

By this stage of my military career, my fellow warrant
officers and I had extremely low opinions of most field
grade officers. We were of the opinion they laid around
most of the day playing with themselves and then strutted
around thinking they were great lovers. (Naturally, I had
a completely different image of my warrant officer buddies who later became field grade officers.) I would bet
money every one of the field grade officers up in the sky
that day received a medal.

The exact location of the downed gunship was evident
from the spiral of smoke rising from the valley floor. At
the far end of the valley, some smoke was still lingering

from the site of the slick crash. The medevac radioed, "Let's give it a try. Will you cover me?" Before I could give any kind of reply, the medevac dove to low level. There was no time to think things over or get nervous. Besides, my friends were on the ground and in big trouble.

Bruce and Aker's machine guns were hammering hard. We were trying our best to drive more than a few nails into some of the commies' coffins. As I dove in low level, Bruce related later that he glanced over at Aker. Aker was shaking his head and twirling his finger beside his helmet to denote my apparent crazy action. The medevac set down, next to Hannah's burnt chopper, and I circled low level overhead spraying the jungle with everything we had. Clearly, the antiaircraft guns were not able to deflect low enough from their position on the side of the mountains to shoot at us while we were at this level. We did not take one hit. With Bruce and Aker working in a furious tandem on the machine guns, the NVA were as busy dodging bullets as they were firing them.

On the ground, Hannah and the others were so close to some of the NVA soldiers, they could hear them yelling and talking. Hannah related seeing the NVA antiaircraft guns firing and watching the soldiers firing them. These particular guns were equipped with shoulder devices that enabled the NVA to turn and aim the large caliber weapons with their shoulders pressing against the turning mechanisms. These were the same weapons that brought down Hannah's ship in the first place. His gunship was seemingly struck in the engine by one of the rounds from the antiaircraft guns. At least one of these rounds ignited the rockets on the chopper and set the fuel on fire. Incredibly, they did not become an airburst! The first memory Hannah had after he hit the ground was the intense heat from the fire burning next to his face.

Hannah was in terrible pain. He did not realize it at the

time, but he had suffered a broken back in the crash. I later asked him, "What did you do while you were hiding on the ground?" He answered, "I just prayed!"

When the medevac reached them, the rescuers threw the three most injured men onto the helicopter and headed for safety. One crew member was left with the LRRP because of his minor injuries. Hannah was laid across the floor of the medevac; and as they took off, the NVA was shooting the crap out of the helicopter. (Apparently, my gunship did not make as many of them duck as I hoped.) Hannah was terrified he had successfully lived so far only to be shot full of holes along with the bottom of the aircraft.

A little over a month after Hannah was hurt, he wrote a letter to Taylor updating him on his condition and thanking Taylor for saving his life. Excerpts from the letter include:

> *I know there were many other people involved who risked their lives to get us out that day, but I want to express my gratitude to you, R.P. [Taylor]. But for your keen eyesight which saw us get out alive, and the swiftness with which you called in help, and your ability in directing the air strikes and other help saved our lives, I am convinced. I knew, during the two hours we were hiding in the jungle with only our .38s that we were going to die. You cannot imagine the relief at being rescued from death, as there are no words descriptive enough to convey the thought properly.*
>
> *Thanks are so inadequate, R.P., but thanks for my life. As worthless as I am, I still enjoy living and hope to attain a ripe old age before I check out. For the rest of my life I will never forget you.*
>   *[Hannah]*

On May 6, the enemy rocketed Chu Lai again. As gunship instructor pilot, I gave six "check rides." I helped a few guys become aircraft commanders, so I could get away faster from the nonsense and go back to flying slicks. That night I flew gunships as LZ Center was again attacked in a ground assault. We flew most of the night.

On May 7, they stacked the Americans in body bags at LZ Baldy like cord wood. The NVA shot down an A1-E and put holes in an F-4 and an A-4 jet.

On May 10, three of our gunships took .50 caliber hits, one in the fuel cells. If that had been a tracer round, the crew might as well have spread their legs, bent over, and kissed their asses good-bye. I took a .50 caliber hit on the nose of my gunship.

While escorting a medevac at night in a different gunship, I took a .30 cal. round through a flak jacket that was lying on the chin bubble. My nerves had totally turned to shit by then. I was more stunned than scared. My body felt numb. Two different times I took hits through the chin bubble into a flak jacket I had thrown down. Both times, it shocked the crap out of me. At night, it felt like an animal jumped up on your feet as the flak jacket jerked from the impact of the bullet.

This time, it took my mind a couple of seconds to figure out what jumped next to my feet, because nothing was supposed to move in that part of the gunship. The more frightened I became, the more flak jackets I would throw on the floor of the gunship. Sometimes, I would travel around with my own version of "four on the floor" of the gunship. Two of them would be in the chin bubble in front of my feet, and two were around the cyclic control below my legs. They were like security blankets. Someone once remarked that I looked like a pack mule lugging all the flak jackets to the flight line. No wonder my gunships could not hover—too much weight from all the flak jackets! I only practiced this habit when we knew the NVA were coming out for a big rumble.

All of our gunships took hits on May 10. Carson was back flying and had an expended .50 cal. (shot from a long distance) bounce off his chickenboard. A gunship pilot out of Da Nang was killed during this action.

General Westmoreland was in the area west of Chu Lai on May 12. At the Kham Duc Special Forces Camp, Americans lost control of all the mountain bases surrounding it. Kham Duc was located in the lower part of a valley. The NVA had successfully positioned mortars and antiaircraft guns surrounding the base. Some intelligent soul decided it was now time to reinforce the base.

The South Vietnamese supposedly wanted to hold on to Kham Duc because that was where the Premier went to shoot tigers. The special forces used the camp to launch attacks into Laos and dubbed the place "Jungle School."

After many of our soldiers were killed reinforcing the place, our generals decided they did not need another boondoggle like Khe Sanh, so they made the determination to charge to the rear. During the evacuation, the Americans aimed their rifles at the friendly mercenaries inside Kham Duc to prevent them from abandoning their positions. The panicked mercenaries were charging the slicks trying to save their skins.

Our aviation battalion had thirty helicopters shot up, with three gunships and two slicks shot down. Two gunships and a slick were total losses. The military also lost two C-130s, an A1-E, two CH-47 helicopters, two CH-46 helicopters (marine choppers at Ngoc Tavak) and an O-2A observation plane on the extraction. Our favorite door gunner, Colonel Buck Nelson, was the last American grunt off the ground. When the brass finally decided to try to reinforce the special forces camp, they brought in Buck Nelson's grunt units from the 196th Light Infantry. When the reinforcement began, Colonel Nelson's men were at the DMZ.

These men were brought in to fight, but the generals then changed their minds and decided to extract everyone because all the high ground had been lost. The weather was also heavily overcast, and it was hard to get air support into the region. The lead helicopter in the first extraction flight was hit with what was believed to be a 37 mm antiaircraft gun. It crashed and burned.

Westmoreland stated that the evacuation of Kham Duc was carried out by US Air Force pilots and was "accomplished with invincible acts of bravery." One even earned a Congressional Medal of Honor for making "the last flight in." Actually, the last Americans evacuated were some special forces troops, with Buck Nelson being the last regular infantry man out. A helicopter from our battalion picked them up and carted them to safety. Our pilots, for this brave, daring act would have at the most been late for dinner back at Chu Lai.

Malek rescued two air force pilots, also on May 12. They were F-4 pilots. The jet jockeys called in a Mayday on the emergency radio frequency. They said they could not see their instruments, because the cockpit was full of smoke. The plane was somewhere between Kham Duc and Chu Lai. Malek flew to the area, and several air force A1-Es were circling the downed plane. As he arrived, he spotted a parachute and went in to pick up the pilot. He then blasted off while receiving intense fire. He began to leave the area, and the jet pilot he had rescued started raising all kinds of hell. He was pointing to the ground and yelling. Malek then realized there were two pilots on the jet when it went down. One was still out there somewhere.

Malek knew they were in deep doodoo then, because he now had to continue circling the spot at low level in or-

der to find the other pilot. One pilot being rescued was
relatively safe. A helicopter could get in and out quickly.
Circling an area low, with Charlie knowing that the chopper will have to land again, was a very dangerous situation.

Malek finally located the other parachute, raced in, and
loaded up the remaining pilot. He flew the men to LZ
Baldy to the Medical Aid Station. He shut down the chopper and shot the bull with the guys for a few minutes
while the doc checked them over for injuries.

After a short time, he told the two jet jockeys it was
time for him to go. They curiously asked him, "What
for?" He told them he had to get back to work, because
he still had about eight flying hours left. The pilots could
not believe he was going back to fly that area all day.
Malek and I agreed later that this was, again, just another
day at the office. A few days after this incident, he received a very nice thank you from the men for saving
their lives. At least, the ones who really counted noticed.
Malek told me about this rescue while we were still in
Vietnam. I thought Malek might get a medal for his actions. All he got was a ten minute break!

Gaither, a friend of mine from our battalion, was shot
down again on May 13. He was the same guy who was
shot between the toes during Tet I. That afternoon, I was
flying gunships at LZ Baldy, and took another .50 cal.
through the radio compartment next to my leg. I believe
that it was this day southeast of LZ West that I thought the
NVA had hauled in a quad-50 antiaircraft gun, four guns
in one. It was either that, or they were shooting straight
tracer rounds. There were too many tracer rounds for one
gun. I practiced my famous "look back tactic" once
again. Again, no friendlies were anywhere around us.

On May 14, Chu Lai came under rocket attack again. I
was still flying gunships. The 196th Light Infantry moved

back into the Que Son Valley. The 198th was about to run
out of grunts.

Parting Shots (Firebird Edition)

Around this time, the slick pilots were giving us trouble,
because, just before dark when they flew into LZ Center,
this one dink would rip off a few rounds at them with a
.50 cal. antiaircraft gun. We assumed it was an old farmer
with an after-hours part-time job. He never hung around
long enough for us to draw a bead on him. He did not
shoot enough for us to find him on the hillside around the
jungle. Someone came up with the brilliant idea that what
we needed was a decoy to fly down the ridge line just before dark. This way we could draw a couple of tracer
rounds from our "friend," so the trail gunship could low
level in and convince the farmer he should have stuck to
his first profession. Another genius also thought that if
the lead gunship had white smoke grenades on the skids
that were set off during a dive after the tracers were fired,
the farmer would stand beside his machine gun and watch
the crash, thinking he had shot the gunship down. This
would expose him for the second gunship.

I must have done a lot of the brainwork on this ingenious idea, because somehow I convinced Carson he
should be the decoy. I certainly had no desire to voluntar-
ily put my own head in the way of Charlie's lead pills.
Anyway, we carried out this crazy plan, and sure enough,
the old farmer shot at Carson. Carson even turned his
lights on, so the dink could get a better shot at him. (To
this day, I wonder if the bullet that grazed his head earlier
had affected his thinking!) I came in behind Carson and
dumped fourteen rockets and about 5,000 bullets on the

dink's dumb butt. I was flying Bruce's minigun ship. Whether I hit him or not, we never found out. But we never had any problems from random fire in that area again. It probably dawned on him that the guys with the red bird on the side of their helicopters were just crazy enough to get serious about flushing him out. If they wanted to go to all of that trouble, they might actually kill him one day. I'm sure he understood the intelligence level he was facing from the guys that dreamed up this brilliant idea and it scared him silly.

I have previously stated my feelings of outrage about our commanders using our soldiers as human decoys. One could note a little inconsistency in my usage of Carson and his crew as flying "skeet." What the heck; Carson and I were just having fun. I had certainly changed a lot from my first days in gunships when I thought all these guys were crazy.

May 16 was the last day I flew a gunship in Vietnam. Carson and I were out in two gunships on a firefly mission. We sank forty-seven sampans, and each gunship took a hit. Now I could go back to being a full-time slick pilot. Now things would be more peaceful . . .

Chapter Four

RATTLER TALES

••

Kucera

I FLEW IN MY FIRST SLICK AS THE PILOT ON MAY 3: I had heard all kinds of stories of flying around hauling "ass and trash" and enjoying the scenery. I was prepared for a nice boring day and ho-hum activity on my part. However, I didn't get my wish.

We were in a flight of seven slicks extracting troops from a PZ and moving them to an area around the Rock Hill. On the last lift, a few rounds were fired at us, so the gunships started shooting up the jungle on both sides of the PZ. Kucera and I were flying lead helicopter with Dillard flying "tail end Charlie." Kucera asked over the UHF radio if the flight was "up." This was a quick way to ask if all the troops were loaded and if the helicopters were ready to leave. Dillard radioed that we were indeed "up." As the flight lifted off, the NVA opened up on us with automatic weapons, but we all got out. Suddenly and frantically, Dillard called over the radio, "I left one." Dillard's helicopter, with all the turbulence from the rotor wash off the other helicopters,

MAY 3, 1968

The governments of Vietnam and the United States finally agreed to have the Peace Talks in Paris.

could not safely lift to a hover while carrying the five or six troops he had loaded. So Dillard did the only practical thing, he chunked a grunt. This was standard procedure when the chopper was loaded down too much to make it safely into the air.

Kucera, as I came to realize more and more in the weeks to come, proved to be undaunted by any predicament. He immediately told the number two aircraft to take over as flight lead and jerked his helicopter around. We went in downwind and landed beside the lonely grunt who was stranded in the rice paddy laying face down in the mud. The only problem we had then was the grunt was absolutely frozen with fear. Water and mud from the commies' bullets were splattering everywhere in our immediate vicinity. Tracers were zipping across the nose of the helicopter. Charlie was toiling very hard to make us permanent residents of this rice paddy.

I couldn't believe this! Flying slicks was supposed to be safe and boring. We sat there, immobile and vulnerable, for what seemed to be an eternity. This eternity was probably five seconds. That was a long time when someone was shooting at you. Fortunately, the NVA were not in position against the edge of the PZ. We would truly have been sitting ducks in that case. The crew chief or another grunt leaped off and dragged the frightened grunt onto the helicopter.

I sometimes wondered about the stark terror he must have felt when he realized he was the only American left behind on the final flight out. I probably would have just keeled over with heart failure as I was tossed from the slick. After we climbed to altitude and relative safety, I glanced back to locate the grunt. He was white as a ghost and possibly close to or in shock. The thankful grunt commander assured Kucera and me he would put us in for a medal as he took our names and identification numbers. We had heard of one helicopter pilot who received a Silver Star for doing the exact same thing.

I always assumed Kucera received his medal for that occasion. A week later, he really did earn a medal. I was just glad I was not with him that day. On May 10, I decided that my fortunes were finally changing for the better. Even though I was back flying gunships that night, I was lucky to be doing so, or I would have been flying slicks with Kucera, earning a Distinguished Flying Cross. He was involved with the evacuation of a small special forces camp, known as Ngok Tavak, in the area of Kham Duc. After dark, the camp came under heavy attack from an NVA unit. Some "friendly" mercenary soldiers, who began the fight with the Americans, switched to the other side in the middle of the battle. When he sat down on the helipad for the last lift, Kucera spotted men scurrying everywhere. He flipped on his landing light in order to see better and immediately noticed that NVA soldiers were the ones doing the scurrying. They carried wire cutters and were cutting the wire to get in the perimeter. I asked him what his reaction was, and he said, "I turned the light off." If this operation alarmed the brave Kucera, they would have probably found me hiding under my stash of flak jackets, suffering from hyperventilation.

The Marines had two CH-46 helicopters shot down at Ngok Tavak during the day. A pilot of one of the CH-46s was hanging or sitting on the skid of an Army slick, as the slick took off. He was shot as the chopper gained altitude and fell to the ground. His body was never found.

Not Kucera

From the 17th to the 28th of May, I only flew with two pilots other than Kucera. They will remain anonymous. One had the unnerving habit of flying the helicopter straight and level and stomping the pedals to get the helicopter swinging back and forth. He apparently performed this stunt just to stop the boredom. Possessing an understanding of the mechanical operation of a helicopter, I realized that this put undue stress on the metal parts. This pilot also loved to do climbs to zero air speed and then kick a pedal turn into a free fall. By that stage of my Vietnam career, I tried not to push my luck any more than I had to unless I was doing something that was absolutely necessary. These kinds of actions made me extremely nervous.

One day, after I made aircraft commander, I was in a small flight of slicks carrying ARVN soldiers at about 1,500 feet. Unbelievably, an ARVN soldier tumbled out the cargo door of a slick. The guy was flapping his arms like wings. The first reaction from the flight was an anonymous radio transmission asking, "Was it a bird, was it a plane?" I was speechless!

Now, this incident could have been a random event. This honestly did occur sometimes, but that guy fell out of the slick flown by the same aircraft commander who got a kick out of stomping the pedals and making the helicopter swing. I honestly did not see any swinging at the time. This ARVN could have just accidentally fallen out, but it was certainly a strange coincidence.

The other slick pilot whom I flew with was the pilot involved in a much talked-about incident that happened in 1968. Much later I read an article in either *Soldier of Fortune* or *Vietnam* magazine that I believe was this event. Bruce related the story of what happened, while I was still in Vietnam.

The pilot was flying a helicopter which was extracting a special forces team from thick jungle west of Antenna Valley. The slick was receiving fire, and Charlie was becoming steadily more accurate. The enemy moved in as the last man was being hoisted up into the slick. The jungle was about one hundred feet high, and the special forces soldier was still about fifty feet off the ground when the pilot decided to take off. When the chopper finally landed, the special forces guy was still suspended from the cable and was badly wounded from the tree branches swiping him. He had a dislocated shoulder, his uniform was in shreds, and he was bloody from head to toe. His only comment was, "Give me a gun, I'm going to kill that pilot!"

Laos

This particular aircraft commander and I made my first flight into Laos on May 20. We went to Hue/Phu Bai and received the standard CIA (Central Intelligence Agency) briefing. As we went into the briefing bunker before the flight, the CIA attempted to confiscate our dog tags and wallets. Because we were about to violate international law, they didn't want us to be identifiable as Americans. All the other helicopter pilots filed in and ignored the agents. Helicopter pilots were independent types.

The CIA guy began to tell us that we were going to fly, in formation, into Laos and land on some hill. Supposedly, some Americans and Cambodian mercenaries were thought to be alive, but we had no concrete proof at the moment. That morning they had inserted a small special forces team into the vicinity, and the entire team was wiped out. Radio contact had not been accomplished since the morning, when the NVA were chunking hand grenades up into the American position. One American was known dead on the ground.

The reason our helicopters were needed was that the Vietnamese helicopter unit, Kingbees, had a helicopter shot down by a 37 mm antiaircraft gun coming off the mountain. One American aboard the Kingbee was killed when it was hit and set on fire in the LZ. This LZ was a mountaintop and not made wide enough for the Kingbee's helicopter, an H-34. The front wheels and tail wheel could not both be set down successfully. The Vietnamese pilot had no choice but to take off into the direct fire from a 37 mm antiaircraft gun. Nearly all of the Kingbees' other choppers had also been badly damaged. The crazy dude giving the briefing proceeded to point out the locations of the hills in the vicinity. They were all manned with 20 mm, 37 mm and .50 cal. antiaircraft positions.

I had been in Vietnam eight months by now, and my proper military attitude was not quite up to speed. As I sat there listening to this briefing, several mutinous thoughts ran through my mind. I figured the CIA had as much chance of getting me to go on that mission as they would have if they ordered me to ride a donkey to Hanoi. Fortunately for all of us, some pilots there were "short-timers," in other words they did not have much time left in Vietnam. They proceeded to tell the CIA representative to take his mission and stick it up his ass. Everybody then joined in an angry chorus and expressed to the CIA dumbass that we damn sure were not going to Laos in flight formation. Furthermore, we had no intention of landing without radio contact, and we would not land with known antiaircraft guns shooting directly into the LZ.

The guy put up no argument and just asked, "What do you propose?" He was advised, by men who actually knew what a mission like this was all about, to obtain some jets with napalm, drop some on the antiaircraft guns, and use a helicopter to drop a radio down into the area to see if anyone was alive to talk to us. We then drew straws to choose the lucky pilot who would take in the radio. The pilot that ended up going had a friend who volunteered, "If you're going, I will fly out behind you and pick you up if anything happens." That was a true friend! I was impressed and relieved at the same time. I was impressed by the friend's generous offer and damned glad I did not know the pilot myself!

We flew out later, with about a mile spacing between us, and the complete mountain had been napalmed. This was also my first opportunity to see a Cobra helicopter gunship in Vietnam. Six of these machines were on this mission and I believe they were from the First Cavalry. As we cruised to Laos, they would race past us, slow down, then race past us again. We were in an old beat-up D-model slick that day. It was a wonder we did not get a ticket for flying too slow compared to the Cobras and the H-models.

This mission showed me that the CIA could get plenty of jets when they called for them. We went in to the top of the mountain, loaded, and never took a hit. We were the second helicopter in, and the special forces soldiers and Cambodians who survived would not leave until we hauled out the dead bodies. We risked our lives for a load of dead Cambodians. I was told these Cambodians were known as KKKs, which was either a Cambodian political group or a bandit group. My gunner, speaking while en route back to Hue/Phu Bai, said over the intercom he could not believe the bodies. I twisted my head around, and he was using his M-16 to push the lips apart on the Cambodian corpses. Every tooth in their heads was gold. He said he was going to help himself to a few, and I instructed him to leave them alone and get back behind the

M-60. I enticed him with the opportunity to swap fire with a 37 mm antiaircraft gun.

When we landed at Phu Bai, a contingent of Cambodians, both men and women, were there to meet the helicopters. The women were crying. After we shut down, I walked over to a special forces sergeant and mentioned my gunner was about to help himself to some gold teeth. The sergeant said that there would have probably been a killing, because that was the family savings account. The first thing the wives did was to remove gold teeth. He then told us that the Cambodians back at the mountain in Laos had already called in and assured this group of mourners that the teeth were all in place. We later learned that the special forces paid the Cambodians with gold. Sixty of the Cambodian KKKs were killed or wounded.

I'm not certain how many times I flew into Laos. I know that on the first of August, I was on a sniffer mission and saw a hospital in an area adjacent to or in Laos. We did not have helicopter gunships supporting the sniffer helicopter. We had two jets and an air force FAC supporting the two slicks. I actually noticed hootches, stretchers, and bloody bandages on the stretchers. I felt certain we were in Laos on a lot of the missions where we had jet support and no gunships. My maps did not go out that far west, and there was seldom anything to see but triple canopy jungle.

Although I enjoyed flying with Kucera, my experiences with the other two slick pilots I was flying with were not all that wonderful. I complained to Captain Castle, my new platoon leader, that there was definitely a conspiracy among his pilots to kill me. Captain Castle knew I had been the instructor pilot in gunships, and because of a shortage of slick pilots, he made me an aircraft commander. I didn't know the first thing about flying a slick.

Shot from Behind

That same day (May 28), I flew again with Kucera in support of the special forces. They wanted us to fly a chopper load of ammo into the camp at Hau Duc, which had been hit with two hundred mortar rounds the day before. Both of us were A/Cs, but Kucera was the boss for the morning flight, and he flew in with a red hot spiral approach and set down on a bunker to the south of the helicopter pad. We successfully dumped the ammo before Charlie could move his mortar tube. It only took a few seconds, and we were gone. I was highly impressed with his diving approach.

That afternoon, I was flying left seat, and they wanted another load of ammo taken in along with a special forces soldier. I remembered from the earlier mission that the mortar rounds were coming from the west. I told Kucera I was going in low level from the east and land north of the pad where a shot-down helicopter had been hit with a mortar. Mortar rounds had been hitting the camp intermittently throughout the day. I came in hot, real fast, and at the last second before touchdown, I noticed plenty of room to turn the helicopter around. I quickly kicked the right pedal and turned the helicopter so that it was facing east. The special forces soldier we hauled in jumped out, stood next to the helicopter, and helped drag the ammo cans out of the helicopter. I saw him flinch several times and glance over his shoulder to the west as he helped unload the chopper. We sat there for twenty seconds at the most. I scanned the chopper that had been hit with the mortar round on the helipad. It must have had two thousand shrapnel holes in it. Charlie obviously used it for target practice after they disabled it. It was a medevac helicopter.

On the way out, I asked Kucera what he thought about

my "hot landing." He said I nearly killed him when I switched the helicopter around. He was sure we nearly hit the tail rotor in the concertina wire. I asked the crew chief next, and he agreed with me that we had plenty of clearance for the tail rotor. Kucera then questioned the gunner, and he agreed with Kucera. We were all joking around because we were happy to have gotten out of there without being killed.

We landed at Tien Phouc Special Forces Camp and shut down. As Kucera and I walked off to get a drink, the crew chief hollered and told us to come look at the helicopter. Some NVA had shot, at the least, a full clip of ammo into the tail boom, straight from the rear of the helicopter. If I had landed facing west, we would have taken a full clip through the windshield. I challenged Kucera to tell me who the dumbass was now!

That special forces guy, unloading the ammo, obviously heard the rounds hitting the helicopter. It took one brave man to stand and unload ammo with a dink shooting on full automatic next to him. We could not count the hits because they ricocheted off the transmission and split. Entry and exit holes were everywhere. I believe they eventually had to sling load the chopper back to maintenance. I know we did not fly it back to Chu Lai.

I always assumed that the Charlie sneaked up to the wire at night and dug in waiting for something to happen. He would have had to have been really close not to hit the American standing behind the helicopter. Remember, the rumor was they earned a bicycle and a thirty day leave for shooting a helicopter down. This guy could have easily shot two clips into the tail of the helicopter. He had plenty of time. The poor slimeball was probably amazed and dismayed when the thing lifted into the air. I am sure his NVA friends did not believe he could be that close and still not knock the helicopter down.

This Charlie was real close to the helicopter when he was burning off a clip or two of ammo at us but not near as close as one story I heard. A pilot in our battalion landed his chopper, and bullets immediately started flying around the inside of the aircraft like mosquitoes. He could not tell where the enemy was as he hastily exited the area. When he eventually landed in a safe area, the crew jumped out to check the chopper. Incredibly, the bottom of the helicopter was covered with powder burns. The pilot had set the chopper squarely on top of a Charlie in a spider hole. The dink was able to stick his gun barrel up to the chopper and blast away. It was hard to miss at that distance!

On May 29, an aviation company in our battalion was hit with a mortar attack. A round hit the top of one hootch where one man was killed and sixteen were wounded.

That same day, Taylor got his private parts caught in the proverbial wringer! He was flying lead in a Frog gunship. As he flew over a tree line, the helicopter received about fifteen rounds of automatic weapons fire. His gunner spotted the exact location where the fire came from, and Taylor circled around to attack the tree line.

Afterward, the crap hit the fan, so to speak. The ARVN alleged that some innocents were wounded in this particular attack. The jerks from the rear echelon stated in writing that the rules of engagement required a person to ascertain the source of the fire, "the source must be positively ascertained as enemy before the target can be taken under attack." Taylor did this. Additionally, the rules require "the aircraft crew must be in jeopardy before fire can be returned." The edict from some remote desk jockey interpreting jeopardy stated "the aircraft crew must be in jeopardy before fire can be returned, and sporadic ground fire would hardly meet the connotation of the word *jeopardize*." Say What?

Ambush

On June 1, Kucera and I were flying together again in a
new H-model slick. Jeffcoat was our crew chief and
Palazzo was the gunner. Palazzo was also my gunner during the Tet Offensive. We were both in gunships at the
time, and he was wounded with a shot to the butt. Years
later, I asked him why he had switched over to the slicks.
He then told me his story.

He spent nine or ten months on a river boat and decided that was too dangerous, so he extended his tour in
Vietnam and took a "safe" job, a door gunner on a gunship helicopter! (Remember, I mentioned earlier that
some of the pilots worried about these door gunners.)
Anyway, he was flying during Tet with the Firebirds right
before he left on his forty-five day leave. (This was the
amount of leave you received if you extended your tour.)
When he took his leave, he left behind a "fine" M-60 machine gun and did not want anyone else to mess with it,
so he hid it on the flight line. Of course, by the time he
returned, water had gotten to it and turned it into a lump
of rust. He was chunked out of the Firebirds and flew as
a slick gunner for awhile until things cooled down. They
eventually let him transfer back to the Firebirds.

Everett Jeffcoat, our crew chief that day, has written
many articles and commentaries since the war dealing
with the issue of PTSD, Post Traumatic Stress Disorder.
One article, "Post Traumatic Stress Disorder—One Vic-
tim's View," covers what happened to us on our mission.

Early in the day, we inserted a special forces recon
team west of Thoung Duc, close to Laos. We received no
fire at that time.

Later, we were flying recon for a convoy of marine
tanks and ARVN trucks taking resupply to the special
forces camp. The camp was at Thoung Duc, west of

Happy Valley and southwest of Da Nang. We flew above the convoy west of Hill 55. This was the marine base where they said President Johnson's son-in-law (now Senator Robb) was stationed. The convoy also included special forces troops. To the west of Hill 55, the road passed over a small hill where a marine artillery base was located.

Kucera was flying left seat, so he was the boss. I do not remember who was on the controls, but we flew through the marine base low level, traveling just ahead of the convoy. Apparently, we blew down a tent, or a radio antenna, or blew some dirt in their beer. An angry jarhead called up on our FM radio frequency and told us that if we would land, he would gladly give us a free ass-kicking. His anger clouded his thinking, and he was fortunate we did not unleash the door gunners on him. We gave him a little lip and bantered back and forth over the radio for a few minutes to break the boredom. I was pretty sure he was wishing us a good day as we went on our way.

Several miles past this base, the road was about fifty feet from the river. The road ran east to west with the river just to the south of it. The fifty feet between the two was covered by a thick growth of trees which extended ten to fifteen feet into the north side of the road. This clearly was a prime location for an ambush. We flew over the area about fifty feet above these trees at a speed of about sixty or seventy knots and looped back over the road to the convoy. Two marine tanks were in the lead, and another tank was to the rear. From the low level helicopter, we did not see anything out of the ordinary, and no one was shooting at us.

As the convoy moved onto the section of the road covered by trees, anti-tank rockets began to explode. The three tanks were immediately knocked out. The entire convoy was hit with a barrage of steel and fire. I witnessed two people blown from one of the tanks by the force of an explosion. They resembled leaves blowing in a strong wind. Within a few hellish seconds, nineteen trucks and three tanks were disabled or destroyed. The commies, with care and cunning, had ensnared the whole convoy in a deadly trap. This NVA unit was well disciplined, because they refrained from firing at the low and slow helicopter. Most of the time, the enemy could not resist the opportunity to fire at any chopper.

We flew in low level over the chaotic scene of the ambush and let Jeffcoat and Palazzo fire down into the enemy positions. Marine gunships were on station within minutes. Kucera and I were flying over the horrific scene at about 300 to 400 feet, but the NVA were too busy with the carnage on the ground to bother shooting at us.

The marine gunship initiated a gun run at about 2,000 feet and broke off at about 1,500 feet. This gunship was doing gravity shots with his rockets. This type of shot happened when a chopper was firing rockets from such a high altitude. He was not actually shooting at a target; he was using gravity to drop them in, because the rocket motors did not burn long enough to get them to the target from that distance. They had Huey gunships with twin-60 machine guns on each side as opposed to the army's more modern C-models with miniguns. They were so far above us; I distinctly remember peering through the Plexiglas above my head to spot them. They had radioed that they were on station starting a rocket run, and I could not find them. They were up with the clouds.

A special forces guy came up on the FM radio and made a desperate appeal for help. He frantically relayed the need for an immediate medevac. Kucera instructed him to throw smoke. Kucera called yellow and dove into the chaotic spectacle. I carefully inspected the woods on either side of the convoy and saw yellow smoke everywhere. The situation was instantly clear. The NVA were on the same radio frequency. South Vietnamese spies had given it to them, and the pukebags were slinging yellow smoke all over the place. The smoke was even up in the burning trucks.

I yelled, "NO!" at Kucera, but he assured me by saying, "Don't worry, this is the right smoke." By luck it was. It was the closest smoke to the north side of the trees. On final approach, both Kucera and I were on the controls in case one was hit. I glanced up and saw, further up the burning convoy, a large flaming object streak out of the mess. Later, I decided it was an enemy B-40 rocket fired at a truck, or at one of the lead tanks, or at us. We took a lot of automatic weapons fire on final, but once we were on the ground, the burning trucks sheltered us. Tracers could be seen flying between the trucks up and down the convoy. The special forces, marines, ARVN, and NVA were pinned down and surrounded, so they were fighting their own World War III right there in a fifty-foot strip of trees.

Palazzo was firing everything he had during our first strafing runs. Kucera told the crew, over all the pandemonium, to get ready; we were going in to land and evacuate some of the wounded. Palazzo's M-60 had been going non-stop. The barrel was red hot, so he grabbed his asbestos glove and pulled out the fiery one and replaced it with a fresh one. With all the craziness around him, he forgot to pull over the lever that held the barrel to the gun.

Kucera, cool and calm, came right in for the landing. The noise was deafening. We were right next to the exploding vehicles. Billowing smoke, relentless fire, and tracer bullets were everywhere. I was so scared that I could hardly breathe. While Kucera was doing his dead level best to get a CMH, Congressional Medal of Honor,

I was positive he was going to get me a CMH, casket with metal handles!

Our guys had fought over to a section just between where the ambush occurred and the edge of the trees to the north. They were trying to secure an area where the wounded could be picked up and taken out. We found out after the fact that there was hand-to-hand fighting in the narrow strip between our helicopter and the road. Both sides were cornered, by different means, and it was a fight to the finish.

As we were setting down in the dense smoke, Palazzo cautiously surveyed the area. Suddenly, at a distance of about ten to fifteen feet, an NVA soldier stepped out from behind a hootch. He was armed with an AK-47.

Palazzo zeroed his M-60 in on the enemy soldier and fired. The dink was staring straight at him. Instead of the burst of bullets he expected, Palazzo heard a "POOF," and the barrel of his gun went flying toward the soldier. The barrel of the machine gun only made it off the edge of the helicopter.

Simultaneously, we "sucked the guts" on that new H-model Huey and roared out of there. Jeffcoat says we took several bullet hits on final approach. We took two more hits to the chopper on takeoff, and Palazzo's startled NVA also burned a clip at us as we left. That dink probably had a religious experience over that incident, if he lived very long. No one would believe him when he told his comrades one of the air gangsters had him in the machine gun sights and then proceeded to shoot the barrel at him. Talk about luck!

Kucera and I evacuated three helicopter loads of wounded from that location that day and hauled them to Hill 55. Because of the extreme nature of the battle, most, if not all, of the wounded were literally thrown onto our slick without bandages or treatment. The marine medevac showed up in an H-34 helicopter. These machines were nothing but a fire hazard. I considered them to be giant, flying Molotov cocktails. The pilot of the H-34 understandably refused to land because of the automatic weapons fire.

I was in a state of shock from all the tracers whizzing around the exploding trucks. After hauling three loads of wounded, I was even more surprised when I heard the jarhead who threatened to whip our ass come up on the FM radio. He was desperate. He had wounded at the front of the convoy who had to come out, or they would die. Kucera told him to move his guys to the back of the convoy where we had picked up the other three loads. By this time, our jets were dropping hard bombs, and we had to watch out for and dodge all the shrapnel from the bombs. The marine said his wounded had been separated toward the front, and we needed to extract them from there.

Kucera did not bat an eyelash. He merely exclaimed, "Let's get them." I made no reply whatsoever. My nerves were in about as good a shape as the convoy. Kucera proceeded to go in low level with tracers zinging around us as thick as flies. Thankfully, one of the smoldering tanks blocked any shot direct to the helicopter once we were on the ground. There was one problem, in that the helicopter was facing west. Kucera, never one to turn the tail around, took off west, and while low level, pulled a hard bank back to the east. During this maneuver, I was just waiting for an NVA to cut the bottom out of the helicopter with automatic weapons fire. We did not receive any direct fire from anywhere but at the ambush site.

When we were finally through with the harrowing experience of the day, we traveled back to the Fifth Special Forces Camp at Da Nang. Kucera and I gladly jumped out of the slick and headed for the bar and some "nerve tonic." We left Palazzo and Jeffcoat behind to clean the chopper and check the bullet holes for permanent damage. I found out years later that the task of cleaning the helicopter that day was a surrealistic nightmare. Blood was everywhere. It had poured out of the cargo compartment, and the rotor wash from the main rotor blades and tail rotor had effectively painted the tail boom and back half of the helicopter with a sticky coat of blood. The clean-up job took a very long time for Palazzo and Jeffcoat. It was a very difficult task in both effort and in what it represented, the maiming of young men just trying to do their duty.

As a pilot who sat in the front of the helicopter, I was not subjected to the regular sight of the mangled bodies that were loaded into my slick. The gunners and crew chiefs were in the thick of it. I certainly never had to clean up the chopper after a mission like this. To this day, I vividly remember the three times I did turn around and view the wounded men. I will carry the images of these men with me forever.

After thinking about this particular mission and the events involved, I more clearly understand the feelings of the men directly subjected to these images day in and day out in Vietnam. I certainly owe a sincere apology to both Palazzo and Jeffcoat for leaving them with that hellish chopper. I wish I had stayed and helped them.

Naturally, we were promised medals from all concerned and never received anything. The special forces colonel did like us and remembered us. Later, he did me a favor that was more satisfying than any medal. They cut me some orders for another R&R to Hawaii, even though I was not really in their unit.

After the escapade with the convoy, I told Kucera he was either the bravest guy I knew or the dumbest. I just could not make up my mind. Twenty-five years later he just says he was brave.

Think About Their Mothers

On June 2, Kucera and I were flying out to Thoung Duc Special Forces Camp. As we passed over the area of the ambush, our now familiar jarhead friend came up on the special forces frequency and told us he had some bodies that had to be taken out of the ambush site. I was flying left seat as aircraft commander. The marine helicopters still refused to go into the site. The NVA survivors had taken flight by jumping in the river at dark. Now the only enemy left near the scene was a bunch of pesky, and potentially dangerous, snipers. Trying to shore up the defenses of the survivors, the marines had moved more tanks into the area.

At first, we told "Jarhead," "No," on hauling the bodies. In response, the marine pulled a fast one on me. This was the first, but not the last time, one of the guys on the ground used an underhanded method to get us to do his bidding. He came back with a statement like, "Hey guys, think about their mothers. Their mothers might want to look at them. You leave them out here in the heat any longer, they can't look at them, or recognize them. Think about it." I took a quick look over, and Kucera simply shrugged his shoulders.

Down we went. I sidled up by a tank for cover and picked up a load of bodies. The marines instructed us to take them to a navy hospital in Da Nang. We were not shot at going in or coming out. At least, we didn't hear anything. The pilots in the marine choppers still would not land. Upon arrival at the navy hospital, we were told to take the bodies elsewhere. They told us that we did not have the proper paperwork. We then carted the bodies to Graves Registration and were again turned away. By this time, I had figured out that the jarhead had been messing with our heads, because with the insufferable heat, no one was going to recognize the bodies anyway. The sweet sickly stench of a corpse in that heat was and still is unforgettable.

We flew back to our first destination, the navy hospital, and were furious by this time. Jeffcoat hopped out of the slick, walked in to an air-conditioned office next to the helipad, and made his point. He unsnapped his holster, placed his hand on his .38 pistol, and quietly threatened, "Paperwork! Try this paperwork, motherfuckers!!" Surprisingly, his eloquent language, his demeanor, or possibly his pistol, convinced them to get off their butts, leave the comfort of the air-conditioned room, and unload the marine bodies from the helicopter. Jeffcoat said we hauled several loads of bodies on this same day. He graphically recalls a crass and stupid comment made by some rear-echelon slimeball, "Save those body-bags for the whole ones. Use the black plastic bags for the pieces." I just remember that bunch of suddenly helpful assholes bursting out the door of the office and quickly unloading the marines' bodies. I was really angry and frustrated because I felt that this was no way for them to treat those brave young men who would never see home again.

Aircraft Commander Carlock

I had been designated an aircraft commander in slicks before I ever landed a troop-loaded slick in formation flight. Consequently I had to teach myself this important skill, and I will never forget my initial experience—it was a definite Romeo Foxtrot.

We were approaching the LZ with about fifteen slicks in a formation called "staggered left." It was "Vs" of three with the right-hand helicopters not there. I had an

old D-model slick with barely enough power to hover
with a load of grunts.

The LZ was a narrow group of small rice paddies. The
gunships were firing rockets, and the left door gunners
were shooting up a tree line. I was intently watching the
other helicopters in the flight since I had never before
done this. My helicopter was located fourth in the flight.
The rotor blades slapped along almost touching one another. The flight lead, in a very steep approach on short
final, radioed, "Pick your spots," and I chose a dike directly under our glide path.

The routine was absolutely "no sweat" and progressing
smoothly, until the dumbass lead reared up his chopper
and decided to land short of the smoke grenade that I assumed he would land on. The second helicopter in front
of me then stole my spot, and the helicopter to my immediate front completely stopped his helicopter to settle in
short of the area where I was on a glide path to land. I
yanked the nose of my helicopter as high as I could, and
pulled all the power I had, while the peter pilot was
screaming over the intercom, "6,000 rpm . . . 6,000 rpm!"
At 5,800 rpm the tail rotor effect is lost, and the helicopter could start to spin opposite of the rotor blades.

As I leveled the nose of the helicopter, I took "pot
luck" on where the helicopter was about to land. My helicopter was falling to the ground wherever I was, which
happened to be in a small rice paddy with my tail rotor
about to hit a dike. I was also concerned that the helicopter behind me was going to crash into my chopper.
The air turbulence from all the rotor wash churned up by
the other helicopters was like a swirling typhoon. Luckily, I'd had a lot of experience flying with low rpm in gunships. At the last second, I jabbed the right pedal, and set
the helicopter on the ground facing due north. All the
other choppers were facing west. One idiot, somewhere

in the flight behind me, quipped, "Way to go!" in a very sarcastic tone. I was shaking and sweating so much, my crew probably thought I had contracted malaria. I was so unnerved when I first touched down, I was not even aware of whether or not Charlie was shooting at us. The helicopters behind me must have had H-models with more horsepower, or else they had enough sense to loosen up the flight and get more distance between the helicopters. They didn't have any trouble.

From that day forward, I do not believe I ever flew in more than two or three flights where I was not "tail-end Charlie." Later on, I would fly lead, if I had someone to make all the radio calls. On a large Romeo Foxtrot, where the battalion staff was observing, a commissioned officer led the flights. Castle led a lot of our flights and did an excellent job when the battalion desk jockeys left us alone. A shallow approach, with a large flight of helicopters, resulted in a lot of disgusted voices over the radio calling the lead an asshole for hanging the flight out on a shallow approach. This type of approach would enable Charlie to shoot the crap out of the big heavy sitting ducks. Too fast an approach often resulted in the type of stack-ups we experienced on my first troop insertion. An approach that was too steep really caused problems. I witnessed helicopters actually "go around" in a troop insertion. They refused to land. That would make the lead look like the idiot he really was. By flying tail-end Charlie, I was able to hang back if I did not like the approach and sort of do my own thing.

Keeping Your Head

Picking up troops could be as tricky as dropping them off. Early in my tour, there was an incident involving a slick and a soldier who was running toward the helicopter. The slick had set down on a slope to pick up some troops. The grunt ran down the slope and straight into the rotating blades of the chopper. He sustained a severe headache and a badly dented helmet. He did maintain possession of his head, unlike other unfortunate grunts who had done the same thing at other times.

While retrieving grunts from a hillside or slope, the rotor head on the chopper has to be perpendicular to the force of gravity, which has nothing to do with the slope of the ground below you. Consequently, the blades would be much lower on the uphill side of the slope. When I was flying slicks, I always radioed the grunt commander and told him to caution his men if we were performing this maneuver on a slanted surface. Part of the problem with these guys running into either the rotor blades or tail rotor came from the fact that they always ran toward the helicopter with their heads down. They were trying to keep the dirt from blowing into their eyes and faces.

One time, I nearly turned over my slick to keep a guy from careening into my rotor blades. I had both skids down on the slope, and the engine at full rpm's, when I spotted the soldier tearing up over the ridge and down the slope. I jabbed the main control that tilted the rotor blades full to the right in order to pull the blades up and over the grunt's head. The left skid, the one on the uphill side, came off the ground completely. The crew chief almost tumbled out of the helicopter, and the grunt unloading the chopper did fall out. Pandemonium reigned. Everyone was cussing and yelling at everyone else. The grunt who caused the whole chaotic mess jumped on the slick and was very nonchalant. He acted like all this was no big deal, so I figured he was either going on R&R or better yet, home.

Prisoners

One vet told the story of how they would sometimes dispose of the VC prisoners they had captured. He said they would throw the guys up into the rotor blades of a chopper that was sitting on the ground. I thought at the time that this would be a very messy solution to the problem of prisoners. It was sort of like pissing in the wind; something was bound to come back on you. I personally doubted the story from the beginning. It sounded like booze talking to me. At least, I always hoped that was all it was.

I heard a lot of stories of grunts pulling all sorts of sordid acts on their captives while traveling in choppers at night. They would supposedly string a blanket up behind the pilot's seats, so the pilots could not see back into the helicopter. They would then have the pilots fly the aircraft over the ocean. Once the chopper was out over open water, the grunts would throw out one prisoner, as another prisoner watched, to make the onlooker talk. I never knew if that was true or not, but I did hear the story more than once. One pilot did tell me that he had witnessed grunts taking bound prisoners and throwing them out from a three-foot hover. This little action helped the captives "visualize" what a two-thousand-foot drop could feel like. Another pilot told me that he watched, in broad daylight, as someone on another chopper threw out several prisoners at over 1,000 feet altitude. Those prisoners received half a helicopter ride. They got a takeoff but no landing.

I once noticed an ARVN interrogator with a large pair of pliers in his back pocket, and I was fairly sure he did not use them to work on his motorcycle. Another time, at either LZ Baldy or Hill 35, an American caught a buddy and me by the arm and led us away from a tent we were near. The ARVN were about to interrogate a prisoner, and he thought it would be a good idea if we were not anywhere around there during the process.

A $250,000 Lawn Mower

On June 4, I was flying as aircraft commander out of Da Nang with the special forces. Accompanying me was a young peter pilot. I had given my gunner the day off. In his place was a buddy of mine from my hometown, Steed, who was in a navy payroll unit and wanted to see what helicopter pilots did. I figured he would be relatively safe, as I'd been told it would be "ass and trash" all day. The crew chief gave Steed a five-second lesson on the use of an M-60 machine gun, and we were on our way. During the day, the special forces asked me to extract a special forces soldier off the side of a mountain. The guy supposedly had suffered a heat stroke. The LZ had been cut out of the jungle with explosives, C-4, about 1,500 feet above the valley floor. I was flying an old beat-up D-model slick, but was not overly nervous about picking up one lone grunt.

For some reason, when the grunts used C-4 to cut an LZ, they always cut the trees about three to four feet off the ground. This created a patch of mangled stumps that forced any helicopter to have to hover instead of actually landing. This LZ was positioned on a small ridge jutting from the mountain. Being an experienced gunship pilot and a novice slick pilot, I surveyed the LZ and determined that it was satisfactory as I flew in and came to a hover above the shredded tree stumps. I did have to mow a little jungle with the chopper's blades on the approach, because the LZ was not quite wide enough. I then noticed something rather unusual and surprising. The grunts had blown a nice entrance into the LZ but had not created an exit path. Straight in front of the helicopter were trees fifty to sixty feet high. Still, since we were going to take on only one grunt, I was not too concerned. However, as we hovered in position, five US grunts crawled into the helicopter. The crew chief began to yell over the intercom that something was wrong. ARVN soldiers were standing to the side hollering and gesturing at the Americans. I was puzzled and beginning to feel a little uneasy about the situation. I told the crew chief to order the extra grunts off the helicopter. The panicky grunts promptly told the crew chief to tell me to get the hell out of the area quickly because the NVA were preparing to attack.

The frantic ARVN soldiers broke toward us then and started climbing on the skids. I shouted at the crew chief and my buddy Steed to stomp on their hands and kick them away, because I was on the "go." The crew chief got rid of several guys. The helicopter then lurched to the right, Steed's side, because the ARVNs were continuing to hang on for dear life. Steed yelled as he finally disengaged the last ARVN, who fell off at about fifteen feet.

The old D-model slick did real well pulling up out of the LZ to about thirty-five or forty feet. The peter pilot called out, "5,900 rpm," and I knew it was time to make a decision, as we were on the verge of losing tail rotor effect—we were about to crash and burn. I had some wonderful choices. I could either set the chopper back in the LZ and risk getting shot to hell by our "allies" and by the NVA, or mow a little timber with the rotor blades. I chose

the latter. By that time, the trees extended ten or so feet
above the rotor blades, and I did not have time to consider
the thickness of the branches. I just tipped the nose and
mowed like a Sears & Roebuck special. The rotor blades
tore into the large tree limbs and each whack sounded like
a small explosion. Luckily for everyone on the slick, the
branches were thin enough to cut through without too
much difficulty. As soon as I spotted daylight, I dove off
the mountain to the valley floor. My heart was beating
wildly, and I was sweating bullets.

I angrily informed the special forces colonel that the
Americans had nearly caused my crew to die needlessly.
We were also extremely fortunate that the ARVN did not
blow us out of the sky. One of the grunts told the colonel
that he understood enough Vietnamese to tell that our allies were seriously discussing changing sides if the NVA
attacked them. The Americans had observed movements
by the NVA scouts in the jungle all day. When we showed
up, the spooked soldiers did not care one way or the other
if their military careers were in jeopardy. They just
wanted to get out of that hellhole and live.

I never found out what became of the five grunts. I
later learned that the ARVN soldiers did manage to make
it out of the jungle that day. Our experience taught me a
valuable lesson about landing in confined LZs, and I
passed the information on to all the peter pilots who flew
with me in the future.

On the way back to camp and safety, some commie
bandit burned a full clip of ammo at us as I low-leveled
in Happy Valley. Needless to say, my buddy, Steed, never
asked to fly with me again. I guess he figured if this was
an "uneventful excursion" for a slick, he did not want any
part of some "real" action.

This mission also taught me something about using
the helicopter as a lawn mower. Many times, the LZs

were too small, and in emergencies, the pilots would just cut their way in and out of the area. If it was a sticky situation, the brass did not gripe too much about tearing up the rotor blades. Bamboo was the worst for cutting up rotor blades. The leading edge of the blades were made of titanium steel, and the remainder was honeycombed aluminum. Being an experienced farm boy from Texas, I soon learned that the helicopter fared much better if the blades were left flat, descending. You should then pop the helicopter up a few inches as quick as it would respond. That way you did not hover on the split ends of the bamboo or tree limbs. At a hover, the blades were slightly tilted, and the soft parts would be damaged.

JUNE 5, 1968

Robert Kennedy was assassinated in Los Angeles.

I frightened plenty of peter pilots, because if I started mowing, I did a thorough job. I would then pull up slightly above the jagged ends. I managed to never cut a blade the whole time I flew slicks in Nam.

Captain Photo

On June 5, I was brought up before the special forces colonel for being disrespectful to a "superior" officer. I landed at a special forces camp that had been receiving random mortar fire. They were taking approximately three to four rounds a day. I believe this was at the Tra Bong Special Forces Camp where some Australians were also stationed. It was generally assumed that the mortars were fired when a VC farmer took a break from plowing on a hot day and decided to have a little fun. He would supposedly shoot a mortar round at the Yankee aggressors, or maybe Aussie aggressors in this case.

I had delivered some "trash" to the camp and instructed the crew to unload it as quickly as possible. A captain, flying as a passenger with us, jumped out of the helicopter to take pictures. I pulled up from the ground to hover, and this idiot just stood still and stared at me. Captain "Photo" came within a split second of being left behind. I screamed out, "Get your ass in!" I suppose he did not appreciate my tone of voice because he turned me in to the colonel.

I explained to the colonel that I considered myself very lucky to be alive this late in my tour and did not appreciate some dumbass pressing my luck. I went on to say that I did not care how brave his captain wanted to appear to others. He could damn well be brave on his own time. The colonel laughed and assured me he would speak to the captain. He recognized me as one of the pilots who medevaced the wounded in the convoy ambush and flew the resupply into Hau Duc Special Forces Camp.

We also got another new CO at the Seventy-First Assault Helicopter Company in Chu Lai.

God Was My Copilot

On the night of June 8, I pulled what was probably the dumbest stunt ever while in Vietnam, even though the turn of events was really out of my hands. It was pitch black and raining lightly. I do not remember why, but I did not have a peter pilot. I was at Da Nang, and a special forces captain (not the one who turned me in to the colonel) came in and said there was an emergency medevac, and we needed to scramble out. I told him I could not

220   F I R E B I R D S

go without a peter pilot. He implored that the wounded
guy would surely die if we did not get him as fast as possible. I asked my crew chief if he knew how to fly and he
said, "Sure." Some crew chiefs could fly. I also inquired
whether he knew how to read the attitude indicator and he
once again responded, "Sure!" The crew chief had more
confidence than I did, so I told the crew to saddle up and
get ready to go. The crew chief sat in the left seat, and I
took the right seat, because it had the best set of instruments, in case we hit some clouds.

We traveled out into Happy Valley and went to an
ARVN unit that had American army advisors. I do not believe they were special forces advisors. Anyway, the
clouds were up to 500 feet, so I flew in the rain with my
lights off at about 300 feet. I touched down, and two guys
ran and jumped on the helicopter. The gunner communi-
cated over the intercom that one of them had a bandage
on his hand. I thought, "This was the one that was going
to bleed to death!" Incredibly, we found out the other one
was going on R&R. The special forces captain later admitted he started to throw the two shitbirds out of the helicopter!

On the way back, the clouds quickly descended, and
the rain started to come down in sheets. I nearly pulled up
into the clouds and flew on instruments back to Da Nang,
which was dangerous enough with two pilots. It was plain
crazy with just one. We were at sea level, so the altimeter
setting of 200 feet was fairly safe. I just knew I would see
the city lights of Da Nang, and the runways if I continued
for a few more minutes. Visibility was basically zero out
of the windshield, but the gunner claimed he could see
the mountains on my left as I headed east, and everything
was okay. I was certainly happy to pop out of Happy Valley and see the lights of Da Nang.

Everybody on the helicopter had spent most of the trip

back discussing various methods of torture and abuse for the two selfish dirtballs who conned us out in the bad weather.

Jolly Greens

On June 9, the NVA rocketed Chu Lai and hit three of our helicopters with shrapnel. During this time period, I flew special forces guys to Khe Sanh numerous times. I would always fly up to Dong Ha and fly out following the old road. I had the radio frequency for an air force air rescue group with the radio call sign of "Sandies." As I flew along the DMZ, I was listening in on their radios. The Sandies flew A1-Es. These planes were able to fly slow enough to escort the Jolly Green Giant helicopters used to rescue downed pilots in North Vietnam. On this particular day, I could hear the Sandies talking, but could not hear the Jolly Green's responses. The one-sided conversation went something like this:

> *"Go up the road . . . Go up the road . . . You will see the chute . . . Go Further . . . Where are you receiving fire from?"*
> *Another Sandie then exclaimed, "Wow!"*
> *The first one said, "What an explosion!"*
> *The second asked, "What are you going to do now?"*
> *The first said, in a resigned tone, "I guess we'll get another chopper and see what we can do."*

I had just listened in as a crew of brave men were instantly killed when their helicopter was blown to bits.

Williams remembered another story about a Jolly

Green helicopter exploding in flight. That incident occurred on September 27, 1968. This is in his own words:

> *We were running a single ship resupply mission early one morning when we heard a Mayday call from an air force "Birddog." The aircraft commander (A/C) looked at the copilot who grabbed the map bag to check for the grid coordinates. He found the location on the map and asked me what we were carrying. When I told him it was a few cases of Cs and some hot chow, he told us to kick them out. We were going to go after the Birddog.*
>
> *Larry Smith was flying gunner with me that day. At that time Smitty and I both had more than two years in country, so we just loaded up the door guns and got ready to help spot the downed plane. Our A/C was pretty good and flew right to the wreckage. We were only about five minutes out. We started into a tight spiraled descent, keeping an eye on the plane and an eye on likely hiding places for enemy fire. The A/C held pitch when we touched down in a flat, very wet field, so we wouldn't settle in too deep close to the downed plane. Smitty and I both started to jump out, but our pilot stopped us. He thought that just one of us should go look for survivors. The downed aircraft was on my side of the ship, so I went. I leaped out and sank into water up to my chest. I grabbed the skid to keep from sinking further. What I had thought was an old wet overgrown rice paddy turned out to be a bog—matted grass and weeds floating on swamp juice, depth unknown. Smitty told the pilot I was stuck, and he picked up into a hover to lift me out of the juice. I started over again, this time crawling on all fours to disperse my weight on top of the floating vegetation.*

The scene looked like the plane had also tried to hit the flat spot where we landed but, instead, overshot and impacted a six-foot-high dirt berm. The impact devastated the small plane. As I approached the wreckage, I spied a bloody hand draped over the fuselage still clutching a .38 pistol. I cautiously rounded the tail of the aircraft to find the photographer, who had been flying the back seat of the tiny Birddog. He was in shock and had numerous serious injuries, including his face which had slammed into the back of the pilot's seat and split wide open. I took the .38 pistol out of his hand, put it in my belt, and took him back to the chopper. By this time, all the racket had brought some VC into the area of the crash site. We were taking AK fire each time I moved across the bog.

I returned to the plane for the pilot and found him also in shock, which was really a blessing because he was hopelessly pinned in the plane by the wreckage. The engine had been forced back by the impact so that both of the pilot's legs were pinned up under his seat. His hands, which he used to try to brace for the crash by placing them on the console, were also pinned in some wreckage which had collapsed on either side. I knew we could not get this guy out since we did not carry any heavy rescue equipment. I returned to the ship and told the A/C that we would need a Jolly Green Giant (air force rescue chopper) to cut the pilot out, then I grabbed a first aid kit. Our A/C called me back to the chopper and told me he would have to get airborne to send a message back for the Jolly Green, and with that he pulled pitch, and I was alone with the trapped Birddog pilot. I crawled back to the plane and tried to administer some basic first aid. The pressure ex-

erted on the pilot by the wreckage was stopping the
bleeding pretty well, so I mainly tried to reassure
him that we were going to get him out.

There were no other choppers over the crash site
yet, but there were some marine F-4s from Da Nang
and some other high performance jets, plus another
air force Birddog. Our buddy with the AK-47 kept
pecking away at us, but we were somewhat protected, as I observed another dirt berm on the other
side of the bog. That was another break, because we
were sitting in a pool of JP4 from the plane. Once, I
was pretty sure I could hear some movement coming
closer to us, so I pulled my .45 and dumped a clip in
the direction of the noise. The FAC who was circling
us must have been watching pretty close, because I
no sooner put another clip in my .45 when an F-4
went over my head about twenty feet off the deck,
scaring the crap out of me. He then cut loose a bomb
load in the direction I had just fired. The bombs went
off very close and shook the ground under me, but I
felt more comfortable knowing that we were not
alone down there with those jet jocks overhead.

I heard some choppers in the distance and hoped
it would be the Jolly Green; this Birddog pilot was
in bad shape and needed help soon. The Jolly Green
appeared overhead just as my chopper was coming
back in to pick me up. We waited on the ground
while the Jolly Green shot his spiraled approach,
and I turned my attention to the inbound flight of
ten slicks and their gunship escort. I heard the un-
mistakable bump, bump, bump, of a .50 caliber, but
this one turned out to be an enemy antiaircraft gun
with green tracers streaming skyward into the soft
underbelly of the Jolly Green. The F-4s made a
rapid approach to the enemy antiaircraft gun, but

too late to help the Jolly Green, as it had just turned into a huge ball of orange flame and a cloud of black smoke. The noise was deafening as the inbound ten slicks touched down, the Phantoms dropped their ordnance on the enemy gun, the Jolly Green wreckage rained from the sky, and my own chopper was running thirty feet away. As the call was sent out for a second Jolly Green, the grunts finally reached the crash site and my A/C called me back to our ship. He was low on fuel and still had to get that photographer from the Birddog back to a hospital. That was how we left that trapped Birddog pilot. I guess I'll never know if he got out of there O.K., but we sure did give it a good try. We flew back to the big navy hospital at Da Nang where Smitty and I carried the guy into the hospital. I unloaded his .38 pistol and left it on the counter.

My aircraft commander said he put me in for a silver star, but I did get an Army Commendation Medal with a V device for valor. I still wonder what that Birddog pilot got—life or death?

JUNE 13, 1968

The Vietnam war became the longest war ever fought by the United States.

On June 15, my attitude about staying away from the helicopter during an attack nearly got me killed. I was flying for the special forces and had landed at Tien Phuoc. The special forces headquarters was located in a hootch built on top of an old concrete French bunker. I told the peter pilot to shut it down while I walked to the bunker for something cool to drink. As I walked, a 122 mm rocket could be clearly heard as it left the side of the mountains to the west. We had plenty of warning, because the NVA had to fire the rocket at an extremely high arc in order to hit the special forces camp below. My crew members, who were in the chopper, were screaming at me to hurry up and fly the helicopter out. I merely waved to them as I sprinted to the bunker.

I now have a picture of myself standing in the hole where the rocket hit. The hootch that was resting on top of the bunker was shaved right off as the rocket exploded nearby. The crew laughed their asses off at me because the rocket nearly hit me. If I had only had put it in gear and run to the chopper I would have been much safer.

A Welcome Break

Because I had flown too many hours, I was "forced" to go to Chu Lai and lie on the beach. I did not have to wash helicopters either. I was off from June 16 through 24. After that I went to Hawaii to meet my wife for the R&R which the special forces had arranged for me, and did not arrive back in Vietnam until July 5. It was a real neat trick not to fly for this long, but my body and my badly frayed nerves needed the rest!

I was certainly glad I was not flying on June 16. West of Tam Ky, we had six slicks and three gunships shot up in a large Romeo Foxtrot. A pilot named Bley made a tape recording of the radio traffic during this Romeo Foxtrot. That night we sat around the club listening to the tape recording of everybody hollering and screaming over the radios. We were mainly trying to figure out who was the most scared. I just knew it was not me, because I had been working

JUNE 19, 1968

The South Vietnamese finally decided to mobilize for war. They began drafting eighteen year olds.

on my suntan all day. I paid as much attention to them as I would if they had complained about a hangnail! Turnabout is fair play, after all!

A peter pilot, on only his third mission, was shot in the leg. Some of the helicopters were shot to pieces. The choppers had landed next to the headquarters of a VC Main Force unit that decided to fight. Castle's first helicopter was shot up as he led the flight into the LZ. Four infantry grunts were wounded as they sat in the back of his chopper. Numerous other grunts were wounded as they rode on the other helicopters. Shortly after this, Castle had another chopper shot to pieces on a flight into the same place.

The story was that a battalion staff officer marked the incorrect LZ by dropping a smoke grenade in the wrong area. The slicks attempted the first landing into one area while the artillery blasted another LZ area that was supposed to be used.

A Rattler pilot named Cotton was killed in the last hours of his last day to fly in Nam. He was supposed to be going on R&R the next morning, and he would have had one week remaining when he returned to Chu Lai. He would not have been required to fly his last week. Cotton had been wounded earlier in his tour and had subsequently been working in the motor pool. For some unknown reason, he decided to push his luck and start flying again. On the fateful day, his peter pilot, Goodman, was flying, and on takeoff from a pick-up zone, Goodman thought the hydraulics went out on the chopper. He immediately made an emergency landing and discovered that the problem was caused when Cotton slumped over the controls, shot dead.

On June 28, the NVA assaulted a refugee village near Quang Ngai. They used flame throwers during the attack, and many women and children were burned to death.

On July 2, Carson wrote a letter to Parsons, who was
still recuperating after being shot down on March 4. It described the action at the time and reveals how the pilots
viewed these actions in letters to each other:

Hello [Parsons],

*First, I would like to thank you for your box of
goodies (everyone enjoyed them), but more
specifically, my new "Firebird 97" shirt.*

*We've been having our knocks every now and
then. You ask about Buzzell and Hannah—they are
both back in the States now, shot down in the
beginning of May. Hannah, I believe, had a broken
neck, Buzzell, broken legs. It was one hell of an
operation getting them out, but somehow we
managed.*

*Remember Cotton—he was shot in the head and
killed about a week ago. Webster was shot down
about a month ago; everyone was OK, but finished
497 [aircraft number].*

*Lt. Burroughs is our platoon leader now. You're
right, Latimer and Leopold are SHORT and will
be leaving for home in a day or so. I have 38 more
days left, and the way things are going, I'll never
make it!*

*The NVA are here, and it gets to the place that
flying turns into a sweat to fight for your life. It
usually happens on the 4th, 5th, or 6th of every
month now, and all hell breaks loose. Just have to
pull the seat belt up tighter, that's all. I'm getting
that short time invincible feeling (like Sutton had).
I killed 15 VC yesterday at about 40 knots and 40
feet! The only people flying that you knew who are
left are Wheeler (gone to maintenance)—he got his
tail rotor shot off a couple of weeks ago, Taylor*

> *(coming back to the Firebirds tomorrow after
> being "suspended" for killing "innocent" dinks).
>   Well, that's the news. Happy (we all are) about
> our "Mop" being uncaged and on the loose again.
> I'll take a spin by your airplane tomorrow with my
> camera.*
>
>   *From all the Firebirds and [Carson]*

Snatch Mission

On July 6, I was back on the job, flying support for the
196th Light Infantry Brigade for several days before I returned to the special forces. During the interval, I pulled
a large "snatch" mission. Two grunt officers rode on my
chopper, and we flew out over the Que Son Valley and
Antenna Valley. I would land the slick next to someone,
and the grunt officers arrested the surprised Vietnamese
by leveling their M-16s at him. When we had gathered
about five or six of them, we flew them to LZ Baldy to be
interrogated.

I had never participated in a snatch mission before this,
so I was not very familiar with the procedure. After they
were finished with their interrogations, the grunts radioed
me to come back and pick up the Vietnamese. We loaded
up everyone, and I asked them, "Where to?" The soldiers
looked at me sort of funny and told me, "It's your job to
take them back." No one had informed me about this portion of the mission, and I had not marked my map with
any of the spots where we had "snatched" the guys. I did
recall two or three of the exact places but could not remember the others. When I returned to the locations I had
kept in mind, the relieved men happily jumped off the
slick. The last two merely shook their heads when I

picked the spots for them. They did not want to get off, but the grunts with us heaved them off the chopper and onto the ground. My gunner and crew chief thought their predicament was real funny. One of them quipped that the dinks would not be shooting at anybody tonight; they would be too busy walking home.

Donut Dollies

One incident I was involved in occurred because of my lack of experience as a slick driver. One day, I was flying two "Donut Dollies" out to LZ West. A Donut Dollie was a volunteer with the United Service Organizations (USO) who helped boost the morale of the troops. Some of the ruder men around nicknamed these gals "Biscuit Bitches." These women played card games that the troops enjoyed, passed out donuts, and mainly just tried to cheer up the guys. I guess the USO expected these young men to satisfy their passions with a donut!

Now, flying in and out of fire support bases was a routine I had performed so many times before, I could do it in my sleep. Since I was mainly concentrating on my aircraft during these times, I had really never inspected or noticed the "ambiance" around one of these bases. Again, I was not paying any attention to my surroundings as I let the women off the helicopter and prepared to swing back up into the air. Apparently, the grunt commander must have glanced out at the helicopter pad about the time the women unloaded, and he went ballistic. Surprised at all the squawking on my radio, I surveyed the firebase and realized, a little late, that these camps, being situated in the boonies, were pretty primitive. Many of the soldiers were taking a leak, or worse, and many were running around the place in their skivvies. In a very abrupt and impolite manner, the grunt commander instructed me to give them some advance warning if I was to ever bring any more females out to the fire base. I got out of there fast and did not stick around to see if the Donut Dollies blushed or swooned.

Hot LZs

Right after I got back from R&R, I was asked to make an emergency medevac in Antenna Valley. The action was a joint ARVN, marine, and 196th operation.

By this time, I had figured out by osmosis some of the tactics used by the NVA. They would set up and hide in certain areas; so that when the Americans attacked them, American artillery would have to be fired either over the American position or directly in front of them. Because of long and short artillery rounds, our guys would hesitate to call in the artillery too close to their own positions. If the artillery happened to be firing from the side, the grunts could call the artillery in very close, and the long and short rounds would not matter. This was one of the reasons why the military always moved the artillery guns around to different fire bases.

In this instance, the Americans were on the back side of the mountains to the northwest side of the Que Son. The grunt commander radioed that his company had walked into a U-shaped bunker system loaded with NVA. His guys had been cut down by enemy machine gun fire. Support from the artillery would be very risky, because some of the wounded were still pinned down in front of the enemy bunkers. The artillery would also have been required to hit the back side of the mountain directly in front of the Americans. A long round would hit the American positions. They desperately needed the choppers to come in and help them evacuate the wounded.

I vividly recall, even to this day, the feeling one experienced as a "hot" LZ was approached. I was detached from reality; the scene was surreal. It was almost like I was watching an action movie, but I was really in it. I knew the enemy was there, and I knew my helicopter would be taking intense fire. Flying into this situation, I was both nervous and calm at the same time. My senses and awareness were acute, but a feeling of resignation descended on me. If this was my "time" to die, then so be it. I felt that whatever was about to transpire was meant to be.

The moments preceding the actual landing were filled with a quiet tension. One's vision became crystal clear. In seconds, the scene was set. The jungle was thick and menacing. All the gunships that could be mustered were on station. Quickly, a pair of Firebirds escorted my slick into the targeted area, firing rockets for cover. I took my new H-model slick directly to the LZ the ground troops had blown out of the jungle. I set the machine down lightly on the bed of fallen trees and concentrated on maintaining my position. The grunt commander, concerned with the grave condition of several of his men, asked me over the radio how many I could carry. I could not look around, but told him to load up as many as he could. Later, I found out four were placed in the floor lying down, and then the walking wounded or the ones that could sit up, were crammed on the helicopter next. The crew chief finally had to tell them to stop. Maimed and bloody wrecks of humanity were wedged in all over the slick. We prepared to lift off and try to get out of harm's way.

I was facing east in the helicopter and up the slope.

This caused me to have to hover straight up above the jungle and do a pedal turn in order to be able to exit to the west. This maneuver caused me to hold a hover facing directly toward the enemy bunkers. Rockets exploded and tracers zipped past like flies. I never heard a sound. All my energy was aimed at getting the helicopter high enough and quickly enough to get out of there. To enable a fully loaded helicopter, even an H-model, to hover up to 100 feet while overloaded required smooth and steady movement on the controls. Any sudden jerking motion on the controls causes a loss of power and lift. Luckily, the NVA had to fire up through the jungle aiming at the sound of the retreating chopper. They missed. As Anton used to say, "There is no greater thrill than to be shot at and missed!" That day my crew and I experienced the "great thrill." I did not even start shaking until we were clear of the area.

I had been instructed to fly the wounded grunts to the Chu Lai Hospital. After we were safely up and away, I gave the controls to the peter pilot. I took a deep breath and laid my hand on my leg. Suddenly, I felt something grasp my arm and very nearly leaped out of my armored seat. If I had not had on the safety harness, I would have jumped three feet easily. A young black soldier, one of the four lying on the floor, had pushed himself up with one arm and grabbed me with the other. His eyes were as big as fifty-cent pieces and filled with pain and fear. He attempted to say something to me as he continued his death grip on my arm. I could not understand him—he was critically injured and somewhat delirious. I screamed at the crew chief over the intercom to do something, anything, and do it fast! The crew chief could not make his way past the other wounded to get up to the guy. Finally, one of the walking wounded reached up to the frantic grunt and gently patted his shoulder. The man let loose of my arm and slowly lay back down. I never did know his name or what happened to him. Sometimes, the look in his eyes and his garbled plea haunt my memory. I am thankful that I had made it my policy not to look back while we transported these fellows. The memories of the few I did actually see will stay with me forever.

During the same general time, when the US grunts and the ARVN were operating in Antenna Valley, I was called in to medevac a load of seriously wounded ARVN soldiers. The Firebird gunships were on station, and I was the second chopper to go into the hot LZ. I believe a medevac chopper (red cross on the side) was the first. Because the LZ was on the side of a mountain, I had to do a straight-in approach. I hated coming in this way and, after much experience, had determined that a hot spiraling approach was the safest way into a hot LZ.

We drew a lot of automatic weapons fire that was once again coming from below the cover of the jungle. The shooters were aiming at the sound of my helicopter, firing blindly at the sky. When I spotted an American standing up in the LZ, I knew I was either safe, or else the guy was an idiot. I often heard that medevac helicopters had a steadfast rule not to land unless a grunt was standing in the LZ with both arms above his head. This was an obvious indication that automatic weapons were not currently firing through the LZ. Personally, however, I saw several medevacs land with no one standing in the open. I have flown into LZs, where on the short final, all the grunts would hit the deck. That was definitely a signal to pull up, fly around, and try it again.

In this case, they loaded the wounded, and I exited the area with no problem. I believe I took the wounded to LZ Baldy. Once we were through with our mission, I hovered off the helicopter pad and shut down to check out the helicopter. As the crew chief walked up to open my door, he motioned for me to take a look at something. I leaned around the armored seat, and immediately noticed that the door handle had been shot off. I pocketed the remaining piece of the door handle and carted it with me to the Officers' Club that night. I thought it made an interesting conversation piece, but nobody cared! My cohorts were totally unimpressed.

While flying on this day or the next, I hauled in a load of ammo to the same area around Antenna Valley. Carson was flying fireteam lead with the Firebirds. Carson had the uncanny knack of continually increasing my "pucker factor" every time he supported my slick. He had the unnerving habit of shooting his rockets right past the door of my slick. He called it "close air support." I specifically remember thinking, as his rockets flashed by my chopper door, that I could have easily reached out and lit a cigar on the back of the passing projectile. Could it have been that Carson was the one who shot off my door handle?

During the course of my tour, I had several "close encounters" during hot LZ landings while flying with the special forces. One mission involved landing after receiving the same cruel statement that suckered Kucera and me into picking up the marine bodies, a surrogate plea from a marine on the radio for the mothers of the wounded. In all the years since my military service, I have always joked that the military does not need a "few good men" for their high risk jobs. What they really need is a few young inexperienced boys. The boys will not know any better than to put themselves in dangerous situations over and over again.

I always prided myself that, while flying with the special forces, I pulled off several missions for the marines that their chopper pilots would not even attempt. I attributed part of the marine pilots' lack of daring to the fact that most were a bunch of decrepit old men. They were at

least twenty-five to thirty years old, and I assumed most
had families. In our army helicopter units, we would have
nicknamed them "Pappy"!

I also heard that the marine chopper pilots classified
some of their missions as "no kid, one kid, and two kid
missions." Supposedly, the older a man was and the more
family he had, the less danger he wanted to face. Heck,
after I got married, one of my friends even told me I was
not nearly as aggressive.

We were flying in Happy Valley. Most of the marine
grunt units in this region had the special forces FM radio
frequency. On this particular day, I was flying a new
H-model and was headed toward the Thoung Duc Special
Forces Camp. As I flew past a mountainous area the
marines called "Charlie Ridge," I viewed a marine H-34
going back to Da Nang with two marine gunships up
around 3,000 feet. A marine at a fire support base radioed
me. (I do not believe it was my old friend who had threatened to kick my butt.) He requested that I come up on the
FM radio frequency of the marine grunts who were up on
the side of the mountain. They were positioned about
1,000 feet up on the mountain. I called the marines on the
side of the mountain and they relayed that they had some
wounded in bad shape and needed them taken out immediately. Since I could hear heavy gunfire in the background of the radio message, I naturally asked if the LZ
was under fire. The marine naturally assured me that they
were not receiving any fire. They must have been very ea-
ger for me to land! One of the passing marine gunships
informed me that their H-34 helicopter had taken hits,
and there were numerous automatic weapon positions directly up the slope from the LZ. I then told the guys on
the ground that I was carrying cargo I had to deliver, had
one special forces soldier aboard, and really could not
help them. That was when the marines "got me." The

ground marine pleaded, "These boys aren't going to make it. Remember their mothers; their mothers want them out of here." When he said that I slumped in my armored seat. What a low blow! I thought, "What a lowlife to say something like that!" I reluctantly told the marine I would attempt a landing, and they should give me as much cover as possible by firing north of the LZ, up the slope. Since I was wary of the NVA listening in on our transmission, I did not inform them that I would be coming in from the south. This far into my tour, even though my nerves were somewhat frayed, I still thought I was quite intelligent. I had figured out that, in the cover of the heavy jungle, the NVA used firing paths and would shoot at anything that crossed those paths. If a pilot managed to stay out of these paths, the enemy had to fire merely at the sound of the helicopter.

Flying in, I could clearly see the LZ the marines had blown. It looked small. The soldier on the radio assured me there was plenty of room to put the helicopter down safely. I circled out over Happy Valley and flew straight at the jungle, 500 feet below the LZ. As I got to the mountain, I pulled the nose up and jerked full power, and the H-model actually accelerated as it went up the side of the hill. I came over the LZ, nearly went past it, and hit the right pedal to turn my tail boom up the hill. I noticed that the slope was too great to set the helicopter down with the tail rotor up the slope, so I kept the pedal in and performed a full 360 degree turn over the LZ. (I have always wondered what the NVA soldiers thought about a crazy helicopter pilot doing aerobatics above a hot LZ.)

I sat in the LZ for what seemed like an eternity, facing directly into where the enemy fire had originated. The marines were blowing the hell out of the jungle in front of me. This was the only time I actually witnessed a grunt hurling a hand grenade at the wall of trees while I sat in the LZ. During intense moments like these, everything appeared to move in slow motion. My actual time on the ground was probably only ten to fifteen seconds, but it seemed like hours. When the crew chief finally yelled, "Up!", I jerked so much power that I actually came up too high above the jungle. I remember thinking, or maybe speaking out loud to myself, "Be calm, settle down!" I did not want to start shaking until I cleared the area. Also, the H-models had so much power that, with a hard jerk, a pilot could blow out the connector between the engine and the transmission, known as the short shaft. I did a rolling turn out of the LZ and flew low level down to the marine bases situated on the north edge of Happy Valley.

That feeling of risking your life and actually getting out of the situation alive was a feeling of joy and elation that only someone who has been through it can imagine. I remember feeling fantastic! As I safely cleared the area, I removed my left hand from the collective control and shot Charlie the finger. Screw them: they could not get me, at least not that time anyway! The marines were making so much noise; I could not tell if we were shot at or not. After we landed, the special forces guy aboard exclaimed, "That was one hell of a chopper ride!"

When taking ammo in under heavy fire, I would have two grunts placed in the back of the chopper, and I would have them kick the ammo out as I flew across the LZ in a quick hover. I would naturally tell the grunts below to duck. One day, I remember flying into a hot LZ where I intended to go out the same direction. This LZ was just south of Million Dollar Hill. We considered this region a portion of Death Valley, but the grunts called it Heip Duc Valley. The LZ had a lot of bamboo around it, along with some trees. I came in red hot, went to a hover, kicked a pedal turn, and took off. Automatic weapons were ripping away, both US and NVA, and I made it out while taking

only one hit in the rotor blade. I confidently asked the peter pilot how he liked that landing, and he answered that
he was worried about hurting the grunts. Somewhat surprised, I asked why, and he explained that I never had the
helicopter below fifteen feet as we unloaded the cargo. A
can of ammo, from that height, would put the lights out
on a grunt if it struck him. The rest of the crew then swore
I never got below twenty feet. I was so scared I would
have bet money I was at a three-foot hover.

During this period, I also flew out of Hue/Phu Bai two
more times into Laos. One mission was the insertion of a
special forces recon team and the other an extraction of a
recon team just around sundown. We took some .50 cal.
fire on the extraction.

Beer with a Nipple

During the action in Antenna Valley, I was flying resupply to some ARVN when the crew chief told me there was
a case of Tiger beer in the load. I asked him to bring me
one. Tiger was the famous Vietnamese beer, and I had
never had one. The crew chief handed it up to me, and I
couldn't believe my eyes. The Tiger beer bottle had a
metal cap on it with a rubber nipple sticking out through
the metal cap about an inch. I had never seen anyone
drink their beer through a nipple, but I already knew the
ARVN did not do things like we did. So, I pulled the old
Bowie knife off my leg, popped the cap, and took a real
big chug. It felt like motor oil as it slid down my throat.

The ARVN flavored their meals of rice with what is
called *nuoc mam*. This concoction was made by taking a
fifty-five gallon drum, punching holes in the bottom, filling it with fish heads and fish intestines, and pouring

ocean water into the barrel. The drippings from the bottom of the barrel was *nuoc mam*. The Vietnamese swore
it was a good source of protein.

The wind blowing around in the chopper had stopped
me from getting a whiff of the contents prior to my chug-
a-lug. But, as I felt the stuff land in my stomach and began to puke all over the instrument panel, it dawned on
me that the beer bottle was really full of *nuoc mam*, and
the nipple was for shaking the drops on the rice. I felt like
I had been poisoned. It was horrible. The crew chief, who
was not the least bit sympathetic, demanded that I help
him clean the helicopter.

How to Avoid Accidents, Part 1

On July 7, I had a resupply mission to LZ East. This was
a fire support base located about 1,500 feet up on the side
of a mountain. I was flying right seat, teaching a young
kid to be an aircraft commander. I was training him even
though I did not have much experience on slicks myself.
He was lucky—I'd had to learn how to land at LZ East all
by myself. I instructed the young pilot to have a grunt
throw a smoke grenade and then watch the hill closely. I
kept reminding the guy to keep looking, as we made the
final approach with the heavily loaded chopper. He was
not responding correctly, so I took the controls and flew
around the area. I asked the "student" to tell me what was
splattered on the side of the mountain, short of the helipad. He responded, "That's a crashed helicopter." I shot
back, "No! That's two crashed helicopters!" One was a
marine H-34.

Once again, I told the pilot to observe the yellow
smoke closely. Finally, he got it. He laughed and stated,

"There is a hell of a down draft, isn't there?" The smoke was traveling level off the helipad and then straight down the side of the mountain. If we had maintained a shallow approach with the heavy chopper, just short of the helipad, the down draft would have splashed our helicopter up on the side of the mountain with the remains of the others.

How to Avoid Accidents, Part 2

The accident record was a big joke around the company. When any accident occurred, it was written up as damage caused by hostile action. One crash concerned an unnamed pilot whose nerves were apparently worse than mine. At the time of his "hostile action" he was sitting on a fire support base in an old D-model slick. The word was that they told him, as he landed, that they were using explosives to blow bunker holes and fox holes. This practice was a whole lot faster than digging the things out by hand. When an explosion went off, the pilot jerked full power, went straight up, lost rpm, and crashed on the helicopter pad. We never did figure out how they justified that as hostile action.

July 8, 1968

THE SEVENTY-FIRST ASSAULT HELICOPTER COMPANY RECEIVED A MERITORIOUS UNIT COMMENDATION FOR GOING TWELVE MONTHS WITHOUT ANY AIRCRAFT ACCIDENTS AND FOR SINKING 1,033 SAMPANS.

The Enemy Within

I really got myself into a lot of trouble on July 22. They were forced to give me a day off because of excess flight time, so I went over to battalion to see a friend of mine. As my friend was searching a file cabinet, I glanced down at his desk and started reading an awards write-up for a Silver Star. This Silver Star was intended for a battalion staff officer who was being written up for the events of June 16, 1968. In this action, our helicopters were shot to pieces and quite a few soldiers were wounded when the helicopters approached the wrong LZ. This guy had marked the wrong LZ, and was now getting the Silver Star for what I knew to be a major screw-up.

Later, back at the Officers' Club after a few brews, I was still angry and started to complain about that desk jockey getting the Silver Star for screwing up and getting people hurt. The more I drank and thought about the situation, the angrier I got. Somebody (I can't remember who) kept prodding me to do something to teach the guy a lesson. He told me I was just the guy to teach the prick that lesson. The gears and cogs in my woozy head were spinning and turning with a good dose of alcohol as a lubricant.

I jumped in the platoon jeep and drove to the division's inspector general (IG). The IG is, by military law, supposed to protect and keep confidential any information given to them. Yeah, right! I unloaded my views and information on him and headed back. As soon as I returned to the company area, a clerk was standing in front of headquarters and ordered me to go see the prick at battalion. Bad news, for me, did seem to travel fast. I went down to battalion, and the guy was very nice. Knowing what I know today, I can now see why he was nice to me. I could have ruined his career and the career of whoever signed the award recommendation. Plus, I could have had the IG person I complained to shot at dawn and probably skinned before he was shot.

The prick asked if I was going to make a career out of the military. I told him no. That was probably not what he wanted to hear. He went on and explained how, "to advance in the military ... certain things were required ... some people merely viewed the same events differently ..." and on and on. By then, the day was hot and stifling. I had sobered up, and all I wanted now was to take a badly needed nap. I had lost all interest in messing with him or the matter. I never dreamed that this wasn't the end of it.

Chapter Five

GETTING SHORT

••

O N JULY 23, THE BRASS BROUGHT ME BACK TO Chu Lai, partly because I had too many flight hours, and partly because I was now a senior aircraft commander, needed to train the new guys. It is also possible that they wanted me back to give me the "payback" for going to the IG.

MACV

I started flying for an army unit that advised the ARVN Fifth Regiment. They were called MACV, Military Assistance Command Vietnam. Finally, I found the job that was right for me. By chance, the first day I flew with them I took four hits. The rotor blade and tail boom were shot up on my chopper. That was not too scary; but it allowed me to go back to Chu Lai and tell them it was a dangerous mission, but I would be willing to fly it in the future. I cannot remember what we were doing when the helicopter was shot. The ARVN would not normally get themselves in too many dangerous positions. It could have well been an ARVN that shot me by accident. I just do not remember.

I flew for MACV for nearly one month. If someone asked for a mission, and no one else objected, they would generally let the pilot have it. Instead of flying "ass and trash" missions for the ARVN, we called it "pigs and rice." Also, the mission didn't require me to be there at daybreak, as a lot of the grunt missions did. The major to whom I reported at MACV was from Texas and each day asked for the pilot from Texas, "Rattler 11" (me).

I warned the peter pilots and crew that I would throw them to the VC if they told anyone about my special mission. Flying the ARVNs was quite an experience. Some of the things they did, I agreed with; they started their days late and ended them early. On the other hand, I was always amazed by the loot that they hauled out of the areas they went into. I never saw the ARVN steal a hootch, but was amazed one time when I did see one come out of a village with a chest of drawers strapped to his back. It was larger than he was. I motioned at him, "No." He grinned real big and kept coming. My crew chief asked if I wanted him to stop the soldier. By this time, I had learned to be careful how I phrased a request or order to my crews about anything. The crew chief might have shot him or shot the furniture off the ARVNs back. This soldier came up to the helicopter, turned and backed up, and his buddies pulled it into the chopper. I made them push it to the middle of the cargo compartment. I could just imagine it blowing out of the aircraft, and me and my crew dying from a stolen chest of drawers knocking off a rotor blade. That would be an interesting accident to explain to the people back home!

Patrick tells a good story about hauling our allies around. They loaded a huge pig aboard his chopper with its front feet tied separately from its hind feet. Everything was smooth until the pig's front feet came loose. The huge pig circled the cargo compartment of the chopper while it was at 2,000 feet and the Vietnamese were trying to hold it down. Luckily, no one fell out. At the last second the pig bolted between the armored seats up onto the instrument console. The pig's nose was next to the fuel switch. Patrick says he nearly had a heart attack as he attempted to fly and hammer on the pig's head with his hand. If that pig had turned off the fuel he was on the way to possibly making his "great escape"!

Malek recalled an ARVN soldier who had a chicken on a string just like a dog on a leash. He thought it was pretty neat to see a guy with a pet chicken. Malek kept gesturing at the soldier to acknowledge his pet. The soldier finally motioned back by rubbing his stomach up and down. He also said the telling words, "Chop, chop!"

The Payback—Sniffers and LRRPs

By August 3, it had been nearly two weeks since I turned in the battalion guy to the inspector general. Castle came into the platoon hootch and casually started asking me how things were going. During this oddly vague conversation, Castle asked me about the missions I had been flying lately. That is when it occurred to me that nearly each morning, before going to MACV, I had been assigned a sniffer, an LRRP insertion, or LRRP extraction each morning. These were considered to be the most dangerous recurring missions a slick pilot faced. I interpreted the vague conversation as meaning that if I would complain, Castle would put a stop to it. I have always felt that somewhere, somehow, battalion sent the word down to teach that "troublemaker" a lesson. Castle did at least stop me from getting a sniffer or LRRP each morning.

I really did not mind flying sniffer missions in slicks because I enjoyed the scenery when I had a chance to see it. As a gunship pilot, I hated them because the upper slick, guiding the one with the sniffer machine, would be looking at a map and would turn you into a cliff. The slick with the sniffer machine could climb up a steep mountain, but a loaded gunship didn't have a chance. The mission had to stop until the slick and gunships could get back in formation again with the gunships set to attack under the slick. One day, I was low level out by Laos, and the upper slick, around 2,000 to 3,000 feet, said, "Get ready for a left turn." When I turned left, my eyes were watching the tops of the trees. Instantly, the peter pilot screamed. I looked up and saw that the upper slick had turned me into a tight valley facing a cliff about 2,000 feet high. I started weaving the chopper left and right and worked myself up the side of the cliff. This maneuver made me lose all my airspeed, which meant my chopper was now a very appealing target. The pilots in the two gunships behind me were cursing up a storm over the radio, because they could not even attempt to climb that high. The turn forced the gunships to climb in the valley between the high ridges, which was dangerous because they also lost airspeed and became instant targets. It was a very easy way to get killed. Taylor said he was one of the pilots behind me in a Firebird gunship. He was plenty mad at that upper slick that day.

LRRP missions were a dangerous matter. A man could get killed doing those things. After I started scheduling, I found we actually had slick pilots who volunteered for the things. When I was scheduling, I gave them all they wanted. Far be it from me to disappoint any of them! After my enlightening discussion with Castle, I did not have that many more LRRP missions.

LRRP insertions were generally fairly safe. I only remember one where I received fire on landing, and the LRRPs never left the helicopter. Sometimes, we would use one slick to fake two or three different landings to attempt to confuse the actual location where the LRRPs exited the helicopter. I also remember having two slicks with one flying behind the other. The first would land the LRRPs and then hurry back into the air to become the second chopper in the formation. I was never really sure if that ever confused the enemy or not.

The extractions were the dangerous part. One morning, low clouds and rain kept us grounded, so I sat around in a tent with an LRRP insertion team at LZ Baldy waiting for the weather to clear. I asked them why it always seemed like they were getting shot at when I was trying to pick them up. The soldiers solemnly explained that it was boring sitting out in the boondocks counting dinks. They knew exactly when one of our slicks was going to show up and would start a little disturbance if there were any dinks within shooting distance. I could not believe it. I reminded them that my aircraft was not an army tank but basically a piece of funny shaped aluminum. The guys merely laughed and said that the Rattlers always came to get them. They then proceeded to show off all their Chinese pistols, watches, and other war souvenirs. Seeing their prizes, I jokingly told them I had a friend at home that wanted me to send him a set of ears. Believe me, I was astonished when one of the soldiers snickered and pulled up a necklace made of objects similar to dried apricots. They all laughed loudly when they realized how truly shocked I was! I hurriedly explained to them that I really did not want to mail a set to my friend or anyone else. The men then began to elaborate on the difficulty of preserving a good set of ears. If the ears were not sun-baked correctly, they would turn black and start to smell. The soldiers complained that, during the rainy season, it was hard to bake them enough. One LRRP even mentioned that he was going to have a toaster sent from home, so he could take ears year-round. By this point in my tour, conversations like this did not even seem that bizarre. A professional psychologist would probably feel otherwise!

Several days later, I went to load up these same men, and they were rudely engaged in a big shoot-out. The Firebirds were on station, and I had to do a straight-in approach to the hilltop LZ as shooting rockets and miniguns fired past my chopper. Once again this type of mission made me nervous, but I was so tired I did not even break into much of a sweat. When I finally got the helicopter to altitude and a semblance of safety with these particular LRRPs, I swung around in my seat. The LRRP team noticed it was me and got a big laugh out of the situation. I personally did not see the humor.

Numerous times I talked to grunts over the radio while gunfire sounded in the background, and the soldiers would often swear they had not had contact all day. Many other times I would be making an approach to land in an LZ to pick up grunts who guaranteed over the radio everything was quiet only to find everyone of them spread eagle on the ground dodging bullets. The grunts must of had some ill-conceived idea that helicopters were completely armor-plated and bulletproof. In emergencies, we called in gunships to help; and if that did not work, we called in artillery and jets with napalm. The grunts really only had a problem when the weather was bad. Then, they could very well be on their own.

Agent Orange

We had one slick pilot who did all the spraying on the Rattler spray missions. He sprayed around fire support bases to kill off all the grass. This enabled the grunts to

AUGUST 8, 1968

Richard Nixon accepted the Republican nomination for President. He said he had a "secret plan" to end the war. I quickly became a Nixon supporter. Being politically naive at this point, I never dreamed he was lying.

safely burn away the dead grass and prevent the dinks from having a close hiding place. It also cleared the area and helped reduce the possibility of having the enemy easily sneak up on them. Agent Orange was the chemical used to kill the foliage. A crew chief once informed me that the rotor blades blew the crap all over the inside of our chopper.

The guy who sprayed this stuff also used it to kill the national bird of Vietnam—the mosquito. The air force routinely used Agent Orange over our entire area of operations. Their motto went something like Smokey the Bear's, but with a twist: "Only we can prevent forests!"

On August 15, battalion declared there would be no more snatch missions. They must have gotten wind of my last one. This was also a great day for helicopter pilots in the area, because a unit from the 196th captured seventeen crew-served .50 caliber antiaircraft guns. I assume that the enemy was moving the antiaircraft guns into the area to use during Tet III, or the Third Offensive of 1968.

Back to the War

On August 19, my gravy train derailed. It would be back to the war for me. That night, I was informed that the CO would be flying with me the next morning. That morning, flying up to the MACV location, I called over the radio three or four times warning them I was inbound with "Rattler 6" aboard. I am sure the CO was wondering what was going on. As I was landing at the helipad, I finally received an answer. It went something like, "Hell Carlock, shut that damn thing down and take a nap." I nervously explained to the CO that the guy on the radio really had some sense of humor. As the CO shut down the chopper, I ran ahead to the air conditioned bunker where I generally took my morning nap. Once there, I pleaded with the major from Texas to find something for me to do. I had to convince the CO that this was an important mission. Unfortunately, the ARVN Fifth Regiment did not have a single soldier in the field that day. I could have gone out with an ARVN officer and flown circles around the ground troops, if they'd had any in harm's way. I then asked Tex if he could get some of them to go to the field. He shook his head and told me that would take a week, at least. Since I could not find a legitimate mission, the CO and I flew from one ARVN camp to another, taking one man here and there. This was the best mission Tex could arrange on such short notice.

Around noon, I was surprised when Tex called me over the FM radio and said, "Come on in, let's go have lunch." I could tell he was ready for his noontime trip to Da Nang for a hamburger, which had become a routine for us and which uncharitable types could see as a waste of the taxpayers' money. I landed and ran in to have a heart to heart talk with Tex about keeping his big mouth shut. I believe we ended up dropping him off at a helipad in Da Nang, while the CO and I went to the PX at Freedom hill. Needless to say, I did not get to enjoy my daily hamburger.

During this same day we were flying around Tien Phouc at about 1,500 feet when the crew chief dropped a bottle of cough syrup on the floor of the helicopter. It sounded exactly like a .50 cal. hitting through the floor. I frantically grabbed the controls and went into a dive to low level out of the area. The CO peered into the back of the helicopter only to see the bottle of cough syrup and remarked, "You're touchy, touchy!" I retorted with, "No, I'm short!" He obviously had not had many .50 cal. pieces of scrap iron pass through his helicopter! On the way back to Chu Lai, the CO said, "I don't believe those people need a helicopter each day." I had the right to remain silent—and wisely did. That night, I decided it was time for me to go back to Da Nang and fly with the special forces. I promptly scheduled myself, and away I went.

Special Forces

On August 21, I was flying a major (I do not believe he was special forces) out to one of the special forces camps west of Quang Ngai. It was an extremely hot day, and at about 2,000 feet, I can only assume I was flying through wind shears. The helicopter was popping 200 to 300 feet at each gust. I had never experienced anything like it. I descended to 1,000 feet, and the buffeting by the wind was not as severe. This wind shear also frightened my crew. I landed, and watched as the major walked over to my window and screamed, over the sound of the helicopter, "You are the worst pilot I've ever ridden with!" That dipstick thought I was making the helicopter jump around like that through my own ineptitude. I had flown a major turd in my whirlybird!

We headed back to Quang Ngai at low level, and the wind was still gusty. However, it was nothing like the gusts we endured at 2,000 feet. We landed, and the crew chief came in to the headquarters where I was and told me we should not be flying the helicopter. When a crew chief told me not to fly, I did not fly.

While checking out the aircraft, the crew chief was able to stick a wooden pencil between the tail boom and the body of the helicopter. It appeared to him that the hardened steel bolts that held on the tail boom had stretched. I did not believe they had stretched, but I thought the tail boom had, in fact, bent. Snake Doctor (Rattler maintenance) showed up on the scene to see for themselves. The maintenance enlisted men were mad, because I refused to fly the machine back to Chu Lai. One of the maintenance pilots threatened to get in the chopper and fly it back himself. After the maintenance people finally inspected the chopper closely and discussed the problems with my crew chief, they too decided it was dangerous to fly. They came to the same conclusion that it was safer to change the bolts before flying it back.

During this period of time, Thoung Duc Special Forces was under a limited siege with intermittent mortar attacks. The strangest combination of circumstances I encountered in Vietnam happened as I flew out there on a mission. I had picked up a full load of Vietnamese at Da Nang. I was flying an H-model and always filled it up until nothing else would fit.

I never had any livestock aboard leaving Da Nang; the chickens, etc. joined us on the trips going into Da Nang. As we flew out, I was monitoring the FM radio, and I heard the special forces guys talking to an air force FAC. As I entered the little valley where the special forces camp was, west of Happy Valley, I advised my crew to watch to the south. I had overheard that two Phantom jets were about to bomb the church with the steeple on it. Someone had spotted a mortar position dug in next to the church, and our guys were about to get rid of it. Incredibly, one of my crew members then told me, "Sir, this priest back here just pointed at that church and says it's his church." I could not believe my own ears. I glanced around, and sure enough, there was a Vietnamese soul saver aboard. The priest had a big proud smile on his face. I turned back around and looked to the south. About twenty seconds later, the first Phantom hit the church with hard bombs and blew it to smithereens. I guess, because I was getting so short, I was beginning to feel like a human again and was actually embarrassed by the bombing of this priest's church. I purposefully never looked around after we let the Vietnamese off at the special forces camp.

As I mentioned earlier, I myself once took a hit from the Catholic church in Tam Ky. The NVA and VC knew that the best way to get the people to hate us was to force us to destroy the things they valued. It was a common practice to set up their gun positions close to something that was important to the local villagers. Many times we also took shots from cemeteries where Buddhist worship shrines were located. When I was flying gunships, we attacked these shrines numerous times. One night, we had a big shoot-out with the VC in a Buddhist shrine southwest of Chu Lai, close to Tra Bong Special Forces Camp. In that engagement, we knocked the whole thing down.

Tet III

In late August and early September 1968, most of the action I was involved in shifted from the Que Son Valley to the area south of Chu Lai. This was west and northwest of Quang Ngai. As a

August 22, 1968

THE ENEMY LAUNCHED WHAT WAS CALLED TET III, THE THIRD NATIONWIDE OFFENSIVE OF 1968.

young pilot, all I knew at the time was that there was a lot of fighting around Quang Ngai. What was really happening was the start of what would later be called the Third Offensive of 1968. The first was at Tet, January 31, 1968. The second was the 150-year anniversary of the birth of Karl Marx (May 5, 1968), and the third was this one in August and September 1968.

The enemy attacked Saigon again at this time. In our area, they attacked Ha Thanh Special Forces Camp on August 22, 1968 to draw American troops away from Quang Ngai City. The first assault did draw American troops into the area. The units we engaged were from the Third NVA Infantry Division. Official records show that Ha Thanh was overrun for three days around August 30. This must have meant the village of Ha Thanh, because the special forces camp was intact. The first prong of the NVA attack was against Ha Thanh, and the second prong went straight toward Quang Ngai City.

On my last combat flight in Vietnam (September 10), we landed in the middle of the second prong attacking force. By September 29, after I left Vietnam, units of the Third NVA actually fought their way into Quang Ngai City temporarily.

When it all started, the special forces had me flying resupply and medevac until 3:00 A.M. The enemy rocketed Chu Lai and killed or wounded sixty-five people. I was in Da Nang during the action and arrived in Chu Lai later in the day to pick up another helicopter. The enemy had just rocketed the area again during the daylight. As I stood at the flight line, the sight was incredible. Looking to the west, in the direction of the mountains, I watched as jets, loaded with napalm, were heavily bombing enemy positions. I watched as a string of airbursts followed behind one of the jets. The dinks were using antiaircraft guns, and the rounds were exploding behind and above one of the jets. One of the maintenance men told me and my crew that everyone had been put on standby, so the helicopters could be evacuated if the NVA attacked. Strongly feeling that I was "too short" for this crap, I saddled up and dashed back to the safety of Da Nang in my trusty slick helicopter. This idea did not turn out exactly as I planned.

The special forces helipad I always used at Da Nang was about a half mile from Marble Mountain. Looking south from Da Nang, along China Beach, the terrain was totally flat. The only exceptions were several huge marble rocks sticking up from the sand. The largest rock was about three hundred feet high. A Buddhist temple is still situated on the side of the rock. On top of the rock, the marines had mounted a recoilless rifle to shoot the enemy. With the special forces, I felt fairly secure.

But my intended day of leisure almost turned into my worst nightmare. Early on the morning of the 23rd, the special forces at Da Nang suffered the worst casualties from one encounter in its history. Seventeen men were killed north of Marble Mountain. At least sixty NVA soldiers got into the base, and many of the South Vietnamese "allies" switched sides and participated in the deadly sneak attack. On the night of the 22nd and the morning of the 23rd, I remember flying wounded out and ammo in during an attack. I was so tired and weary, my memory is gone as to the exact locations I was landing.

Some helicopter pilots reportedly barricaded themselves in their hootches and fired randomly at the slightest sound. I never determined what unit the pilots were with who shot through the walls of their hootch, but it wasn't us. Malek points out that we could not have shot through the walls of our reinforced hootch, even if we wanted to—they were made of concrete and were four or five inches thick.

By the afternoon of the 23rd, helicopters were being used to shoot the dinks off of Marble Mountain. Thoung Duc was under heavy attack, and I flew out there several times during the day. The base at Marble Mountain was retaken during the afternoon. That night, the enemy regained control once again. I was never told about all the special forces guys being killed; I assume they tried to keep it quiet. They must have used trucks instead of helicopters to move out the bodies the next day.

I managed to sleep through the second attack on Da Nang on the morning of August 24. No one woke me up during the attack until a decision was made to move all the helicopters. They came looking for the pilots and found me. In the action, the dinks captured the marine base on top of Marble Mountain for the second night in a row and were shooting from the top of it into our special forces camp. Several enemy soldiers were able to sneak into the base itself. It was my understanding that there were two perimeters set up in this camp, with our helicopters located in the second one, further away from Marble Mountain. The attack began late at night, but it was morning before they came to get me.

I was seriously worried that I would only finish my tour in this hellhole and end up in a rubber room back in the States.

On my return trip in 1993, it was easy to see how the VC captured the base at the top of the mountain. The Vietnamese now have a sign posted there which states that there was a VC hospital set up inside the mountain itself at the same time the marines were on top. We Americans were barred from going inside the tunnels of the mountain during the war, because the site supposedly housed a Buddhist shrine or holy place.

General Impression

In August, I hauled my first and only general on my helicopter. I had the impression he was not a special forces general, because he had a big beer belly. I always suspected that he needed a medal, so he had us haul him in to Thoung Duc Special Forces Camp so he could get one. The commies were shooting mortar rounds every time they saw movement. From prior landings there, I knew the rounds were well aimed and were hitting the helipad, which was positioned on the west end of the camp. I called the camp and told them I was going to let the general off on a bunker on the eastern end. I knew there were no radio antennas on this bunker. The general had three staff officers accompanying him. I told one of these officers I was going to put them off on the eastern bunker. I instructed him to just jump off that bunker and head to the one with the antennas. I also strongly suggested they move at "double time" (don't walk). After a few moments, the staff officer came back and said, "The general desires to land on the pad!" I looked around at the general and grinned, because I thought they were making a joke. The general stared at me with his fat face contorted in contempt as if my crew and I were just a bunch of piss ants. I quickly decided to teach the pompous fool a lesson. I would follow his orders! The peter pilot implored, "No, no, don't do it!" I replied, with gritted teeth, "Yes, yes!" The peter pilot just shook his head dejectedly. I calmly told the staff officer, a captain, they better jump from the helicopter fast, because I was going to sit there for two seconds at the most.

As we got to the west end of Happy Valley, I went down low level and cranked the chopper wide open. The mortars were coming from the south, where the Catholic church used to be, so I flew around and came in from the north. I did a real hot cowboy landing and touched down to the west of the pad. Sure enough the little group hopped off quickly with the peter pilot muttering, "No, no!" I blasted off and went in a tight spiraling climb intentionally staying away from the pad. The staff officers had apparently seen the writing on my window that said I had a little over thirty days left in Vietnam and must have assumed I knew what I was talking about, because they hastily dashed across the helipad into the bunker. I was totally amazed as I observed that the general, going after that medal, calmly strolled across the pad. I could not believe anyone was that stupid. Apparently, the dumbass commie, operating the Bolshevik mortar tube, had taken a smoke break, because the general walked across the pad and had taken five or six steps when a grayish white flash hit dead center on the pad. The flash was followed by a dark circle that moved instantly out from the flash. The general received his expected hot reception. Charlie was trying to pin his own version of a medal on our idiot general. The big-stomached general suddenly beat feet like he was trying out for the Olympic Team. He had certainly decided it was time to save his precious skin and did not wait around for any brass bands to escort him to the bunker. My crew started laughing big time, and I laughed so hard I nearly wet my pants. Once I composed myself, I called the special forces and tried to inquire sincerely about the new arrivals' safety. It was obvious that the radio operator wanted to laugh too. He radioed that everyone was okay. That afternoon I picked them up below the camp on the north side. No one mentioned the general's warm reception.

To this day, I never could decide if it took total stupidity or ignorant heroics for that general to walk across that helipad. In 1968, as a young warrant officer, I just assumed the general had sat farting in his fancy armchair too long. Charlie certainly came close to putting a hole in his beer belly.

Moving Targets for NVA Gunners

Williams told about a mission in October 1968 into Thoung Duc Special Forces Camp. This was after I let the general off and after Ericsson was shot down. This is the only time I have heard of B-52 bombers giving "close air support." This is in Williams's own words:

> Around the same time that our Firebirds (gunships) were working the Phu Bai TDY (temporary duty assignment), the slicks got a Da Nang Fifth Special Forces support TDY. I volunteered because I knew it would be interesting. I felt kind of invulnerable about this time in my tour; I had been in country about two years. I had grown into a firepower freak, and I was flying with twin-60 door guns. One was my normal mount gun and the second was a free gun (infantry type) M-60 that I would lay on the brass bag of the first gun. I also carried a tommy gun, a .45 caliber, and about twelve frag grenades. Hell, I didn't have to hump it so it was easy. The mission enabled me to see the DMZ for my first time, and I flew into camps that you only heard about in books because of one huge fire fight or another.
>
> One of these camps, Thoung Duc, became the scene of some of the hairiest flying I ever participated in. We overheard a lot of talk about a big action that was going on west of Da Nang at a camp that was surrounded by an estimated ten thousand

NVA. But talk was always going on about some action, so we didn't give this any more attention than normal.

In the afternoon, the bird "kernal" in charge of the Fifth Group and the Mike force (Vietnamese Special forces) at Da Nang requested a hurry up meeting with all flight crews. I thought it would be a hot extraction of an LRRP or a hot medevac, something we were already familiar with doing. It turned out this would be very different than anything we had ever flown before. First, we would not be using helicopter gunships for cover, but our ship would go in with two Phantom (F-4) jets (that's a major speed disparity), and second we would try to go down the high valley to Thoung Duc while a B-52 strike (Arc Light) would be dropping on the ridges that formed the valley. Normally, all aircraft were given a warning to stay two miles clear of all Arc Light. Finally the "kernal" promised that the pilots and crew would be put in for decorations if they would volunteer to just try to dust off some of the more critically wounded Green Berets. Now, I knew that this was a very serious situation—nobody tells you ahead of time that, if you try this, they'll put you in for a decoration.

We found another catch when we got the ship ready to leave. Battalion had called and advised us to leave behind all of our ship's radios except what we needed to contact the camp and all personal effects including pictures, letters, etc. About this time, I was wishing that I was a cook or something. I was thinking that they were confident that we were not coming back from this ride.

Well, we took off after another briefing about antiaircraft guns all along both ridges leading

down the valley to Thoung Duc and a lot of other
stuff I really didn't want to hear about. The thought
of being a cook was starting to sound like a great
idea to me. We flew west until we were about two
miles from the mouth of the valley. Still no F-4s, and
we climbed to about 5,000 feet, which was about
even with the top of the ridges, and went into a little circle waiting for the Arc Light.

We had been briefed on the two chopper pads at
the special forces camp, one called the high pad,
because it was at the high end of the camp and
other was a low pad. The fact that was bothering
our crew was that we had been told that both pads
were zeroed in by the NVA gunners, who could be
expected to drop the first round on the pad about
five seconds after we made known our approach to
whichever pad. We looked up and could see the slip
streams of the B-52s, almost right over us now, and
started up the valley.

Just then the two F-4s blew by us so fast we could
barely make out what they were. A few seconds after their first pass the F-4s blew by again. This time
they made a move toward the south ridge. I guess
they acquired a target that we hadn't seen. Then the
thunder started as the B-52's ordnance started to
impact the ridge line. We got distracted by the
bombing and missed what actually happened next,
but we noticed only one F-4 on the next pass and
looked around to see two parachutes gliding gently
toward the south ridge. We mentally marked the spot
and continued down the valley, wanting to take full
advantage of the Arc Light. We started a rapid descent toward the valley floor when we could just
barely see the special forces camp. From 5,000 feet
it would take a little time to lose altitude, and we

needed a visual identification of the two helicopter pads in the camp from as far away as possible so our aircraft commander could strategize his approach.

Looking outside the wire of the camp, we could see the burned-out remains of a Chinook (CH-47) and a deuce and half (two-and-a-half-ton truck) that had both gotten smoked in an earlier attempt to outfox the NVA gunners. The CH-47 had flown low level down the valley, and at the last moment, the Green Berets had thrown all of the wounded on a deuce and a half and drove through the main gate down the road toward the village. The Chinook was already landing beside that road outside the compound. The move was supposed to happen so fast as to confuse the NVA gunners who had the chopper pads zeroed in. The net result of this bold maneuver was worse than the original problem. During the transfer of the wounded from the truck to the CH-47, it only took the NVA gunners three rounds to score a direct hit on the Chinook. It cost an additional four KIAs (killed in action) of the chopper crew, and some of the WIAs (wounded in action) also became KIA. Several more WIAs made their way back inside the wire with the help of those only slightly wounded.

We spotted the two pads, and the aircraft commander informed the Green Berets that we would touch down at the lower pad after a fake approach to the high pad. This was where another Huey, which didn't do so well getting off in five seconds, still sat as a silent reminder of the proficiency of the NVA gunners. Our ship was just ready to touch down on the high pad, when the pilot jerked the collective and headed to the lower pad. The copilot started an audible count on the ship intercom as soon as we touched the lower pad. We frantically shoved out the boxes of ammo and medical supplies while wounded were loaded onto the ship. We heard the crump of a mortar round hit the high pad. I guessed they took the fake. Then, I heard the copilot say, "Five," and the aircraft commander pulled the collective. Before the tail of the chopper cleared the lower pad, the second round dumped onto the lower pad, peppering the tail boom with minor shrapnel hits.

We came out low level and flew toward the south slope gradually picking up altitude. When we hit about two thousand feet, we could see the area where the F-4 pilots went in, and we headed to a very small opening in the jungle close to the downed pilots. We couldn't land because of the angle of the ground, so the pilot held the front of the skids on the ground in a hover as we covered the jungle with our M-60s. It seemed that we were there for a half hour, but was probably two minutes, before we spotted two gray flight suits bounding into the opening. All I can remember about those two F-4 jocks was that their eyes were the size of manhole covers with fear . . . Yeah, like we were calm and collected! They loaded on with the wounded, and once again, we were flying the friendly skies toward Da Nang.

Inbound on that flight to Da Nang, we learned that we had the camp commander of the Green Berets with us. He had been wounded on the first day of the battle, and again on two more separate days, and was forcibly loaded on our ship only because he had lost so much blood he was too weak to resist being evacuated any longer. Well, we never

> *did get our promised decoration for that, but it was one hell of a day's work—at least a pucker factor of "9."*

Moving Targets for US Gunners

Around the end of August, I flew my last mission for the special forces, other than a brief ammo resupply. After this, I decided I would do something different to attempt to change my luck. Until sixty days before the end of August, I had never had much hope of getting out of Vietnam alive. I just took it for granted that I wouldn't make it. With about thirty days left, I began to think seriously about going home and started to worry about getting killed. This happened to be one of those days I thought I was destined for an untidy demise.

I was flying right seat and had the peter pilot in the left seat. Before a peter pilot was made aircraft commander, he had to be approved by at least one or more senior aircraft commanders. On this flight, I had a device like a clipboard strapped on my leg to keep notes, so I could brief the younger pilot on how he did.

We left An Hoa, a marine base southwest of Happy Valley, and headed for Da Nang, across what the marines called Go Noi Island. We had to be flying an H-model, because it was packed with Vietnamese. They had suitcases and bags, but I do not remember if we had ducks and pigs aboard. There were some children with us. The young pilot had never seen that many people packed into a helicopter and was somewhat distracted by all the commotion. When he took off, he forgot to call and get clearance from the artillery.

In Vietnam, no one flew anywhere unless he had the ra-

dio frequency for artillery control to insure that an aircraft did not fly into an artillery round. I looked to my
right as I made a note on the pilot's mistake and stared directly at the marine artillery. They had the big guns
mounted on a track device. I think they were called 175s.
The barrels were parallel to the ground, and I noticed
people standing around them. I decided not to call, because we were already up to about 300 ft. (I later learned
that they lay the barrels down to put the shell in them and
then jack them back up into firing position.) We had
climbed to around 1,500 to 2,000 feet and were probably
six or seven miles out of An Hoa, when it sounded as if
five or six freight trains were running past the chopper. It
was the artillery! The marines had a fire mission in the direction I was flying.

I grabbed the stick and went into a twisting dive to the
north. Running east and west was a small river or creek,
and I was diving just past it to pull up and low-level away
from the impact of the artillery once we spotted it. At
about 100 feet, I saw an unbelievable sight. Peeking out
from the edge of a tree line, and holding cigarettes in their
hands, were thirty or forty NVA soldiers. I was close
enough to observe their smoking cigarettes. I could only
guess at the number of guards they had posted, but it must
have been five or six with AK-47s at the ready. My helicopter was diving so fast, and was so loaded down, that I
did not get an immediate response as I jerked the power
and cyclic to get away from them. I was in the right seat
and pulled right, which exposed the bottom of the chopper even more. I was in a slight dive to the right anyway
and Da Nang was in that direction. A left turn would have
taken me further away from civilization, but there was no
question a left turn would have forced the NVA to shoot
through the trees. I am sure the NVA were as shocked as
I was about seeing a fool dive straight on them and about

how they could shoot so many holes in a helicopter and not be able to knock it down.

The helicopter was utter pandemonium. The NVA automatic weapons were chattering, and a hail of bullets just kept hitting the helicopter. The bottom of the helicopter made a nice target right in front of them. One of the crew started screaming, "Some fell out!" One was screaming, "I've been hit!" The peter pilot was screaming, "We've got wounded." And I was screaming above them all, "Read the instruments, put me on guard, put me on guard!" (Guard is the radio frequency for emergencies—you flip a knob and you're ready to transmit.) I was unable to look down at the instruments, because I was low level and weaving, trying to stay over trees. I was not about to go down again, especially in Happy Valley, without a "Mayday" radio call. I frantically yelled, "Mayday, Mayday, army helicopter, Happy Valley between An Hoa and Hill 55." I would call out my message, then scream, "Read the instruments!" to the peter pilot. Out of the corner of my eye, I spotted the master caution light flashing like a beacon. It apparently began to blink when a fuel pump warning light came on. A bullet probably hit one of them. I noticed that the fire light was not on.

As I low-leveled, some persistent enemy dirtball shot at us again several miles from where the first gunfire had taken place. The peter pilot called transmission and engine gauges in the green, and an air force plane answered my Mayday. I requested that the air force plane relay, "Rattler 11 Mayday, Mayday, Happy Valley, An Hoa, to Hill 55." I knew some Rattler in the Que Son Valley would pick up the transmission and come to my aid in a few minutes. The air force plane relayed back that a Rattler had picked up the Mayday and was en route.

I set down on the helipad at the marine base, crawled out of the slick, and stumbled over to a bunker. I sank down on the ground and leaned back on the sandbags. I never looked at the Vietnamese and never asked how many fell out. I never asked how many Vietnamese were hit, but the helicopter was awash in blood. My heart was stuttering like a machine gun, and I actually thought I was about to have a heart attack, or at the very least, pass out. I did not walk back to inspect the helicopter.

Ham and Lima Bean Injuries

While I was trying to collect myself, one of the crew came over with white stuff covering his fatigue shirt. He thought he had been hit. On the slick M-60 machine guns, the wind would blow the ammo belt against the gun and cause breaks in the linked ammo as it was pulled at a ninety degree angle into the gun. The army had made a device to hold a C-ration can just below where the belted ammo entered the gun. This way, the ammo belt came across the top of the can instead of a ninety degree turn.

The crew member had taken a round directly in the C-ration can. He had ham and lima beans blown on him. The crew member thought it was his brains.

A Rattler soon landed and relayed that "Snake Doctor" was en route. I told a marine officer that our maintenance crew would be there in about thirty minutes to check on the chopper. I climbed in the Rattler slick, took off, and never went back to Happy Valley.

I took the next day off and have absolutely no idea as to why I did not go to the flight surgeon and tell him I had had it. I think it was the age, the macho atmosphere, or else we had all gone completely nuts; I still can't decide. I was sure I still had nearly four weeks of flying left, assuming I stopped flying for a week before I left. As it happened, however, I turned in my wings sooner than that.

Bruce also had an interesting story dealing with a "ham and lima bean injury." He was in a Firebird chopper over some inland waterways. A Vietnamese in a sampan waved as they passed over. At the same time, someone else, from a tree line nearby, fired at their helicopter with what they believed was a recoilless rifle. The round made an airburst next to the aircraft, wounding both the peter pilot and Bruce.

Bruce had his M-60 machine gun rigged with one of the cans of ham and limas. No one could eat the crap, so it was used for

AUGUST 28, 1968

The Democratic Convention was held in Chicago. Hippies, shagheads, and dopers were out in force. The streets were chaos, as they rioted. One of the jerks must have been a Civil War buff, because he used a weapon from that war designed to injure the police horses. I personally felt the police did not need horses; they needed gunships.

other purposes. As the gunship circled the tree line, he shot all his door gun ammo at the hidden target. The heat from the gun cooked off the beans. With all the action going on, Bruce knew he was hit. All of a sudden, slimy stuff started to drip off the visor on his flight helmet. Bruce only thought, "What the hell?"

The pilot quickly flew the injured men to Chu Lai. Once there, the doctor just stood and stared at the injured Bruce. The doctor obviously could not determine the origin of the ham and lima beans. I am sure the wounded door gunner looked like he had just stepped off of an aircraft from the planet Pluto with all the lumpy muck dripping all over him!

Parting Shots (Rattler Edition)

For the next eleven days, I flew my last missions—ass and trash in the Que Son Valley, with an occasional combat assault.

August 30, 1968

UNITS FROM THE AMERICAL DIVISION FOUND AND CAPTURED THE LARGEST ENEMY MOTOR POOL THEY HAD EVER FOUND. IT WAS AROUND HA THANH SPECIAL FORCES CAMP. THEY CAPTURED SEVENTY-FIVE BICYCLES AND A LOT OF INNER TUBES.

On August 31, I flew another sniffer mission near or into Laos. We passed over a clearing, surprising a group of NVA soldiers. The jets flying behind my chopper blew them up before they had time to jump back into their holes.

I believe it was during this time that they had several helicopters west of Hau Duc Special Forces Camp searching for an air force FAC airplane that had crashed into the thick jungle. We looked for a hole in the trees where the plane had penetrated the thick jungle, but could not find one. Both the pilot and the airplane disappeared; it was as if they had been swallowed whole by the jungle!

I remember one large combat assault into a valley southwest of Chu Lai. The flight had fifteen slicks or so in it, and I was tail-end Charlie. I remember the cloud cover driving us lower and lower, until we were finally down to 500 to 600 feet. Flying in formation through enemy territory at 500 feet did not have a very calming effect on a short timer. To add to my anxiety, I had never flown into this area.

The lead slick made a nice left turn between two mountains and then a fairly abrupt right turn. I was watching the flight and not paying any attention to the terrain. Suddenly, I heard the lead as he stated, "Pick a spot." When I looked down, I thought, "What a nice place to land." The landing area appeared to be concrete or asphalt with grass growing through the cracks. As I touched down and looked to the left, I was completely surprised. There was an airport building. We had landed at an old French airport that was not marked on our maps. The terminal building had all the windows knocked out, but it appeared that a fixed wing aircraft could still land on the runway. One of the grunts later told me the place was an old cinnamon plantation. The entire area was beautiful.

On one mission, we had a combat assault, and I was positioned up in the flight for some reason. We must have had some real short timers flying that day to get farther back than me.

We landed in an area I had not been into before, south of Chu Lai. As I set down, I looked out the window and was amazed to find myself sitting in the middle of a peanut field. My dad was a peanut farmer way far away, back home in Texas. I screamed over the intercom for the crew chief to jump out and pull up a few vines for me. He responded, "Screw you, let's get the hell out of here!" From all the noise caused by the helicopters, gunships, and the grunts jumping out, I did not know if Charlie was shooting into the LZ or not. The crew chief clearly must have felt they were. We did not get hit, and I never got any Vietnamese peanuts.

I remember one day I landed early in the morning at a grunt company east of Highway 1 in VC territory. They had some mamasans (old women) with them. A grunt told me they forced the mamasans to spend the night so their sons, the VC, wouldn't attack.

On one particularly broiling day, we sat in the shade of our choppers as they were gathering slicks at Duc

Pho for a large Romeo Foxtrot. As we were sitting there shooting the bull, an H-23 helicopter landed. These were the small bubble jobs that were used in flight school. A guy jumped out of the chopper who was truly a sight to behold. He spotted me talking to some grunts and ambled over. Now, when I first arrived in Vietnam, for the first day or so, I acted like I was John Wayne. This guy could have put my act to shame. He was a captain and wore spit-shined paratrooper boots. He was also decked out in pressed and starched jungle fatigues and was sporting two pearl handle pistols. The pistols were crossed over his chest in the style of Pancho Villa. I carried a Bowie knife on my leg, but this cowboy's large Bowie knife was hooked on the straps with his pistols. I was impressed. The grunts' mouths fell open.

I only saw a few H-23s while I was in Vietnam, and someone said later they thought this guy must have been with an artillery unit. The man asked where the flight was going, so I pulled out my map and showed him. He then asked if I knew anything about the area, and I told him no. I did say that the grunts were sure the whole region was full of Charlies, and a big fight was expected. After digesting the information we shared with him, "John Wayne" declared he would head on out ahead of us and check the area. I was astonished. The thing he was flying was made of plastic, with the gasoline tanks positioned behind his head. The man's intentions did not seem prudent at all.

Once the flight began, I was tail-end Charlie. As we turned into the valley heading toward the LZ, about three miles from our destination, we passed nearly directly over the crashed and burning H-23. I never found out whether "Captain Cowboy" made it out of the flaming debris alive.

On September 6, the battalion had a helicopter shot down in action west of Quang Ngai.

On September 7, the battalion had a helicopter shot down in action west of Quang Ngai.

On September 8, the battalion had a helicopter shot down in action west of Quang Ngai.

The Medals Flow Uphill

Also on the 8th, I was awarded several medals at a company formation. As I walked away after the little ceremony, I was confronted by Palazzo, the gunner who was shot in the butt on the 31st of January, during the beginning of Tet. He stepped directly in front of my path and muttered, "Why do you officers always get the medals, and all we get is the shit shot out of ourselves. You guys just sit up there in your armored seats." I was speechless and did not say one word. I was also as embarrassed as I had ever been in my life!

What he said was true. If I thought I was screwed over as a warrant officer, the enlisted men really had something to complain about. By way of example, I will relay one more story from Crew Chief Williams:

> *Our crew drew a single ship support mission one morning, where we found ourselves airborne, directing an artillery strike for ground troops. On board, we had three passengers, an RTO (radio-telephone operator), a sergeant, and a second lieutenant, who were all running the artillery mission. Suddenly, we heard an urgent plea for assistance. A medevac was needed for a grunt who had stepped on a mine and was in immediate need of evacua-*

tion. The A/C informed the grunt lieutenant that he was going to go after the WIA who was in our immediate area, and the lieutenant agreed.

We found the hill, asked for smoke, and then shot our final approach to the smoke—nothing out of the ordinary. The grunts jogged toward our ship with their WIA, and then all hell broke loose. An AK-47 barked a loud burst, and all three artillery grunts on the front seat hit the floor in an ever widening pool of blood. Spatters of blood and small fragments of metal and plastic started flying around everywhere in the cabin. I heard the distinctive, "thunk . . . thunk" as rounds started hitting other parts of the ship. Simultaneously, we opened up with both door guns, laying down suppressive fire. Luckily, our gunner got the VC with the AK, who was standing about twenty-five yards away. In a reflexive move, the A/C pulled pitch, and we all found the cabin spinning faster than the rotor blades. Our A/C immediately figured out that we had lost the tail rotor and bottomed the collective, only to land on a mine which peppered my gunner in both legs with shrapnel. The wounds were serious enough to get him a ticket back to the States because the shrapnel had penetrated the bone as well.

The gunner and I went forward, opened the pilots' doors, and pulled their side chickenboards back, so they could get out. I helped the three wounded grunts get out to cover in the brush on top of the hill. Our A/C got off a "Mayday" with our location before he left the ship. Our gunner and I next removed the mount guns from the ship. The artillery grunts started to treat each other's wounds, which were not as serious as it first looked. One had a long grazing wound to the chest, another was shot through the forearm, and the third was hit in the hand. The grunts whom we originally set out to help, dispersed down the hill to set up covering positions. They left their wounded on top of the hill with the other wounded grunts.

We were on top of a hill, in the neighborhood just south of the Song Tra Bong River, so we were pretty close to Chu Lai. Within five minutes, we could hear the distinctive popping of Hueys headed in our direction. I strained to see the birds that I knew were getting close, but I could not spot them until one burst up from the valley below the hill summit and damned near hit us, it was so low. I still remember the two gunners on that Firebird gunship. They were positioned entirely outside the ship as they overflew us looking at us almost eyeball to eyeball. Gunships are pretty impressive when they are parked on the ground, or if you ever see them making a gun pass, but let me tell you, when you are on the ground and these Firebirds fly directly at you about four feet off the ground, that is a sight you will never ever forget.

Well, with those mothers in the AO, we knew the shooting part of our day was over. We watched them circling our hill like huge birds of prey, daring someone to give them an excuse. Next to arrive was the medevac, and as soon as it touched down, I grabbed the guy we first came for and threw him on the medevac and went back for the other wounded and got them all aboard. As the dustoff pulled pitch, I turned and covered my face from the dust when the rotor wash moved a bush and set off another mine that blew me flat on my face. I thought I was dead, or at least wounded, but did not have a scratch. I had just moved back to my machine gun in the brush when a Rattler landed to pick up the rest of us, but this slick A/C was smart enough to rest the skid on a boulder, knowing the hill was heavily mined. We all piled on, including the original grunts who had moved back to the top of the hill after the Firebirds had arrived. When the A/C of the slick pulled pitch, he yelled to his crew chief that someone would have to get off as he was overloaded. Since I had taken an outside door position sitting on the floor with my machine gun, I bailed out to wait for the next ship. The slick pulled pitch and took off, and I turned to find my A/C had also jumped out. We stood alone on the hill back to back afraid we would step on another land mine and waited for the next slick, and a ride home.

They recovered my ship with a CH-47 later that day after the minefield was cleared and the hill secured. We took four hits in the tail boom, one of which had severed the tail rotor cable and caused it to wrap around the tail rotor drive shaft.

I still would like to know where everybody went to when I was running back and forth through the mine field putting the four wounded on the dustoff. My two pilots and my gunner got the Distinguished Flying Cross for that action. I wasn't put in for any award, but I think I had a pretty good day anyhow.

Final Missions

My next to last mission was a resupply of the special forces camp northwest of Quang Ngai, Ha Thanh Special Forces Camp. I flew into the special forces camp three or four times that day. The army had moved some units into the area. I guess someone from our aviation battalion was circling up above my helicopter that day. This observation was based on a copy of a battalion directive to the aviation companies telling them to advise their pilots not to do what I did that day.

For some unknown reason, two Shark gunships were on station to escort me into the camp. The Sharks were from another company in our aviation battalion. They reported that a slick going in had been shot at and hit on final. Also, the camp was being mortared. They seemed very insulted when I informed them I was going to spiral in and land on a bunker. I had been in those special forces camps dozens of times under fire without a gunship's support, and I was not about to do a straight-in approach now. I made it in and out on each mission during the day without taking any hits.

The battalion directive I later saw reported that some slick pilots were refusing gunship support in order to do spiraling approaches to hot areas. The companies were instructed to tell pilots it was safer to make straight-in approaches with gunship support. Right!

I flew my last combat mission on September 10.

Dillard and I were set to leave Vietnam around the 24th of September. Most aviation companies allowed pilots to quit flying a week early. In our case, that would have made our target date somewhere around the 17th or 18th of September. On the 10th, Dillard and I, flying separate choppers, landed at the 176th Aviation Company, a company in our battalion. We were waiting on other slicks to arrive, so we could then go to a PZ close to Quang Ngai.

Dillard and I asked some guys where two of our friends were that came to Vietnam the same day we did. We were told they were drunk in bed, because their CO had let them quit flying. I looked at Dillard as he stared back at me. It was crystal clear we were having the identical thought. We should not be flying!

In a large flight of slicks, we picked up some grunts and were briefed (I believe over the radio) that our guys had lost radio contact with another group of grunts. I later learned that there were fifteen of them and all fifteen were found dead. It must have been a grunt recon team.

During the interval between the loss of contact with the grunts and the discovery of their bodies, no one had any idea where they were. Therefore, it was going to be a no-fire LZ to insure that we would not shoot any Americans on the ground. There would be no artillery pounding, no gunships firing, and no door gunners firing from the slicks. In other words, it was going to be pretty damn quiet, at least on our part. I carefully ordered my crew not to fire the machine guns without my specific orders. I was tail-end Charlie, and Dillard got stuck up in the flight.

Our LZ was west of Quang Ngai north of the river. The NVA attack at the special forces camp was to draw Americans away from Quang Ngai, so the remaining NVA could strike the city. We were about to land in the midst of the attack units of the NVA without the help of any outgoing fire. We flew south of the river to the west past the LZ. I could only assume that our illustrious commanders wanted the enemy to have plenty of time to get a good look at us, so they could be ready to give us a "warm" reception.

As we turned our choppers north, I looked down and spotted a burning gunship lying on its side on a sandbar next to the river. I instantly thought, "Oh shit, I'm too short for this!" A gunship pilot from the 176th Aviation Company was killed that day, and the downed gunship could well have been one of theirs. We flew on, and a crew member told us to look down. I saw a crashed observation helicopter, either an H-13 or H-23. My pucker factor went up to the max!

We flew further, made a slow looping turn around to the east, and landed in the LZ to the south. On final, I again reminded the crew of the "no fire," because we could not accurately determine where the friendlies were. As my helicopter skids touched down, a machine gun began to blast away. I was flying left seat and looked over my left shoulder. I keyed the intercom mike to order a "cease fire" to my gunner. As my finger hit the mike, I glanced around, and the gunner was gawking straight at me with eyes as big as manhole covers. The NVAs machine gun was so close, the muzzle was practically kissing my helicopter. Because of the gun's proximity to us, I thought it was my door gunner initiating the shooting. It was hidden in a bush-covered bunker only a few feet from my chopper. Luckily, for me, the NVA shooter picked the chopper in front of me for his intended target. I could only assume the enemy soldier thought the chopper ahead was going to set down in front of him or else his bunker was turned slightly toward the length of the LZ. My aircraft was at the extreme end of the LZ. I heard grenades or rockets explode, as I turned my helicopter to the west and broke out of the LZ. The grunts aboard my slick jumped out, nearly landing on top of the enemy bunker. Dillard related that he started turning to the west to escape, but the lead helicopter finally got a move on it to expedite to the south. Every helicopter there was hit, except mine, with the one ahead of me not even being able to get out of the LZ.

Dillard and I flew back to the Snakepit and shutdown. I told him not to let me down; and if we stuck together, there was nothing they could do to us that was worse than what we had just lived through. We marched straight in before the CO and told him, in no uncertain terms, "We quit." We disclosed to him that the 176th had let their guys who were "short" quit. We also reminded him we were way in excess of ninety hours flight time over the past thirty days. Enough was enough: we were not going to fly anymore. He blurted out, "You can't quit!" We just smiled at him and stood our ground. Without uttering another word, I think he knew we had had it. We had reached our limit and quite possibly pushed Lady Luck way past hers.

He hesitated and finally spoke some golden words, "O.K., I have a helicopter to be picked up in Cam Ranh Bay. You two can go get it." It was like divine intervention! God, it was an intoxicating feeling. I had made it. I was happier than a pig in slop. I had served my tour and was going to go home alive!

SEPTEMBER 20, 1968

The government released a report stating that Agent Orange would not hurt anyone.

EPILOGUE

....

The Long Ride Home

I WAS NOT ALONE ON MY TRIP BACK TO "THE World." They were there with me, going home, staying in my heart and mind; they were a part of my life now—visions of my buddies and strangers I haven't even mentioned in this account running through my head over and over: the dead soldier with the St. Christopher's medal just like mine, the old Vietnamese man carrying several bodies back to his village, the black soldier who gripped my hand in terror and pain as we flew in the chopper. And where were Anton, Lewis, and Pfister? Were they alive? Would I ever see them again? Was all this pain and suffering in vain?

My initial reaction upon taking my seat for my plane trip home was—I made it! I was alive, and as a bonus, physically whole. I was lucky; I was blessed. My mind was a mass of confused thought.

For the first time in almost twelve months, I was in the air without the fear of being a target. I was overwhelmed with a myriad of emotions including incredible relief, haunting sadness, and an all-consuming anger.

For months, I was a part of harrowing missions on an almost daily basis. I saw friends shot down, friends maimed and killed, and even friends carried off to God knows where. In the early days of my tour, I honestly figured I would never make it through. As my days grew "short," I once again began to think about getting out of the whole mess and getting on with my life. After being numb with fatigue, I was almost numb with the relieving feeling of safety.

I carried with me a certain sadness, a sadness that has softened only somewhat through the years. Time does heal emotional wounds, but the images remain, lurking in the back of the mind only to seep out at the most unexpected moments. A certain smell, a particular sound; and suddenly, I am propelled back in time to a sense of stress and uncertainty. I have feelings of regret and guilt, regret that so many died and guilt that I was happy it was not me.

In spite of the ridiculous rules, handed down by some small men with big ranks, my fellow soldiers and I carried on with our duties. The vast majority of American military personnel performed honorably and bravely under extremely difficult circumstances. Our goals were neither political nor philosophical. Our goals were to take care of one another and try to make it out of the nightmare of war alive.

Return to Nam

In July 1993, I returned to Vietnam. Touring much of the country in a battered old Russian helicopter, I flew over many of the areas of our former operations. Every location, every site, brought back memories of my friends.

I saw the location where Hannah was shot down in flames. I saw where Buzzell heroically struggled to run, after suffering two broken legs, in order to save his crew from the burning gunship before it exploded. I saw where Anton, Lewis, and Pfister were captured, and observed the river Carson jumped into to escape from the North Vietnamese soldiers. I located the mountain where the medevac pilot, later awarded the Congressional Medal of Honor for his actions, hovered his helicopter down the cloud enshrouded mountain in a sideways manner to reach the soldiers wounded in combat the same night Anton was captured. I saw the mountain ridge where Parsons, crippled by a broken back, miraculously carried his crew chief, Reynolds, over his shoulder to safety after their chopper was shot down. I found the area where Leopold, Bruce, Aker, and I crouched down in the Vietnamese grave to hide while we waited for McCall to come to our rescue. I saw the mountain ridge I was flying over when the irascible marine beseeched me to haul out the dead and wounded soldiers, because their mothers would want me to help them. This landscape is etched in my memory and will always remain with me.

I also gazed across the Que Son Valley and observed numerous, huge Vietnamese military cemeteries covering the valley. It was indeed "Death Valley" for both sides. (Our interpreter said most of the white headstones did not have bodies under them but were put up so pictures could be sent to the parents.)

Not surprisingly, many of the locations mentioned in this book have changed over the decades, but others are still familiar. To this day, LZ Ross has nothing growing on it because of all the oil we sprayed on it to hold down the dust. The Vietnamese erected a statue there to celebrate their victory. Flying right over LZ Baldy, I had difficulty finding the runway where we used to land. I finally realized that they had built houses down the runway. It would be difficult to land anything on it now. There is also no growth on LZ East—probably also due to the oil we sprayed. All along the sides of this steep mountain, hungry Vietnamese have dug numerous holes, scavenging for discarded C-rations.

I also visited the War Crimes Museum in Saigon. One of the outspoken interpreters there questioned me about a photograph that supposedly showed a helicopter in flight as a Vietnamese prisoner was shoved out of the aircraft. They were aware that I had been a chopper pilot. I could tell that the interpreter realized that the Communists had lied many times concerning incidents in the war and other matters. They were actually questioning the validity of the picture, which happened to be cut from a Chicago newspaper.

I didn't know whether the picture was real or not and could only say that bad things happened on both sides. Later, I found out that this particular photo was a phony. The body was really an already dead NVA soldier, and the event had been staged. A crew member sent the picture to a girlfriend, and she sent it on to a newspaper.

Anton had asked me to take a picture of his ring at the Hanoi War Museum. Years before, he had seen a picture of his dad's Air Force Academy ring that he was wearing when he was captured. The Vietnamese had it on display at the Hanoi Museum. I went two different times to the Museum and never could find the ring. I even sent a Vietnamese lawyer there, offering a sizable donation for the ring. The lawyer told me I could have the whole museum for a reasonable price. The guy running the place had been there for seven years, and said he had never seen any rings. They did say that if I had a picture of it or could draw it, they would have one made for me in twenty-four hours.

Some of my most memorable experiences from this trip took place at Marble Mountain, the hill at Da Nang with the VC hospital inside. I made the mistake of telling my tour guide there that I was a helicopter pilot during the war. She looked like she was twelve years old and gave tours after school. Apparently she told some other tour guides that I was a helicopter pilot. When I finally climbed into the VC hospital inside the mountain, with buckets of sweat pouring off me, I noticed six or seven of the little girls (tour guides) following us. The inside of the former VC hospital has bullet holes in the marble rock where the marines and VC fought it out inside this huge cavern. One of the other little girls stepped up to me and pointed at the sign noting it to be a VC hospital and the date of the battle and asked, "Were you here then?" I made another mistake when I pointed in the general direction of the special forces camp and stated, "I was there." All of the little girls at the same time asked, "Were you the helicopter pilot that bombed our hospital?" After some discussion, they were adamant that a helicopter bombed the hospital. Some bomb fragments were still inside the cavern. Apparently, a jet blew out the top of the VC hospital and a helicopter hovered over and dropped diesel or foo gas inside the hospital, which was then ignited.

A real pretty tour guide looked me right in the eye and said, "VC killed lots of Americans!" I started to say, "The VC were as lethal as little girls throwing marshmallows," but I figured she wouldn't understand the word "marshmallow." Then I started to tell her to ride south to Death Valley and count the cemeteries and she could figure out who killed who, but I merely replied that "VC were very brave." I find it interesting that the sign in the VC hospital has the wrong date on it. They say the battle took place on August 21, 1968. The battle was on August 24, 1968, after the VC captured the top of the rock on the mornings of August 23 and August 24.

The tour guides at Marble Mountain make money selling carved marble objects (Buddhas, jewelry boxes, etc.). After my guided tour, I purchased several items. My little guide looked at me after I purchased several jewelry boxes and with tears in her eyes told me, "My daddy beats me if I don't sell lots of marble." I thought, here I am, accused of bombing hospitals and now I am going to cause this little girl to get a beating. So I purchased most of her trinkets. On the final steps coming down from Marble Mountain she was laughing and jumping around while I was so tired I could barely move, and she said, "Come here GI, I want to introduce you to my daddy." I said, "Is this the dad that beats you?" The little girl laughed so hard she could barely walk. They are still playing the Americans for a bunch of suckers!

Reflections

My return to Vietnam reinforced my opinion that our involvement in that war was justified, if not well-conceived. Regardless of the shortcomings of a nation struggling to learn democracy, Communism has obviously not been a good alternative for them. The government has had to battle with its own people during various food riots throughout the country. In Hue, there have been many protests because the Communists cannot feed their own citizens. Even though the citizens of Hanoi and Ho Chi Minh City appeared to be well fed during my visit, the small towns in the countryside are experiencing difficulties due to a severe shortage of fuel for the motorized fishing fleets. They cannot travel out into the ocean to work, and the local fishing areas are badly depleted because of over-fishing. I noticed the obvious absence of the overpowering aroma of *nuoc mam*, fish sauce. This odor permeated the air in 1967-68, and the sauce was a vital source of protein for the locals. Many Vietnamese have resorted to eating small snakes in order to supplement their diet. I noticed many bicycles outfitted with small cages used to haul the snakes. I never saw this in 1968. From the discussions I had with the Vietnamese who felt comfortable talking to me, they all mentioned the difficulty they had in feeding their children with any food other than rice. Many, who understood the English word protein, explained it was common for children to die, because most of the general population could not routinely afford any source of protein. Communism has brought starvation and hardship to the majority of its people. While I was in Hanoi, a famous Vietnamese writer from Hanoi wrote that the people in the south were better off when the Americans were there.

On one occasion, I was seated at the table with a Vietnamese gentleman who is currently an executive with a large American company. He then went on to say that the saddest part of his many trips back to his homeland was the conditions at some of the military cemeteries. Many of his friends and family fought and died for the ARVN and were buried in these cemeteries. Once they had control of the country, the Communists came in and obliterated the headstones on the graves of their adversaries. The locations of the graves were lost and hidden from the survivors forever. He went on to say that the only pleasure he derived from his return trips to the region was the complete satisfaction that both he and the government officials he encountered knew that he had fought and supported the "correct" side in the futile war. Off the record, the government representatives he deals with readily admit that communism was and still is a disaster for Vietnam. It is slowly, but surely, failing in that country. The people of Vietnam are still fighting their own quiet bat-

tles against an oppressive form of government. They still
have not won, but times are changing the climate of this
oppression.

I hope that we learned a lot about how not to fight a
war. Our military actions in Vietnam were dominated
much more by politics than by sound tactics. The North
Vietnamese knew this and used it as a powerful and ef-
fective weapon against American troops. During a cocktail party I attended in Hanoi, a group of Vietnamese
generals conceded that they would never have fought and
won against the US military if it had not been shackled by
American politics.

Daily reports of protests, bombings against our government at home by leftist extremists, and the actions of
some politicians, strengthened the resolve of the enemy.
The Communists could not outgun us, but they did out-
last us. The resolve of our citizens and leadership was
weak, at best. Decisions were made by men and women
who had no idea of the ramifications that would be suffered by the men in the field, who were merely doing
their duty. Never again should we put our troops in harm's
way without making sure that our goals are truly in the
best interest of our nation, that we have given them the
means to win, and that they have our support. It is particularly unfair to ask any soldier to give up his or her life
for a cause that is not supported at home. Our young soldiers should never again be sacrificed so uselessly.

If anything beneficial has come from the Vietnam
Conflict, it would be that the lies and distortions suffered
then have caused people to reassess their attitudes toward
government and people in positions of power. This is an
open society, and questions should be asked. The prevail-
ing cynicism concerning government today is due, in
large part, to actions taken at the time of the Vietnam War.

It seems more than a little ironic to me that many of the

people in charge of our government in the mid 1990s, and in favor of big government, were the same people marching in the streets, here and in other countries, against our government during the '60s and '70s. These people should not forget that they questioned the government at one point in their lives; and should expect to be questioned themselves.

The greatest disgrace of this war has been the injustice done to our young people who fought there—injustice not from the enemy, but from home. Many Vietnam vets have related horror stories of the treatment by their fellow citizens upon their return stateside. They were spat upon, cursed, and treated with an incredible disrespect simply because they served their country. I am thankful that I lived in a part of the US where I was never insulted or treated poorly because I wore the uniform and served in Vietnam. It is hard for veterans of this war to accept such irresponsible behavior by people who had no idea what went on during this combat. In this telling of my story, and the story of those around me, I have tried to show the courage and determination of these men. They will always have my respect and my undying gratitude. The Vietnam period was a time of question and tragedy, but it gave me the most priceless friendships of my life. When it came down to it, all we could count on was each other. But in my case, that was enough.

PURPLE HEARTS

....

Awarded to Firebird Gunship Pilots
November 1967–May 1968

McCall, Gary   *shot down*

Carlock, Chuck   *shot down*

Anton, Frank   *shot down & captured*

Carson, Frank   *shot down*

Hannah, Shawn   *wounded, leaving bunker for booze (Oops, they took it away!)*

Parsons, Bob   *shot down*

Litchfield, Lou   *shot down*

Hannah, Shawn   *shot down*

Buzzell, Steven   *shot down*

Sutton, Andrew   *wounded in leg*

Latimer, Wilber   *wounded in leg*

Leopold, Mark   *wounded in face*

Twelve pilots were assigned to this platoon during this period.

WHERE THEY ARE NOW

....

Aker, Michael: Married, living in Nevada. Still has problems with injuries incurred in the military. Is a Little League Baseball official.

Anton, Frank: Retired warrant officer and still married to the lovely woman he met shortly after he was released from the Prisoner of War camp. Currently a pilot with a major airline.

Beck, Gary: Married, living in Florida. Retired as a colonel from the army and has occasional problems with his wounds.

Bootle, Charles "Bill": Retired softball pitcher, retired warrant officer, still married to his flight school sweetheart, Molly. Currently runs his own business in South Carolina. That baby boy he had in flight school is now a colonel in the army.

Bruce, Joe: Eventually, Bruce's luck ran out. He was shot down and spent about sixteen months in military hospitals. Bruce was trapped under the transmission of the crashed helicopter, and the hot oil slowly dripping out nearly cooked him. They finally X-rayed his arm and discovered a bullet in it. Bruce's hips and legs were also crushed by the weight of the wreckage. Today he lives in Oklahoma and is in management in an aviation company, having made a good recovery from his injuries.

Burroughs, Bob: Was a lieutenant in Vietnam and currently is a warrant officer still on active duty—one of (if not the) most senior combat helicopter pilots in the army. He was awarded the Silver Star in Iraq. He's married and lives in Kentucky.

Carlock, Chuck (author):   Is still married to Kathy, the beauty he left the Tet Offensive to go marry in Hawaii. He has three lovely daughters, two of them college graduates, and one in the process of graduating. He is a Certified Public Accountant and Director of Taxes for a prominent Texas family.

Carson, Frank: Just retired as a full colonel. Currently building a home in Florida. He is still married to the wonderful woman who gave him a son while we were in Nam. He still has an occasional eye problem from the Plexiglas incident of May 2, 1968.

Castle, Bob: Is married and living in Virginia. He is a retired army major and currently teaches at an academy.

Cervinski, John: Is married and living in California. He is in law enforcement and has apparently recovered fully from being hit by the flare cap.

Collins, Jim: Is married and living in Florida. He's a retired air force major and is currently a pilot for a major airline.

Ericsson, Jerry: Is married, living in Texas. Currently a colonel with the Texas Army National Guard and has his chickenboard with the bullet hit hanging in his office. My daughters think he is the hottest looking guy they have ever seen.

Foley, Ray: Is married, living in Florida. He is in the sheet metal business and flies airplanes in his spare time.

Fox, Carl: Lives in Florida and still has problems with his injuries suffered in Nam. He is a hero to us.

Hannah, Shawn: Lives in Texas and is still married to the lovely lady who nursed him back to health from his May 5, 1968 injuries. He is a retired warrant officer and currently is an air traffic controller.

Hines, Les: Married, living in Iowa. Even though not mentioned in the book, he furnished the military records and information that made this book possible. He flew out of Chu Lai during the war.

Jeffcoat, Everett: Lives in South Carolina and is active in veteran's affairs and matters concerning Post Traumatic Stress Disorder. He is a hero to us.

Kucera, Roger: Lives in Oregon and is still married to the Texas girl he married in flight school.

Latimer, Wilber: Although Latimer quit flying gunships shortly after Leopold and I asked for a transfer, he later went back to Nam for a second tour. Unfortunately, he never made it through his second tour. He was one of many who just pushed his luck a little too far.

Leopold, Mark "Buddy":   Lives in Florida and has just retired as a colonel from the army. He is still married to the lovely lady whom he married prior to going to Nam. She currently has him playing "Mr. Mom" while she works.

Lewis, Robert: Is married and a retired army sergeant. He appears to be doing well physically after his time in the POW camp. He lives in Texas and is currently in aircraft maintenance.

Malek, Jim: Is married, living in South Carolina. He flies for the FAA.

McCall, Gary: Died in a helicopter crash during an emergency medevac as I was writing this book. He has a son who looks exactly as McCall looked in Vietnam. McCall taught me how to stay alive.

Miller, Jim: Is married to the fine woman he met after he returned from Nam. He is a lawyer in Arkansas (and doesn't work for the Rose law firm).

O'Quinn, David: Is married and retired as an army major. He is currently building a home in South Carolina.

Palazzo, Greg: Lives in Texas and is an insurance company executive.

Parsons, Bob: Lives in Tennessee and is a stock broker/financial consultant. He is still married to the sweetheart he had while in Vietnam. I confirmed that it was Sherry's picture that he kept in the Firebird hootch. This picture was "wounded" during the rocket attack that hurt Hannah as he was going for booze. The frame broke and cut the picture. They still have the picture.

Rogers, Mike: Lives in Alabama and is vice president of a large corporation.

Seabolt, Ron: Is married and lives in Texas. He works for the Post Office and is the president of our reunion association. Without him and the wonderful support of his wife, Kay, our association wouldn't exist and this book wouldn't have been written.

Taylor, Richard P: Is a retired army major and an investment banker in West Virginia.

Webster, Rick: Is married and lives in Florida. He went from being a helicopter pilot to a rocket scientist.

Wiegand, Ken: Is married to the lovely lady (Donna) he married shortly after his return from Vietnam. He is a retired army major living in Virginia and is in aviation management. Besides nearly scaring me to death, he also taught me how to survive.

Williams, R. J.: Is married, living in Pennsylvania. He is a phone company executive. He is the only guy that carried a larger Bowie knife than I did. He still has his.

Zbozien, David: Married, living in Tennessee. He is in the restaurant franchise business.

GLOSSARY

....

A-1E   propeller driven support aircraft

A/C: aircraft commander

AO   a unit's area of operations

APC   an armored personnel carrier, a track vehicle used to transport troops or supplies, usually armed with a .50-caliber machine gun

ARVN   South Vietnamese regular army; officially the Army of the Republic of Vietnam

Autorotation   A procedure for landing a helicopter without engine power. The weight of the falling helicopter creates a "pinwheel" effect that turns the blades. The pilot gets one chance to use the "pinwheel" effect to safely touch down the helicopter.

B-40 rocket   an enemy antitank weapon

B-52   US Air Force high-altitude bomber

Battalion   a military unit composed of a headquarters and two or more companies, batteries, or similar units

Body bag   a plastic bag used to transport dead bodies from the field

Boom-boom   slang for sex

Bouncing Betty   a land mine that, when triggered, bounces waist-high and sprays shrapnel

Brigade   a tactical and administrative military unit composed of a headquarters and one or more battalions of infantry or armor, with other supporting units.

CA   combat assault

Cav   Cavalry; shortened term for First Cavalry Division (Airmobile)

C-model   UH-1C, Huey gunship

CO   commanding officer

Cobra   an AH-1G attack helicopter; also known as a gunship, armed with rockets and machine guns

Combat Assault   large helicopter insertion of troops led by company officers. If battalion staff were involved, we generally called the insertion an RF, Romeo Foxtrot, or Rat Fuck.

Company   a military unit usually consisting of a headquarters and two or more platoons

Concertina wire   coiled barbed wire used as an obstacle

C-rations   combat rations; canned meals for use in the field

Dink   derogatory term for Viet Cong or NVA soldier

D-model   Huey slick with 1,100 horsepower turbine engine

DMZ   Demilitarized Zone; the dividing line between North and South Vietnam established in 1954 by the Geneva Convention

.50 cal.   either a machine gun used by Americans or a term used by our pilots for the enemy's .51 cal. or 12.7 millimeter antiaircraft gun.

FAC   Forward Air Controller; a person who coordinates air strikes

Fire base   an artillery firing position usually secured by an infantry unit; also, fire support base

Fire team   two gunships in attack formation

Gunship   an armed helicopter

H-model   Huey slick with 1,300 horsepower turbine engine

Hootch   a hut or simple dwelling

Hot LZ   a landing zone under enemy fire

Howitzer   a short cannon used to fire shells at medium velocity and with relatively high trajectories

Huey   nickname for the UH-1 series helicopters

I Corps, II Corps, III Corps, IV Corps   the four military regions into which South Vietnam was divided, with I Corps the northernmost regions, and IV Corps the southernmost delta region

KIA   killed in action

Lead   lead gunship in a Fire team

LRRP   long range reconnaissance patrol; an elite team usually comprised of five to seven men who would go deep into the jungle to observe enemy activity without initiating contact

LZ   landing zone; where helicopters land to take on or discharge troops or supplies

M-16   the standard US military rifle used in Vietnam; successor to the M-14

M-60   the standard lightweight machine gun used by US forces in Vietnam

M-79   a US military hand-held grenade launcher

MACV   Military Assistance Command/Vietnam; the main American military command unit that had responsibility for and authority over all US military activities in Vietnam; based at Tan Son Nhut

Medevac   medical evacuation from the field by helicopter; also called a dustoff

Miniguns   similar to Gatling guns. Operated by the peter pilot on gunships—fires 6,000 rounds per minute

Mortar   a muzzle-loading cannon with a short tube in relation to its caliber that throws projectiles with low muzzle velocity at high angles

NVA   North Vietnamese Army

Peter pilot   copilot

Pop smoke   to ignite a smoke grenade to signal an aircraft

Purple Heart   a US military decoration awarded to any member of the armed forces wounded by enemy action

PX   Post Exchange; military store

PZ   pick-up zone, area from which troops are extracted from combat

R&R   rest and relaxation; a three- to seven-day vacation from the war for a soldier

Recon   reconnaissance; going out into the jungle to observe for the purpose of identifying enemy activity

RF Romeo Foxtrot—"Rat Fuck"—large helicopter combat assault when battalion staff officers were involved

RPG a rocket-propelled grenade; a Russian-made anti-tank grenade launcher

Satchel charges pack used by the enemy containing explosives that are dropped or thrown and is generally more powerful than a grenade

Shrapnel pieces of metal sent flying by an explosion

Silver Star a US military decoration awarded for gallantry in action

Slick troop-carrying helicopter

Spectre AC-130—large airplane with miniguns

Spider hole a camouflaged enemy foxhole

Spooky AC-47—large airplane with miniguns

Tet Buddhist lunar New Year; Buddha's birthday

Tet Offensive a major uprising of Viet Cong, VC sympathizers, and NVA, characterized by a series of coordinated attacks against military installations and provincial capitals throughout Vietnam. It occurred during the lunar New Year at the end of January, 1968.

Tracer a round of ammunition chemically treated to glow or give off smoke so that its flight can be followed

Tree line a row of trees at the edge of a field or rice paddy

Victor/Victor Charlie/Mr. Charles/Chuck/Charlie Viet Cong, the enemy

Warrant officer military rank between commissioned and non-commissioned officers. Most army helicopter pilots were warrant officers

WIA wounded in action

Willy peter/willy pete/WP white phosphorus; an element used in grenades or shells for incendiary purposes

Wing second gunship in a fire team

The fascinating true stories behind these extraordinary public figures

IT DOESN'T TAKE A HERO: *The Autobiography*
by General H. Norman Schwarzkopf with Peter Petre

Rarely does a figure appear of such compelling leadership and personal charisma as to capture the imagination of an entire nation. Now, in this candid, outspoken, and eagerly awaited autobiography, General Schwarzkopf reveals the full story of his remarkable life and a career spanning nearly four decades. ____56338-6 $6.99/$7.99 in Canada

I COULD NEVER BE SO LUCKY AGAIN
by General James H. "Jimmy" Doolittle with Carroll V. Glines

Confidant and adviser to presidents and winner of virtually every medal his country had to offer, Doolittle's life is a story of the successes and adventures, the triumphs and tragedies of a true American hero whose courage, devotion, and daring continue to make their influence felt to this day. ____29725-2 $6.99/$8.50

YEAGER: *An Autobiography*
by Chuck Yeager with Leo Janos

From his humble West Virginia roots to his role as the test pilot who first broke the sound barrier, this is the story of the man who rose to lead America into space. ____25674-2 $7.50/$9.99

MARINE! *The Life of Chesty Puller*
by Burke Davis

This is the explosive true story of the most courageous and controversial commander of them all--the only marine in history to win five Navy crosses. Here is the fabulous tale of a real-life hero. ____27182-2 $6.99/$8.99

ABOUT THE AUTHOR

••

After leaving Vietnam, CHUCK CARLOCK served as a helicopter flight instructor, earned a college degree, and became a partner in a national accounting firm. He is currently the Director of Taxes for a prominent Texas family and structures some of the nation's largest business deals.